Eugene A. Nida is Executive Secretary for Translations of the American Bible Society. Anwar S. Dil is Professor of Language Science and Communication at the United States International University, San Diego.

Language Structure
and Translation

Language Structure and Translation

Essays by Eugene A. Nida

Selected and Introduced
by Anwar S. Dil

Stanford University Press, Stanford, California   1975

Language Science and National Development

A Series Sponsored by the
Linguistic Research Group of Pakistan

General Editor: Anwar S. Dil

Stanford University Press
Stanford, California
© 1975 by Eugene A. Nida
Printed in the United States of America
ISBN 0-8047-0885-1
LC 75-183

P
27
.NS

Contents

Acknowledgments

The Linguistic Research Group of Pakistan (LRGP) and the General Editor of the Language Science and National Development Series are deeply grateful to Dr. Eugene A. Nida, Associate Member of the Group, for giving us the privilege of presenting his selected writings as the eighth volume in our series established in 1970 to commemorate the International Education Year.

We are indebted to the editors and publishers of the following publications. The ready permission on the part of the holders of the copyrights, acknowledged in each case, is a proof of the existing international cooperation and goodwill that gives hope for better collaboration among scholars of all nations for international exchange of knowledge.

Analysis of Meaning and Dictionary Making. International Journal of American Linguistics 24, 4. 279-292 (1958), with permission of the Editor.

Principles of Translation as Exemplified by Bible Translating. On Translation, ed. by Reuben A. Brower (Cambridge, Mass.: Harvard University Press, 1959), pp. 11-31, with permission of the publisher. © 1959 by the President and Fellows of Harvard College.

Linguistic and Semantic Structure. Studies in Languages and Linguistics in Honor of Charles C. Fries, ed. by Albert H. Marckwardt (Ann Arbor: The English Language Institute of The University of Michigan, 1964), pp. 13-33, with permission of the publisher.

Difficulties in Translating Hebrews 1 into Southern Lengua. The Bible Translator 18. 117-122 (1967), courtesy of the United Bible Societies.

Science of Translation. Language 45. 483-498 (1969), with permission of the Linguistic Society of America.

Semantic Structures; with Charles R. Taber. Studies in Linguistics in Honor of George L. Trager, ed. by M. Estellie Smith (The Hague: Mouton Publishers, 1972), pp. 122-141, with permission of the publisher.

Indigenous Pidgins and Koinés; with Harold W. Fehderau. International Journal of American Linguistics 36, 2. 146-155 (1970), with permission of the Editor.

Communication Roles of Languages in Multilingual Societies; with William L. Wonderly. The Bible Translator 22, 1. 19-37 (1971), courtesy of the United Bible Societies.

Varieties of Languages. The Bible Translator 23, 3. 316-322 (1972), courtesy of the United Bible Societies.

Words and Thoughts. The Bible Translator 25, 3. 339-343 (1974), courtesy of the United Bible Societies.

Linguistics and Christian Missions; with William L. Wonderly. Anthropological Linguistics 5, 1. 104-144 (1963), with permission of the Editor.

Implications of Contemporary Linguistics for Biblical Scholarship. Journal of Biblical Literature 91, 1. 73-89 (1972), with permission of the Editor.

Dr. Afia Dil of the San Diego State University; Mr. Paul C. Clarke, Ms. Leila Wright, and Miss Marguerite Eldredge of the American Bible Society; and Mr. Curt R. Douglas of the United States International University, San Diego, deserve our gratitude for help in many ways. Typing of the camera-ready manuscript has been done by

Mrs. Margo Oliver of San Diego. She certainly deserves a word of appreciation for a job well done.

The Editor would also like to record his thanks to the language scholars who are working with him in the preparation of further volumes in the series.

This volume is affectionately dedicated to ALTHEA NIDA, the author's life companion and constant helper on his many journeys.

EDITOR'S NOTE

These essays have been reprinted from the originals with only minor changes made in the interest of uniformity of style and appearance. A few changes in wording have been made in consultation with the author. In some cases bibliographical entries and notes have been updated. Footnotes marked by asterisks have been added by the Editor.

Introduction

Eugene Albert Nida was born in Oklahoma City on November 11, 1914. During his high school days in Southern California he became interested in the Greek, Latin, French, and German languages. For his undergraduate work he went to the University of California at Los Angeles, where in 1936 he received his bachelor's degree with a major in Greek. At this stage he developed a love for the Bible and the Church; he also became associated with a linguistic mission to Mexico, which later developed into the Summer Institute of Linguistics. In 1939 he earned a master's degree from the University of Southern California, where he immersed himself in the University's extensive collections in patristic literature and specialized in the study of the New Testament in Greek. His growing interest in Christian missionary work led him to pursue linguistic studies at the University of Michigan. Most of his work there focused on descriptive linguistics, cultural anthropology, intercultural communication, and the study of Greek, Gothic, and Old English. His Ph.D. dissertation on English syntactic structures was completed in 1943 under the guidance of Professors Charles C. Fries, Leonard Bloomfield, and Edgar H. Sturtevant. The same year he was invited to join the American Bible Society, where he has continued to serve as Executive Secretary for the Translations Department.

Dr. Nida has had rich and far-reaching experience as a language scientist with the American Bible Society. His work has taken him to more than seventy-five countries around the world, where he has conducted field surveys, research, and training programs involving more than two hundred languages. He has been a regular contributor and member of the editorial board of The Bible Translator since it was founded in 1948. More recently he has taken on additional duties as the Translations Research Coordinator of the United Bible Societies, and is currently working with a team of some fifty translation consultants in over five hundred languages. In recognition of his meritorious work in the field he has been awarded honorary degrees of Doctor of Divinity by the Eastern Baptist Seminary (1956) and the Southern California Baptist Seminary (1959); Doctor of Theology by the University of Münster, West Germany (1966); and Doctor of Literature by the Heriot-Watt University, Edinburgh, Scotland (1974). Dr. Nida has been a visiting lecturer at a number of universities. In 1968 he was President of the Linguistic Society of America.

Dr. Nida's international reputation as a specialist in Bible translation lies in his series of articles and books resulting from his application of insights gained from linguistics, anthropology, communication, and related branches of modern knowledge. In Bible Translating (1947) he first elaborated a set of principles and procedures for assisting missionary workers in handling problems of translating the scriptures with illustrative data, all of this based on his own field observations and manuscript-checking in the files of the American Bible Society, and the experiences of his colleagues in Latin America and other parts of the world. His continuing growth as an authority in the field can be seen, for example, in the following books: God's Word in Man's Language (1952), Customs and Cultures (1954), Message and Mission (1960), Religion Across Cultures (1968), Communication of the Gospel in Latin America (1969), and A Translator's Handbook on Paul's Letter to the Romans (with Barclay M. Newman, 1973). What impresses me particularly in these and other publications of Nida is his attempt at an integrated application of contemporary knowledge to the transmission of the Christian message in the cultural idioms of our time. His work establishes the need to occasionally reword the content of the scriptures in order to accommodate the sociocultural changes (especially the diachronic linguistic changes) and the discovery of new materials relevant to biblical studies.

Dr. Nida is well known for his work in semantic structure and translation theory. His first published article, "Linguistics and Ethnology in Translational Problems" (1945) has been widely acclaimed and included in Dell Hymes's standard reader, Language in Culture and Society (1964). His first book, Morphology, The Descriptive Analysis of Words (1946, second revised edition 1949) remained for over a decade a basic textbook in linguistic courses. In 1947 he published his popular Linguistic Interludes, whose informal dialogue format even today attracts the reader to its usefulness as a general introduction to the basic principles and methods of descriptive linguistics and the importance of linguistic study in the broad context of human culture and society. Similarly, his Learning a Foreign Language (1950, revised edition 1957) is a simple but sound handbook on the subject. His dissertation, A Synopsis of English Syntax (1964), though dated because of its use of the immediate constituent model, remains a useful reference work for its comprehensive lists of words functioning as syntactic classes. Nida's major linguistic contribution so far is best represented in Toward a Science of Translating (1964), The Theory and Practice of Translation (with Charles R. Taber, 1969), and Translation Across Cultures (in press), which broaden his earlier approach to a more comprehensive sociolinguistic view of translation with focus on the role of the receptor. Exploring Semantic Structures (1975) extends his analysis of the meaning of nuclear structures and the relationships between such units, and Componential Analysis of Meaning (1975) explores the referential aspects of meaning and supplementary aspects of connotative and emotive meaning. Publications in preparation include a volume on lexicography and a dictionary of the Greek New Testament based on a classification of some fifteen thousand meanings identified and arranged under more than two hundred fifty domains.

Nida's work has richly extended multi- and intercultural awareness not only for the missionary workers and Bible translators but also for all students of cross-cultural studies. He has made notable contribution in recent years to the creation of a climate of more open-minded acceptance of the fact of cultural diversity among the peoples of the world, as a first step toward better human communication and understanding. Underlying this approach is Nida's deep conviction, amply justified by his research, that anything that can be said in one language can be said in another with reasonable accuracy by establishing equivalent points of reference in the receptor's culture and matching his cognitive framework by restructuring the constitutive elements of the message. Communication across languages and cultures is thus viewed as a process of translational equivalence of messages in appropriately reconstructed formal and semantic structures. As I see it, this perspective on intercultural communication offers more optimistic possibilities of human understanding than is promised, for example, by the Sapir-Whorfian hypothesis of linguistic relativity, according to which cognitive organization is "constrained" by the linguistic structure of a particular community. Further, the realities which affect intercultural communication as illustrated by Nida's work in translational equivalence could serve as useful signposts in skirting various roadblocks to international understanding. Seen in this context, the relevance of Nida's work to the broader task of human development across belief systems and ideologies is worthy of far more attention than has been given to it to date.

Anwar S. Dil

United States International University
San Diego, California
March 17, 1975

Language Structure
and Translation

Part I. Semantic Structure and Translational Equivalence

1 | Analysis of Meaning and Dictionary Making

Meaning, the indispensable helper, but often repudiated friend, of science, is at last coming into her own. Information theory, the advance of anthropology into the realm of personality and group psychology, the inevitable necessity of structural linguists to deal with meaning (despite its lack of structural neatness), and political events in our present world have all joined to force upon us an awareness of the necessity, importance, and scientific basis of communication. An essential part of investigations in semantics is reflected in dictionary-making, a highly specialized process, which, however, too often reflects only a meager appreciation of some fundamental problems involved in the analysis of meaning.

1. Types of dictionaries

Dictionaries are essentially descriptions of the distribution of language units (usually words) in terms of linguistic and cultural contexts, though in general the cultural contexts predominate. By linguistic context we mean the phrases or sentences in which such words are or have been used (in general this means citing literary sources). By cultural context we mean the description of a process or object as a part of the culture. As long as a dictionary is written in the same language as the words it is describing and is prepared for people who participate fully in the culture which is being described, the problems of analysis of meaning are appreciably simpler than in the case of dictionaries in which the language of description is different from the language being described. Furthermore, when there are serious lacunae, the reader can supply what is lacking by virtue of his knowledge of the cultural context. However, as soon as one

undertakes to prepare a dictionary of a foreign language, the problems
seem to increase with geometric proportion, depending upon the
degree of linguistic and cultural diversity. That is to say, a dictionary
of French words written in English is relatively simple (because of
the essentially similar languages and cultures) in comparison with a
dictionary of Zulu in English. Too often, however, compilers of
dictionaries are not sufficiently aware of the profound structural differences between languages and between cultures or they take for
granted that the reader will infer the essential distinctions.

There are, of course, a number of different kinds of dictionaries, depending upon the purposes for which they are designed,
but if we omit from consideration those dictionaries which are produced solely for commercial purposes and include only those dictionaries which are designed to provide scientifically useful data,
we are left with three fundamentally different types of dictionaries:
(1) a list of words with identifying glosses, (2) a list of words with
more or less full treatment of types of occurrences drawn from text
material, and (3) a list of words with more or less exhaustive treatment of the kinds of cultural contexts in which such words occur. In
the first instance the list of glosses, which serve primarily as identificational tags, assists one materially in an analysis of a text and in
the working out of structural relationships. The second type of dictionary consists of a compendium of usage in which words are classified and illustrated on the basis of linguistic contexts. The third
type is essentially an "ethnolinguistic dictionary", in that it relates
linguistic units of semantic relevance to the total context of cultural
behavior. There is little value, for example, in saying that a word
means female puberty rite if there is no available ethnological data
on the culture in question. Similarly, to say that a word means goodbye is also relatively useless, unless we know under what circumstances it is uttered: at what time of day or night, in anticipation of
how long an absence, to what classes of people, after or before other
words of parting, combined with what variety of gestures, intonation,
or voice quality, etc.

In actual practice most dictionaries are a blend of the three
basic types, with differing proportions of data depending upon the
practical needs of the intended users.

2. Problems of traditional methodology

No doubt much of our difficulty in dealing with bilingual and bicultural dictionary problems has been the inadequacy of certain traditional methods of semantic analysis and the tendency to mix classificatory criteria and to shift methodology depending upon the ease of treating any particular word. The two most commonly employed techniques have been based upon (1) historical lineage and (2) central-peripheral plotting.

Where there is abundant historical data and where the line of descent seems relatively clear, one encounters few difficulties. For example, the Greek word k^{h}aris means <u>outward loveliness, kindness</u> (as a quality of personality), <u>favor</u> (an act), <u>gift, delight</u>, and <u>thankfulness</u>. This can be treated as a lineal development: appearance-character-action-object-response. However, even here we are not sure of the details in the historical development, despite a rather extensive literature, for we cannot be certain of usage during those periods represented by gaps in available data, nor can we ascertain the developments in the colloquial use of this word. Furthermore, we cannot assume that the histories of the literary and colloquial usage are strictly parallel. Synchronic functioning constantly "remakes" the historical patterning. We know, for instance, that historically the <u>by</u> in <u>bylaw</u> is not the same <u>by</u> as the <u>by</u> of <u>bypath</u> and <u>byproduct,</u> but for the average speaker of English there is no such distinction. The historical method is, of course, utterly inadequate for languages which have no available historical record, for there are no inviolate laws of semantic development. For example, one of the most generally accepted principles is that in instances of related object and process words, the latter are derived from the former, but that is not always the case. In Tarahumara the words mičuruku <u>shavings,</u> rituku <u>ice,</u> pačiki <u>an ear of maize</u>, and opačaka <u>garment</u> are derivative formations from the underlying forms mičuru <u>to make shavings</u>, ritu <u>to be icy</u>, pači <u>to grow ears of maize</u>, and opača <u>to be dressed</u>.

For anyone working with aboriginal languages the historical method obviously has its strict limitations, except where certain reconstructions seem warranted on the basis of comparative data. As a result the tendency has been to substitute a 'logical arrangement' of meanings, on the basis that certain meanings can be logically derived from each other. This logical framework, however, as useful as it may be for certain classificatory purposes, does not necessarily reflect either the historical development or the relationships between different meanings as they may be understood by native speakers of the language.

The so-called logical method of analysis and arrangement of meanings is, however, very difficult to apply, for categories which are familiar to us as foreigners often seem incapable of application to the array of meanings of words in foreign languages. Furthermore, the more one becomes intimately familiar with a language, especially one with widely different linguistic and semantic structures, the more it becomes evident that logical criteria drawn primarily from one language-culture complex cannot be easily or validly applied to another.

Accordingly, rather than attempt a logical ordering of meanings, those preparing dictionaries tend to describe meanings in terms of central and peripheral meanings, though usually these distinctions are not explicitly stated. What often happens is that the first meaning given is assumed to be central and that the meanings which follow are arranged more or less in terms of successive distances from the center. Despite certain serious problems encountered in the application of this method, it must be recognized that it is distinctly superior to the practice of trying to state the fundamental "core" or the "common denominator" of meaning, sometimes described as the "central idea" inherent within each meaning and one from which the related meanings are presumably derived. Nevertheless, even the arrangement of meanings in terms of central and peripheral involves two fundamental limitations: (1) the multi-dimensional relationships of the data (which cannot easily be squeezed into what is essentially a two-dimensional analysis) and (2) the false assumption that words should or always do have "central" meanings. In many instances it simply is not possible nor useful to try to describe a series of meanings of a word in terms of any central meaning and peripheral uses. But this should not unduly alarm us. We have had to abandon a similar practice on a morphological level. For example, we no longer feel compelled always to choose one allomorph as the basic allomorph from which all others are descriptively derived. Of course, if in a series of related forms one allomorph can be selected so as to make possible the accounting for alternative forms by certain generally applicable morphophonemic statements, we should set up such a central form. However, when the data do not justify any such selection, we must be content with the facts of the language as they are and not impose any arbitrary categories upon the material. Something similar exists in the case of the classification of what we may call the allosemes of a sememe.

We do not wish to imply that the techniques of historical, logical, and central-peripheral analysis and description are not useful. They are. But their usefulness is strictly limited and, as I hope to point out in the rest of this paper, there are certain other techniques which seem to provide more fruitful results, both in terms of analytical methodology as well as a descriptive arrangement.

3. Basic principles

Though in general those who compile dictionaries are supposedly aware of the basic principles of semantic correspondence (or lack of it), some dictionaries are formulated with apparent disregard for the three fundamental presuppositions which must underlie all adequate semantic analysis: (1) no word (or semantic unit) ever has exactly the same meaning in two different utterances; (2) there are no complete synonyms within a language; (3) there are no exact correspondences between related words in different languages. In other words, perfect communication is impossible, and all communication is one of degree. The statement of equivalences, whether in dictionaries or in translations, cannot be absolute. We are faced, therefore, not with a problem of 'right or wrong' but with 'how right' or 'how wrong.' Perhaps, because of the essentially negative character of these principles and the difficulties of application, the compilers of dictionaries react in favor of describing what is known rather than what is not known. Nevertheless, the essentially negative elements in the basic principles of semantic equivalence must be constantly recognized if one is to deal adequately with the broader ethnolinguistic relationships. Furthermore, though dictionary compilers cannot attain an absolute definition of a term in another language or culture (or even in the same language or culture—for that matter), nevertheless, they can give very useful approximate descriptions.

4. Relationship of language to culture

Whatever we may personally think of structural analysis as divorced from meaning or of the influence of grammatical categories on thought processes, we certainly must admit the close relationship between language and culture. Language cannot be properly treated except in terms of its status and function as a part, a process, and, to some degree, a model of culture, with a high degree of reciprocal reinforcement. Though one may not wish to go all the way with Whorf, nevertheless, one cannot escape the fact that language seems to provide the 'grooves for thought' in the same way that cultural patterns constitute the molds for more general modes of behavior.

An illustration of a close tie between language and culture is provided by the two 'possessive' systems in New Caledonian.[1] These may be roughly distinguished as 'intimate' and 'non-intimate' possession. The first class includes such nouns as those meaning mother, liver, and descendants, while the second class includes father, heart, and personal life. The apparently arbitrary character of the distinction can only be understood if one realizes that New Caledonian society has been traditionally matrilineal, that the liver has been regarded as symbolic of the entire person (the liver is used in sacrifices as symbolizing the victim), and that one's descendants have a more intimate, continuing relationship to a person than even his own life. However, with the rapid breakdown of the old cultural patterns (including the complex series of religious beliefs), this grammatical dichotomy is losing its synchronic validity and rapidly becoming another linguistic 'fossil', with which all languages are strewn. That is to say, this tie between formal language structure and cultural behavior is breaking, but, as in all languages, there are other newly emerging formations which reflect current cultural developments.

When one proceeds from the level of grammatical categories (which are largely implicit) to the level of words, which are symbols for dynamic and explicit features of the culture, one is obliged to interpret the meaning of such linguistic units in light of the cultural context. That is to say, the meaning of a unit must be described in terms of the sum total of what it signals in all the contexts in which it is used. Note that we specifically reject meaning as 'a common denominator' or 'what is common to all situations in which a term is employed.' If, for example, we analyze the use of <u>charge</u> in the following contexts, we will find that a common denominator would be precious little indeed. It would be only a small part of the total meaning signalled by <u>charge</u> in the various contexts: <u>charge into the line of players</u>, <u>charge the gun</u>, <u>charge the battery</u>, <u>charge the pencil</u>, <u>charge the man ten dollars</u>, <u>charge the culprit with the crime</u>, <u>he gets a charge out of it</u>, <u>a charge of electricity</u>, <u>he is in charge</u>, <u>he is a public charge</u>. The only way to 'define' the meaning of <u>charge</u> is to describe (usually by illustrative phrases or sentences) the distribution of the word.

When, however, we speak of 'the distribution' of a word we must distinguish between (1) the specific linguistic context, which gives a form a linguistic meaning, and (2) the practical-world (non-linguistic) context, which provides what is more generally understood by the meaning of a word. Obviously, the so-called 'function words,' (following Fries' usage) have predominantly linguistic meaning.

The cultural distribution must, however, reckon not only with objective events but with evaluations of the events and the corresponding symbols. The emotion which a patriot feels when he uses the phrase 'Old Glory' is utterly unintelligible to a Nuer of the Sudan, who neither has nor understands banners. But when he dances before a favorite bull and calls out its name, he experiences a similar 'thrill' in having uttered an emotionally charged expression.

We can say that the cultural event symbolized by a word provides the denotative meaning, while the emotional response experienced by the speakers in the culture (and modeled by the culture) is the basis of the connotative meaning. Since there is no speech without speakers and no speakers without subjective evaluations (absolute objectivity is an illusion, for we are parts of as well as students of culture), there are no words without some measure of connotation. Even apparent neutrality of meaning may be regarded as connotatively significant, by virtue of its apparent lack of emotional coloring.

5. Totality of language-culture correlation

The correlation between language and culture is perfectly obvious when we are dealing with isolated words which reflect unusual cultural objects, activities, or attitudes. For example, the Shilluks of the Sudan speak of forgiveness as spitting on the ground in front of a person, a description of the manner in which forgiveness is formally indicated. The Uduks, also of the Sudan, employ a phrase to meet snapping fingers again (a concise description of the cultural event) in contexts where we would use the term reconciliation. The Cuzco Quechuas call the year tying up the sun, an obvious reference to the ancient use of quepus. However, some of the significant correlations between language and culture are not these more obvious correspondences of individual semantic units (whether single words or whole phrases), but involve whole sets of vocabulary. These correlations may be summarized as follows:

(1). The vocabulary relating to the focus of the culture is proportionately more exhaustive than that which refers to nonfocal features. That is to say, the extent of vocabulary relating to any phase of culture is directly proportionate to its cultural relevance.

(2). Subcultures have proportionately more extensive vocabularies in the area of their distinctiveness.

The proportionately greater vocabulary in the area of the focus of a culture is almost a truism, but nevertheless a fact which is not infrequently overlooked. For the Nilotic Nuers cattle are the central fact toward which almost all the rest of the culture is oriented and in the light of which most behavior has meaning. Accordingly, one finds many hundreds of words which describe different colors (including distribution of color), sizes, shapes, breeds, behavior, and values of cattle. The English language has nothing even remotely approaching such specialized 'cattle' vocabulary. On the other hand, the Nuer language may be regarded as very 'deficient' in words for mechanical artifacts, of which the Nuers have relatively few, while English abounds in names for gadgets, a reflection of the fact that mechanical technology is the focus of our culture. The Ponapeans have an extensive vocabulary to describe different forms and varieties of sweet potatoes, for the growing of these tubers is one important focus of their culture. For us sweet potatoes are a very minor feature and accordingly possess no specialized vocabulary. Similarly, the abundance of terminology relating to maize: its kind, stages of growth, parts, cultivation, harvesting, and preparation as food, is a readily understandable feature in the various Mayan Indian languages of southern Mexico and Guatemala. It is easy to understand why so many dictionaries prepared by outsiders to a culture tend to omit a high percentage of the foci vocabulary, for such words are difficult to elicit and extremely hard to describe, due to the lack of corresponding words and traits in the compiler's language and culture. In going through such dictionaries, one is likely to receive the impression that the languages in question are quite deficient in words, while actually the apparent scarcity of words results in large measure from a failure to give adequate treatment to foci vocabulary.

Since the extent of vocabulary is roughly reflected in the degree of cultural relevance of the referents of the semantic units, it is obvious that such vocabulary is not necessarily a permanent feature. For example, in many of the Mayan languages of southern Mexico there is a significant lack of indigenous terms for juridical processes and government, which must certainly have existed before the conquest and for which there is adequate evidence in the Popol Wuj. However, with the destruction of patterns of indigenous government and the superimposition of foreign authorities, this vocabulary largely disappeared. In its place there came into usage a rather meager vocabulary drawn from Spanish and reflecting the nature of the contacts with the Spanish-speaking rulers. A similar shift in the extent of vocabulary is taking place in Anuak, a Nilotic language of the Sudan, in which there are, for example, eight different terms to describe various methods and stages in the grinding of corn, but up to within the last few years only one word for anything made of metal, whether a screwdriver or an airplane. However, with the rapid increase of contacts with people using metal tools and machines, there is a sizable increase in the number of borrowed words and coined expressions which are being rapidly introduced into the language, in order to designate these new, culturally valuable objects.

These principles relating to the size of vocabulary in proportion to the cultural relevance of certain objects or modes of behavior are true not only for cultures as a whole, but for subcultures, where the relationship between extent of vocabulary and cultural specialization seems even more striking. For any specialized subgroup within a culture the extent of vocabulary is proportionately greater in the area of distinctive specialization, since such an area

of activity is generally the focus of the subgroup and hence has much
greater cultural relevance for those people. For example, people in
the fishing villages of Newfoundland have an abundance of words relating to the sea and their work, while the farming people of the interior
areas are conspicuously lacking in such terms. The same principle
holds for all occupational subgroups within a culture—including linguists, who find it difficult to speak without _-eme_ words.

The significance of these correlations between culture and
the extent of vocabulary should make the dictionary compiler not only
more aware of the probable volume of words in the different areas of
the culture, but also more alert to reflect in any abridged dictionary
(and most dictionaries are drastically abridged) a truer picture of the
proportion of words in the different phases of the culture.

However, though there are broad correlations of a statistical
nature between culture and vocabulary, the principle of selectivity
operates so extensively in semantic structure that we cannot anticipate
the manner in which a particular language will treat any given phenomenon. Cultures may possess the very same traits, but identify and
describe them in utterly diverse ways. This is particularly true of
psychological characteristics. For example, the Habbes of the French
Sudan speak of sorrow as having a sick liver. The Bambaras, somewhat to the west of the Habbes, say that sorrow is having a black eye.
The Mossi people, just north of the Gold Coast, insist that sorrow is
having a rotten heart, while the Uduks in the Sudan describe sorrow
as having a heavy stomach. Psychological phenomena are not, however, the only features which illustrate the unpredictability of means
of symbolization. We speak of the eye of a needle, but the Kekchi
Indians of Guatemala call it the face of the needle, the Lahu of Southeast Asia and the Piros of Peru speak of the nostril of the needle, the
Haka Chins of Burma call it the mouth of the needle, the Tiddims of
Burma refer to it as the ear of the needle, the Mitla Zapotecs in
Mexico say the face of the needle, and the Amuzgos, likewise of Mexico, talk about the hole of the needle.

6. Frequency of semantic units

Information theory has provided us with some very important
concepts for making quantitative (and to some extent, qualitative)

judgments concerning semantic phenomena. The fact that information is in inverse proportion to redundancy gives us important clues to the relationship between certain aspects of frequency and meaning, though we must not make the mistake of assuming that information as used in communication theory is the same as information when used in the popular sense of the extent of meaning which some particular word might have in a particular context. For example, if a translator is unable to employ some indigenous term to describe a foreign object, e.g. phylacteries as spoken of in the Scriptures, and so chooses to employ a borrowed word, the unpredictability of such a term within the context means that it carries a heavy informational load, but it actually does not mean much to the reader. On the other hand, words such as thing, matter, object, datum, and item have such a high frequency of usage in some types of writing (e.g. in scientific papers, where there seems to be a premium on generalizations or dullness), that they really contribute very little to the meaning of a passage. They mean so much that they end up meaning very little in many contexts.

This problem of meaning and frequency should be more fully recognized by compilers of dictionaries. For example, in all dictionaries of Classical Greek with which the writer is acquainted there are rather full descriptions of connectives such as de, kai, and oun. From the nature of the lengthy statements of their use one tends to infer that such words are quite important, and that they are at least equivalent in semantic value to the corresponding English conjunctions but, and, and therefore, by which they are usually translated. The truth of the matter is that these Greek conjunctions occur so frequently that they mean much less than their English correspondents. A brief comparison of frequencies will make this evident. Of the first forty sentences in Plato's Republic all but six have some type of connective, of which de, oun, and kai are the most frequent. Of these six sentences, two begin sections (including one which begins the book) and four are direct discourses, which are more or less interruptive in nature. In the first twenty sections of Isocrates' On the Peace every sentence but the first has some type of conjunction either as the first word or as postpositive to the introductory expression. Of the 55 paragraphs which make up the treatise On the Peace all but the first begin with some type of connective, of which de occurs in 22, oun in 12, and other connectives in the remaining 20 paragraphs.

No writer of English in any way approximates this type of frequency.
In some selected writings of John Ruskin (reproduced in Twelve Centuries of English Poetry and Prose, published by Scott, Foresman
and Company) out of the first 35 sentences only four begin with connectives, and each of these begins with and. Out of a total of 32 paragraphs, 26 begin without connectives, two begin with and, two with
now (in a conjunctive, not temporal, use), and one each with for and
however. James Truslow Adams in his book The Adams Family
(published by Little, Brown, and Company, 1930) employs conjunctions
to begin only two sentences out of the first 32. Of the first 66 paragraphs only 8 have connectives.

Our Greek dictionaries, however, go on repeating the traditional statements about Greek conjunctions, but they do not indicate
the differences in relative frequency between the corresponding Greek
and English conjunctions. As a result, the average user of a Greek
dictionary is badly misled in his judgments about the relative importance of such conjunctions in the respective languages.

7. Size of semantic units

Semantic analysis begins with the morpheme and concludes
with the discourse. For the dictionary maker, however, the derivational layer of word formation has generally been regarded as the
minimal unit. Between the morpheme and the 'dictionary level' there
is the great no-man's land which the structural linguist usually refuses
to touch, and which the dictionary maker regards as beneath his level
of analysis. It is very true that the meaning of sub-word units is hard
to define and describe, for the meaning is primarily determined by
the linguistic context. For example, bad, good, kind, and full can
be described in terms of their cultural contexts, but -ness, which
may be suffixed to bad, good, kind, and full, but not to well, cannot
be so easily defined.

Above the level of the word the dictionary compiler is generally not in too much difficulty as long as the combinations in the
language are largely endocentric in semantic structure, that is to say,
if the meaning of the whole can be determined by adding up the meanings of the parts (which is true of most utterances). However,

so-called idioms are a problem precisely because the meaning of the whole is not the meaning of the sum total of the parts. Such expressions are exocentric—and in varying degree. The expression <u>he is in the house</u> has only an endocentric meaning, but the slightly different expression <u>he is in the doghouse</u> may be either endocentric, if it refers to an animal, or exocentric, if it means a man. Of course, there is the possibility of a man being inside of a doghouse, but that is an extremely unlikely meaning for the sentence.

Idioms have very often been overlooked by dictionary compilers, for they are hard to 'alphabetize' and are too frequently judged to be slang or transitory. However, they often play a major role in the process of communication. The actual inventory of different words in some of the so-called primitive languages of the world may not be conspicuously high, but the number of highly exocentric idioms is often very great. For example, if one were to construct a dictionary of Anuak along traditional lines, the language would appear to be almost devoid of terms to describe psychological states and attitudes, while as a matter of fact, the language abounds in such expressions. However, most of these are exocentric phrases containing the word cwiny <u>liver</u>: he has a cwiny (<u>he is good</u>), his cwiny is good (<u>he is generous</u>), his cwiny is bad (<u>he is unsociable</u>), his cwiny is shallow (<u>he gets angry quickly</u>), his cwiny is heavy (<u>he is sad</u>), his cwiny is stubborn (<u>he is brave</u>), his cwiny is white (<u>he is kind</u>), his cwiny is cold (<u>he will not be impolite in eating ahead of others</u>), his cwiny is burned (<u>he is irritable</u>), his cwiny is sweet (<u>he is happy</u>)—to mention only a few.

It may be argued by some that for the Anuak such phrases are not exocentric, but endocentric, that is to say, they constitute language myths which have 'objective reality' for the people of that culture. No doubt to some extent this is true (even as it is somewhat true for comparable idioms in all languages), but on the whole the Anuak people cannot be accused of being appreciably more naive about their idioms than are English-speaking people, who readily recognize that one cannot insist on a literal word-for-word objectivity in such phrases as <u>dead tired</u>, <u>drunk with power</u>, and <u>nothing but horsefeathers</u>.

However, having recognized the importance of idioms, we must not assume that all languages have the same type or employ them with the same degree of frequency. Cuna, spoken by the San Blas Indians of Panama, is a language which not only has an abundance of semantically exocentric expressions and uses them with high frequency, but also readily admits borrowed metaphors from other languages. On the other hand, the Tarascan language of Mexico not only falls considerably below the average in the number and frequency of metaphors (in comparison with most languages in Mexico) but does not readily admit the introduction of idioms from foreign languages.

Any accurate semantic analysis (and, accordingly, adequate dictionary) of a language must reckon with the various sizes of meaningful units and describe the semantically exocentric combinations. Without this one cannot know the extent or nature of the semantic resources of a given language.

8. Methods of investigation

One of the most serious problems encountered by any field investigator is the exploration of a 'semantic field,' an area of semantically related terms. The problem is not too complex in the case of a more or less well-delineated series such as kinship terms, for one can plot the various components, e.g. sex, age, ascending and descending generations, consanguinity, affinity, etc. , which may be evident in any particular system and then fill in the 'holes'. Similarly, in the case of the color spectrum, it is possible to provide informants with the entire range of colors and elicit the corresponding terms, thus providing a complete nomenclature for such a limited semantic field.

However, the problems become much more complex when one is dealing with a series of terms which seem to have no such easily definable limitations and in which there appears to be a considerable area of overlap. Recently, for example, in a conference of linguistically oriented field investigators we were attempting to study some of the problems involved in terms for shaman in some of the Mayan languages in Guatemala and southern Mexico. The comparison of lists of terms submitted by the various participants in the conference revealed what were either (1) obvious omissions or oversights on the part of the linguistic investigators or (2) strange lacunae in the linguistic usage of the language in question.

Once, however, the problem of exploring the semantic field has been accomplished, there still remains the difficulty of trying to relate the various meanings of individual terms so that the area of meaning covered by a word or semantically endocentric phrase may be understandably relatable to the culture in which it is employed. Moreover, one must also be in a position to attempt to determine whether two apparently different meanings are relatable at all, or whether one must classify the forms as two homophonous expressions.

These diverse, but closely related, problems require several different investigative procedures, which we may describe as (1) componential plotting of a semantic field, (2) diagrammatic plotting of semantic distinctions, and (3) componential analysis of the meanings of individual terms.

9. Componential plotting of a semantic field

As in the case of the terms for shaman, noted above, it seemed wise to attempt to determine the number of words or phrases which might be employed in any one language and how they could be related to one another. This was done by placing in the vertical listing all the names for shaman which had been found by the investigator in any one language. For example, in a chart for Aguacateco there were eight different terms in the vertical listing, while in the description of the Kekchi data there were only four. In the horizontal listing we placed all the functions of shaman, regardless of what word might be employed, e.g. healing sick, casting spells, foretelling the future, determining the cause of drought, burial of the dead, dedication of new buildings, officiating at weddings, performance of rites before planting and harvesting, and consulting with the spirits of the dead. The next step in procedure was to ask informants which type of person as given in the vertical listing performed which type of functions which had been noted. This procedure produced two results: (1) the clarification of functions for the titles employed and (2) the addition of other titles to designate functionaries not already properly included. Moreover, rather than find a neat division of labor between the various types of such socio-religious functionaries, it was discovered that there was a quite unsuspected degree of overlapping in certain functions.

At one stage in the investigation, however, we became almost
hopelessly confused because of an unsuspected error in the horizontal
listing, for we had introduced not only functions, but techniques, e.g.
burning of copal, use of candles, reciting of prayers, going into a
trance, speaking in a strange language, dancing, use of rock crystals,
making of medicine bundles, counting red beans, and changing oneself
into the form of an animal. This confusion of function and techniques
resulted in a hopeless arrangement of data, but a separation of the
two soon revealed some interesting correlations between techniques
and functions. Moreover, it soon became quite evident that some of
the names used for shaman were primarily technique terms, e.g., aj
pom master of the copal (Aguacateco, Quiche). Others identified primarily a function, e.g. aj cun brujo, witch-doctor (Aguacateco,
Quiche). Still other terms might be derived primarily from a technique, but be applicable principally to a function, e.g. the Aguacateco
term aj wutz mes medium, who always employs a table, as implied
in the title, which includes a borrowing of Spanish mesa.

By means of a componential plotting of the semantic field,
even though all the various functions and techniques might not be known
at the time, it is possible   to achieve a high degree of satisfactory
eliciting of data. This is, of course, not substantially different from
what is done when one is attempting to elicit morphological forms by
filling out paradigmatic sets. The only difference here is that we
are dealing with the possibilities of the occurrence of certain terms
within a delimited series of semantic functional positions, rather than
testing the occurrence of morphemes in a specific series of morphological combinations.

There is, of course, a degree of artificiality about such an
approach to a semantic field, for the discovery of such terms in text
material would be preferable, but the same problems apply here as
in the case of morphological analyses: we cannot always wait for the
chance occurrence of a form which seems necessary to fill out a crucial spot in the structural analysis.

10. Diagrammatic plotting of semantic distinctions

Once we have explored any semantic field by the processes
of componential plotting, it becomes immediately evident that a single

term may exhibit a wide diversity of meanings, but within this range there are certain clearly recognized relationships, generally reflecting certain culturally significant facts. For example, the Biblical Hebrew root *kbd occurs in a very wide range of linguistic-cultural situations, giving rise to a number of so-called 'meanings', listed in an English dictionary as heavy, much, many, slow, abundant, burdensome, difficult, grievous, sluggish, dull, riches, respect, honor, and great. One may regard the meanings as given in English as designations for classes of contexts in which the root *kbd may occur. Such glosses, therefore, constitute a kind of grid by which we may describe the range of occurrence, while recognizing two essential facts: (1) the English glosses stand only for a cluster of closely related contexts in Hebrew and (2) despite the faithfulness of such a grid to the linguistic-cultural contexts in Hebrew, there is an inevitable degree of skewing by virtue of the differences between English and Hebrew. Nevertheless, the analyst, who must generally make use of a foreign language in at least the initial stages of study, can with profit—and care—employ the foreign language glosses as a useful investigative tool.

For example, in the study of the range of meaning exhibited by the Hebrew root *kbd, one will immediately note four different classes of glosses, as determined by the nature of the referents and the value judgments involved: (1) those which designate quantity (but without any value judgment) in terms of mass and number, e.g. heavy, much, many, abundant, (2) those which describe certain aspects of inertia, slow (without evidence of value judgment) and sluggish and dull (with disapproval), (3) those which specify certain culturally valued features, e.g. riches, respect, honor, great, and (4) those which denote abundance as a source of features which have only negative value: burdensome, difficult, and grevious.

This division into four classes suggests certain relationships. The first class is neutral (or central) to the two poles of positive and negative values. The meaning of slow seems to fall somewhere between the neutral series and the culturally disfavored ones, since the meanings sluggish and dull, being closely related to slow, are disfavored.

We may plot certain of these relationships diagrammatically in the manner shown in Diagram A.

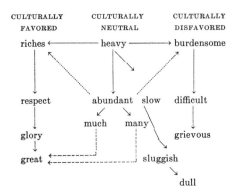

DIAGRAM A

Diagram A is not intended to reflect the relationship between these glosses as they are used in English, but as they are employed in Biblical Hebrew, in which the nomadic background of the people was an important factor in giving rise to a series of meanings in which a quantity of substance could be either the basis for wealth if it had cultural value or the cause of great inconvenience if it were relatively valueless. The arrows are intended to show the presumed direction of derivation, on the basis of what we know about such patterns of life and language usage, and the two types of arrows, solid and broken, designate two degrees of semantic relationship.

Such a diagram has the advantage of permitting a valuable organization of diverse data into a relatively small compass, thus allowing for the study of otherwise overlooked relationships. On the other hand, such a diagram includes a number of serious limitations: (1) the representation of the relationships between the meanings is overly simplified (several planes, plus a dimension of time would be necessary if one were to diagram all the factors accurately), (2) the arrows imply a kind of etymological descent, which may or may not be true, (3) instead of two degrees of interrelationship, there are actually several, with a considerable reciprocal reinforcement, which cannot be shown in such a diagram, and could not even be fully ascertained from the available evidence, and (4) despite all attempts to make such a diagram conform to what we know of the cultural and linguistic situation reflected in the Bible, it is inevitable that the language employed as a grid will tend to skew the data. This last fact should not, however, unduly alarm us, for at certain stages in the semantic analysis of any language the influence of the language of investigation must be reckoned with. The same type of problem confronts the phonetician, who brings to his study of a new language a background of language experience which inevitably colors his investigation and introduces judgments which can only be corrected by later phonemic analysis in which the data is analyzed on the basis of the self-contained system. In the case of semantic analysis we must do substantially the same thing, but in the past there has been the tendency to use the glosses provided by foreign languages without recognizing either their arbitrary character or their limitations.

11. Componential analysis of individual terms

Rather than attempt to diagram all the relationships which exist between words, it is often more meaningful to analyze the various meanings from the standpoint of the glosses and the cultural components which are to be found in such uses of words. Diagram B consists of the same meanings of the Biblical Hebrew *kbd charted with five culturally relevant components.

	heavy	much	many	abun-dant	great	riches	re-spect	glory	slow	slug-gish	dull	bur-den-some	diffi-cult	grie-vous
Physical weight	+	±	±	±	±	+			±	±		+	±	±
Inertia	+	±	±						+	+	±	±	±	
Culturally desirable		±	±	±	+	+	+	+						
Culturally undesirable									±	+	+	+	+	+
Increased degree				+	+			+	±	±				+

DIAGRAM B

The meanings listed along the top of diagram B really represent certain classes of contexts in which the root *kbd may occur. It is not necessary to use such meanings in English, or any other language, for we could simply identify different contexts, but there would be a great many such columns, e.g. <u>heavy</u>, as a stone over a

grave, <u>much,</u> as of water in flood, <u>many,</u> as of men in battle array,
etc. By using the English terms <u>heavy, much, many,</u> etc., we group
contexts together. Moreover, this is done here on the basis of distinctions peculiar to English. If we should use another language, the
"grid" would, of course, appear somewhat different.

The components are selected on the basis of (1) their cultural
relevance and (2) the number of contexts in which they occur. The
choice of components is subject to the same dangers of subjectivity
as the determining of the themes of a culture. The ultimate validation
of either the cultural themes or the semantic components lies in the
degree to which they help describe (and hence to explain) the complex
nature of the multi-relational data. By applying such a componential
analysis to the semantic problems of a number of languages, we
should be able to refine our procedures and reduce the degree of subjectivity, but despite the recognized risks of subjectivity the advantages of such a technique seem to far outweigh its limitations.

The above diagram does not, of course, indicate all the
components which occur with these meanings (e.g. nonphysical dominance, as in <u>great</u> and <u>respect</u>), but only those which reveal the
broader patterns of relationships.

The plus sign means that the feature in question occurs; the
symbol ± means that the feature may or may not occur. A blank
indicates that the feature does not occur, but there is no attempt to
state whether the absence of such a feature is relevant in the context.
The occurrence of these symbols depends upon the cultural data of
the language in question. In this particular instance the close relationship between the meanings <u>heavy, riches,</u> and <u>burdensome</u> can
be readily understood if one considers the early nomadic culture
which gave rise to the use of *kbd in these diverse ethnolinguistic
contexts. The same heavy objects could be <u>riches</u> as well as <u>burden-
some,</u> depending upon the viewpoint.

One of the very evident problems involved in any type of
componential plotting which employs a grid dependent upon a foreign
language is an inevitable degree of skewing, despite all cautions which
may be taken. Hence, in order to appreciate somewhat more fully
the value of such an investigative and analytical procedure, we need

to apply it to the uses of a term in which there are no corresponding terms in the language of the analyst. Furthermore, there are many instances in which one cannot line up a series of so-called meanings as based upon distinctions in a foreign language, but one must employ a series of contexts as the basis for any horizontal listing.

A profitable example of the application of componential plotting to such a series in which we must speak of cultural contexts, rather than glosses, is provided by the use of jwok in Anuak, a Nilotic language of the Sudan. The following ten contexts include all the principal uses of the term in question, for which in most instances there is obviously no possible corresponding English gloss:

1. "The one who made the world and everything in it is jwok." In this type of context jwok is always referred to as a person, but any traits of personality are mentioned only in rather vague terms.

2. "The juu piny must be placated by offerings and sacrifices." The juu piny (juu is the plural form of jwok) are literally gods of the earth, most of whom seem to have been borrowed from the neighboring Nuers. For the most part they are malevolent and they differ in activity and power. The relationships (1) between the juu piny themselves and (2) between the juu piny and the creator jwok are not defined.

3. "The family shrines are jwok." Small village and family shrines mark places where the juu piny are propitiated by offerings and sacrifices.

4. "That grove of trees is jwok." A few places are regarded as jwok. They are not numerous, are generally quite isolated from any village, are for the most part avoided, and seem never to be the site of any community ritual.

5. "The medicine man is jwok."

6. "The white man is jwok." Any person who has special abilities (something which is regarded as true of all white men) is spoken of as jwok.

7. "Radios, cars, airplanes, phonographs, and electricity are jwok." Any object whose functioning is inexplicable in terms of the Anuak frame of reference is jwok.

8. "Anything startling is jwok." The one exception to this is the appearance of a ghost (spirit of a deceased person), which is called tĭpo.

9. "The sick man has been taken by jwok." In this type of context the creator jwok may or may not be implied.

10. "What can we do now? It all depends on jwok." When people give up hope, as in the case of apparent fatal illness, they insist that the outcome is up to jwok, but there is no evidence that they always have in mind the creator jwok.

The variety of these ten contexts in which jwok may be employed is so great that it seems almost impossible to 'define' jwok, if by definition we mean the traditional type of summary statement which will include all the attributes and functions. The word jwok not only includes what we generally regard as God (context 1), but also demons (context 2), mana (contexts 3, 4, 5, 6, 7, and 8), fate (context 10), the sacred (contexts 3 and 4), and the mysterious (contexts 8 and 9). At first glance the use of jwok seems to imply confused and inconsistent thinking, or at least a serious incapacity for analytical judgments. But this is not the case. From the Anuak viewpoint jwok is employed very consistently, for by it the Anuaks express clearly their view of the supernatural. A componential analysis of the meanings of jwok reveals some of the essential coherence and unity in this term (see Diagram C).

COMPONENTS	CONTEXTS									
	1	2	3	4	5	6	7	8	9	10
Extraordinary power	+	+			+	+	+	+	+	+
Personality										
non-human	+	+							±	±
human					+	+				
Fear	±	+	+	+	±	±	±	+	+	±
Respect	+	±	+	+	+	+	+		±	+
Unfamiliar cause-effect sequences							+	+	+	+
Objects			+	+			+			
Processes							+	+	+	+

DIAGRAM C

We have not indicated all the components which are present
in the various contexts, but we have listed those which are more significant and which indicate the unity and consistency of the Anuak
point of view. We have purposely omitted such components as ethical
vs. nonethical and secular vs. sacred for the very reason that these
distinctions in their traditional formulations are not particularly
valid or important in Anuak religious beliefs. It is true that the
creator jwok is usually benevolent and the juu piny are for the most
part malevolent; and yet the benevolent or malevolent characteristics
are not primary nor absolute, and they are never related to ethical
or nonethical standards. Similarly, though there is a sense in which
the Anuaks recognize a distinction between the secular and the sacred
(contexts 3 and 4), nevertheless, this distinction is very poorly defined and, in so far as it is employed, shows no one-to-one correspondence with jwok. In contexts 5 through 9 there is no special
evidence of taboo, and even in contexts 3 and 4 there is practically
no ritual avoidance nor any abrupt lines of demarcation.

According to the traditional method of defining meanings
there would be endless questions as to whether jwok meant a personal
God or an impersonal power. Componential analysis makes it possible to reject such an 'either-or' proposition in favor of the more
culturally relevant 'both-and' statement. The meaning of jwok cannot
be stated by means of any simple formula, but only in terms of the
culturally relevant component features which occur in different combinations in the diverse contexts.

NOTE

[1] Maurice Leehardt, Do Kamo: La Personne et le Mythe
dans le Monde Mélanésien (Paris: Gallimard, 1947, pp. 21-24).

2 Principles of Translation as Exemplified by Bible Translating

In terms of the length of tradition, volume of work, and variety of problems, Bible translating is distinctive. Beginning with the translation of the Hebrew Old Testament into Greek in the second and third centuries B. C. and continuing down to the present time, the Scriptures have been translated, at least in part, into 1,109 languages, of which 210 possess the entire Bible and 271 more the New Testament. This means that the major part of the Christian Scriptures exist in the languages of at least 95 per cent of the world's population. Moreover, most of this work has been accomplished in relatively recent times. By the time of the invention of printing, approximately 500 years ago, only 33 languages had anything of the Bible, and even by the beginning of the nineteenth century only 71 languages possessed anything of the Scriptures. However, within the nineteenth century more than 400 languages received something of the Scriptures, and during the first half of the twentieth century some part of the Bible was translated into approximately 500 more languages and dialects. At present the volume of translation and revision is of such magnitude that within the next twenty-five years as much will be published as within the entire nineteenth century, for more than a thousand persons are giving all or a major part of their time to the translation and revision of the Bible in various parts of the world.

The unparalleled range of Bible translating, including as it does not only all the major languages of the world but hundreds of "primitive" tongues, provides a wealth of data and background of experience in the fundamental problems of communication which constitute the basis of the following article.

Practical Nature of Problems in Bible Translating

Whereas for some people translating may be primarily a matter of theoretical interest, the Bible translator must face up to certain immediate problems. For example, if he attempts to translate literally the expression "he beat his breast" (speaking of the repentant publican, Luke 18:13), he may discover that, as in the Chokwe language of Central Africa, this phrase actually means "to congratulate oneself" (the equivalent of our "pat himself on the back"). In some instances it is necessary to say "to club one's head."

It is assumed by many people that the repetition of a word will make the meaning more emphatic, but this is not always the case. For example, in Hiligaynon (and a number of other Philippine languages), the very opposite is true. Accordingly, one cannot translate literally "Truly, truly, I say to you," for to say "truly, truly" in Hiligaynon would really mean "perhaps," while saying "truly" once is actually the Biblical equivalent.

Quite without knowing the reasons, we usually insist that, in rendering in another language a sentence such as "he went to town," one must use an active form of the verb meaning "to go." However, in many of the Nilotic languages of the Sudan it would be much more acceptable to say, "the town was gone to by him."

In still other instances one encounters what is regarded by some as a completely distorted orientation of experience. For example, in the Bolivian Quechua language it is quite possible to speak of the future, even as it is in any language, but one speaks of the future as "behind oneself" and the past as "ahead of one." When pressed for an explanation of such an expression, Quechuas have insisted that because one can see "in the mind" what has happened such events must be "in front of one," and that since one cannot "see" the future such events must be "behind one." Such a perspective of the past and the future is every bit as meaningful as our own, and it can certainly not be condemned as distorted. It is simply different from ours.

Accordingly, in such areas as (1) behavior as described by language (e.g., "beating the breast"), (2) semantic patterns (e.g., repetition of constituents), (3) grammatical constructions (e.g., active

vs. passive), or (4) idiomatic descriptions of "perspectives," the Bible
translator is faced with acute problems demanding answers. He knows
full well that reproducing the precise corresponding word may utterly
distort the meaning. Accordingly, he has been obliged to adjust the
verbal form of the translation to the requirements of the communicative process.

Underlying Principles

Though in many instances the principles underlying Bible
translating are only partially recognized or formulated by those engaged in such work, nevertheless the results of any accurate translating reveal the following basic principles:

1. Language consists of a systematically organized set of
oral-aural symbols. By oral-aural we are simply emphasizing the
fact that such symbols not only are uttered by the vocal apparatus of
the speaker but are also received and interpreted by the listener.
The writing system of any language is a dependent symbolic system
and only imperfectly reflects the "spoken-heard" form of language.

2. Associations between symbols and referents are essentially arbitrary. Even onomatopoetic forms bear only a "culturally
conditioned" resemblance to the sounds which they are designed to
imitate. For example, the equivalent of our tramp-tramp is kú·kà·
in Luvale, a Bantu language of Central Africa, and mingòdongòdona
in Malagasy.

3. The segmentation of experience by speech symbols is
essentially arbitrary. The different sets of words for color in various
languages are perhaps the best ready evidence for such essential arbitrariness. For example, in a high percentage of African languages
there are only three "color words," corresponding to our white, black,
and red, which nevertheless divide up the entire spectrum. In the
Tarahumara language of Mexico, there are five basic color words,
and here "blue" and "green" are subsumed under a single term. The
comparison of related sets of words in any field of experience—kinship terms, body parts, or classification of plants—reveals the same
essentially arbitrary type of segmentation. Since, therefore, no two
languages segment experience in the same way, this means that there

can never be a word-for-word type of correspondence which is fully meaningful or accurate.

4. <u>No two languages exhibit identical systems of organizing symbols into meaningful expressions</u>. In all grammatical features, that is, order of words, types of dependencies, markers of such dependency relationships, and so on, each language exhibits a distinctive system.

The basic principles of translation mean that no translation in a receptor language can be the exact equivalent of the model in the source language. That is to say, all types of translation involve (1) loss of information, (2) addition of information, and/ or (3) skewing of information. To understand clearly the manner in which such "distortion" takes place we must examine the ethnolinguistic design of communication.

Ethnolinguistic Design of Communication

By adopting the simpler components of the communication process and relating these to the entire communicative context, we may construct an ethnolinguistic design of communication as shown in Figure 1.

Figure 1

In the diagram of Figure 1 <u>S</u> stands for source (the speaker as source and encoder). <u>M</u> is the message as expressed in accordance with the particular structure (the inner square in this instance) of the language. The message may include anything from a single word to an entire utterance. <u>R</u> is the receptor (including decoder and receiver), and the outer square (designated by <u>C</u>) represents the cultural context as a whole, of which the message (as a part of the language) is itself a part and a model (compare similarity of shapes).

It is quite impossible to deal with any language as a linguistic signal without recognizing immediately its essential relationship to the cultural context as a whole. For example, in Hebrew the root *brk is used in the meaning of "to bless" and "to curse." Such meanings would only be applicable in a culture in which words in certain socio-religious contexts were regarded as capable of either blessing or cursing, depending upon the purpose of the source. Similarly *qdš, which is generally used in the sense of "holy," may also designate a temple prostitute, an association which would be impossible within our own culture, but entirely meaningful in a society which was well acquainted with fertility cults.

This emphasis upon the relationship of M to C must not, however, constitute an excuse for unwarranted etymologizing, in which meanings are read into words from historically prior usages, for example, treating Greek ekklesia "assembly" or "church" as really meaning "called out ones" (a contention of some Bible interpreters) because of an earlier use of the compound word.

Despite the recognition of the close connection between the M and C (that is, between the realities symbolized by the inner and outer squares), we must at the same time recognize the fact that every S (source) and every R (receptor) is a different individual in accordance with his background and is hence somewhat diverse in the use and understanding of M (the message). If we may describe each person's encoding-decoding mechanism as a kind of linguistic grid based upon the totality of his previous language experience, we must admit that each grid is different in at least some slight degree. This does not make communication impossible, but it removes the possibility of absolute equivalence and opens the way for different understanding of the same message.

In the communicative process, however, S and R generally recognize these matters of difference and tend to adjust their respective grids so as to communicate more effectively. For example, a speaker adjusts himself to his audience (if he wishes to communicate with any degree of effectiveness) and the audience, in turn, makes allowances for the background of the speaker. Furthermore, each participant in the S-M-R process is aware of such adjustments and tends to make reciprocal compensation so as to comprehend more

fully and correctly.[1] Communication is thus essentially a two-way
process, even though one person might be doing all the speaking.

One of the essential tasks of the Bible translator is to reconstruct the communicative process as evidenced in the written record
of the Bible. In other words, he must engage in what is traditionally
called exegesis, but not hermeneutics, which is the interpretation of
a passage in terms of its relevance to the present-day world, not to
the Biblical culture.

One interesting problem in exegesis which may be treated by
the method of reconstructing the communicative process is the formal
differences between the phrases "kingdom of God" (used exclusively
in the Gospel of Luke) and "kingdom of heaven" (used in most contexts
in the Gospel of Matthew). Most Biblical scholars have regarded these
two phrases as essentially equivalent, but there are some persons who
insist that they refer to two different "dispensations." The answer to
such a problem consists in reconstructing the facts of the communication: the Jewish taboo avoidance of Yahweh (and by extension other
terms referring to deity), the substitution of words such as "heaven,"
"power," and "majesty" for Yahweh, the Jewish background of the
writer of the Gospel of Matthew, the evident Jewish audience to which
the Gospel of Matthew is directed, the Greek background of Luke, the
Greco-Roman audience to which the Gospel of Luke was directed, and
the complete lack of any substitution device (such as "heaven" for
"God") on the part of the Greco-Roman community. These factors in
the communication process when considered in the light of the total
cultural context make the identification of the two phrases entirely
justified.

Two-Language Model of Communication

Up to the present time we have been discussing the translator's task in terms of the Biblical languages, but assuming, for the
sake of greater simplicity of statement, that the translator was a part
of the Biblical culture. This, of course, is not true, for though he
may be well acquainted with numerous aspects of this culture, he is
not, nor can he ever be, anything like a fully participating member.
Not only can the culture not be fully described, but it can most

certainly not be reproduced—despite Alley Oop's time-machine experiences.

The fact that English (the language which we shall, for our present purposes, assume as the language of the translator) is the means by which information concerning the Biblical culture is directly or indirectly gathered, e.g., through commentaries, dictionaries, and learned journals, is described diagrammatically in Figure 2.

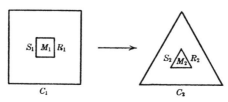

Figure 2

In this diagram the squares represent the Biblical language (for the sake of our diagram it makes no essential difference whether we are speaking of Greek, Hebrew, or Aramaic) and the triangles represent the "equivalent" communication in English. The subscript numerals help to identify the different components in these parallel instances of communication. A translator of the New Testament into English assumes the position of R_1, even though he can only approximate the role of a New Testament receptor. At the same time this translator becomes S_2, in that he reproduces M_1 as M_2, so that R_2 may respond in ways essentially similar to those in which the original R_1 responded.

Where there is a time gap between C_1 and C_2 the translator (S_2) can only be a kind of proxy R_1. However, a bilingual translator who participates fully in two linguistic communities may fulfill a dual role by being quite validly both R_1 and S_2.

Figure 2 serves also to emphasize two significant factors: (1) the essential differences in the form between M_1 and M_2, and (2) the relationship of M_1 and M_2 to their respective cultural contexts. Of course, the actual situation is not as simple as the diagram would imply, for nothing so complex as a language-culture relationship can possibly be reduced to a few lines. However, the differences are present and real and can be noted in all phases of the communicative

procedure. A few of these differences will enable one to understand
more fully certain of the broader implications of what we are only
able to hint at here.

Though as English-speaking people we employ a language
which is relatively closely related to Greek (certainly in comparison
with the differences between English and Hottentot), there are numerous basic differences. In the meanings of words, for example, we
have relatively few close correspondences. We use love to translate
certain aspects of the meanings of at least four different Greek words:
agapaô, phileô, stergô, and eraô, but these words also correspond to
such English meanings as "to like," "to appreciate the value of," "to
be friendly with," "to have affection for," and "to have a passion for."
Even a first-year Greek student will give the meaning of logos as
"word," but the Liddell and Scott dictionary lists more than seventy
different meanings—and these do not do full justice to the specialized
Biblical usage. However, Greek also has two other words, epos and
rhêma, which are likewise translated as "word" in many contexts.

The incommensurability between Greek and English is quite
evident in the differences between tense and aspect, a problem which
gives constant difficulty to a translator of the New Testament. This
problem is made all the more acute by the fact that the Hebrew of the
Old Testament employs a tense-aspect system which is quite different
from that of the Greek, but which is often reflected in the distinctive
Semitic coloring of many New Testament usages.

In the matter of arrangement of words, especially in the
marking of long series of dependent phrases and clauses, the English
language simply does not have the structural potentialities of Greek.
Accordingly, a stretch of speech which may be a perfectly good Greek
sentence (consisting, for example, of verses 3-14 of Ephesians 1) can
only be rendered intelligibly by several sentences in English.

Whether, then, in terms of the meanings of words or idioms
("heap coals of fire on his head," "bowels of mercy," or "the reins
and the heart") or of the grammatical categories or arrangements of
words, M_2 differs from M_1. However, this is not the whole story,
for most Bible translators are faced not with a two-language but a
three-language communication problem.

Three-Language Diagram of Communication

By means of one's own language—which in the case of English bears a close cognate relationship to Greek and reflects a considerable historical connection with the Biblical culture, even as Western culture took over much from the Judaeo-Greco-Roman world—one not only explores the Biblical languages but in large measure tends to mediate these data in communicating into another language. Accordingly, we may diagram this process (Figure 3).

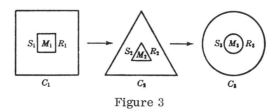

Figure 3

Of course, there are a number of translators who translate "directly from the original languages," but even then a high percentage of their responses to the forms of the original languages tend to be colored by the medium of study and analysis, namely, their own mother tongue. Their task, however, is to communicate the M_1 in terms of M_3, with the least possible skewing as the result of M_2. The problem is made more difficult in most instances by virtue of the fact that most languages do not have any historical connection with the Biblical languages, either by being members of the same language family or because of historical and cultural associations. However, there is one interesting fact, namely, that the so-called Biblical culture exhibits far more similarities with more other cultures than perhaps any other one culture in the history of civilization. This is not strange, if one takes into consideration the strategic location of this culture in the Middle East, at the "crossroads of the world" and at a point from which radiated so many cultural influences. This fact makes the Bible so much more "translatable" in the many diverse cultures of the world than most books coming out of our own contemporary Western culture. This essential similarity to the cultures of so many peoples helps to explain something of the Bible's wide appeal.

Definition of Translating

A definition of translating will inevitably depend in very large measure upon the purpose to be accomplished by the translation in question. However, since in Bible translating the purpose is not to communicate certain esoteric information about a different culture, but to so communicate that R_3 may be able to respond to M_3 in ways substantially similar to those in which R_1 responded to M_1, a definition of translating which is in accord with the best traditions of Biblical scholarship could be stated as follows: "Translating consists in producing in the receptor language the closest natural equivalent to the message of the source language, first in meaning and secondly in style. "

This type of definition recognizes the lack of any absolute correspondence, but it does point up the importance of finding the closest equivalence. By "natural" we mean that the equivalent forms should not be "foreign" either in form (except of course for such inevitable matters as proper names) or meaning. That is to say, a good translation should not reveal its non-native source.

It is recognized that equivalence in both meaning and style cannot always be retained—in the acrostic poems of the Old Testament, to cite an extreme example. When, therefore, one must be abandoned for the sake of the other, the meaning must have priority over the stylistic forms.

Differences of Formal Structure

In comparing the form of the Biblical message (M_1) with the corresponding form that must be employed in any other language (M_x), we are immediately impressed with the marked formal differences. We cannot, however, consider all these contrasts. Nevertheless, a brief statement of such problems as diversities in (a) word classes, (b) grammatical categories, and (c) arrangements of words can be illustrative of the basic principles involved in determining what is the "closest natural equivalence" in any given situation.

Word Classes

There is a great deal of difference between languages in respect to the word classes that are used to express certain ideas, for so often what is a noun in Greek must be rendered as a verb in other languages, and what is a pronoun in Greek or Hebrew frequently must become a noun in another language. Furthermore, adjectives in Greek or Hebrew are often verb-like words in other languages. Nevertheless, behind this apparent wide discrepancy in the word classes of various languages there are some astonishing similarities. In the first place, most languages described to date have been found to have "object words" (usually treated as noun-like words), "event words" (generally designated as verb-like), and at least some other classes, often pronouns, adjectives, and/ or relational particles. What is therefore more significant than the apparent differences between Greek and other languages (such differences are much more evident in New Testament translating than in the Old Testament) is a fundamental agreement between languages as to classes commonly called nouns and verbs.

What we designate as noun-like words and verb-like words are predominantly those which are (1) "object words" with more or less fixed figures or forms, tree, stick, hill, river, grass, rope, stone, sun, moon, star, canoe, dog, cat, head, foot, and (2) "event words," run, walk, jump, swim, see, hear, fight, hit, talk, make, and fly. It is possible that Gestalt psychology can provide certain important clues as to the reasons for this basic dichotomy in languages, though it is recognized that in many languages there is considerable overlapping of classes and shifting of terms from one class to another. The well-defined figure, as compared with the ground (to use Gestalt terminology), could provide us with the core of noun-like words (the so-called "object words"). The less well-defined figures representing movement, becoming, passing, or "eventing" would then be represented by the "event words," namely, the verbs. Certain characteristics held in common by various "object words," for example, red, yellow, true, good, kind, one, and two, would provide the abstracts generally designated as adjectives, and those designating common features of events, fast, suddenly, slowly, once, and twice, for instance, would correspond to adverbs, though in this there is also considerable overlapping and shifting of class membership. In addition to the word classes designating objects, events, and abstractions, there are the relationals, which describe relations between objects or between events. If such words are used primarily as relationals between objects, we call them preposition-like words, and if they indicate relations between events, they are generally classed as conjunctions, but here again there is a great deal of overlapping and shifting from one class to another.

The preceding paragraphs must not be interpreted as a defense of the Indo-European word class structure, nor of the fatal error of descriptive methodology in defining a noun as "the name of a person, place, or thing." Furthermore, we are not suggesting that these semantically important classes represent any inevitable direction of development for any language. In the Mayan languages, for example, the equivalents of English adjectives are for the most part a formal subclass of verbs, and the prepositions and conjunctions are predominantly noun-like words, though of a very restricted class. In Tarahumara certain object words (as judged in terms of the present semantic values) are certainly derived from event words, for example, pačiki "an ear of corn" (from pači "to grow ears of corn") and remeke "tortillas" (from reme "to make tortillas"). Nevertheless, despite such divergencies there is in most languages a sizable core of words which reflect distinctions explicable in terms of Gestalt psychology. Moreover, whether as major or minor classes, languages do tend to have four principal groups: object words (roughly equivalent to nouns), event words (roughly equivalent to verbs), abstracts (modifiers of object and event words), and relationals (roughly equivalent to prepositions and conjunctions in the Indo-European languages).

For the Bible translator the most serious problem relating to word classes is created by the fact that in Greek, and for that matter in most Indo-European languages, there is a marked tendency to use event words without reference to the objects or persons that may participate in such events. For example, in Mark 1:4 there is the clause "John preached the baptism of repentance unto the forgiveness of sins." All the nouns except John are essentially event words, but the participants in the events are not made explicit, and the relationships between the events are very ambiguously indicated. When, as in many languages, this type of expression must be translated not by a series of nouns but by verbs, the problem is difficult, for not only

must the participants be explicitly indicated (as required by verb constructions in question), but the relationships between the events must
be more explicitly stated. This means that such an expression in
many languages must be rendered as "John preached that the people
should repent and be baptized so that God would forgive the evil which
they had done. "

Similarly, it is quite impossible to say in many languages,
"God is love. " The word indicating "love" is essentially an event
word, and it cannot be combined as a kind of predicate complement
to a subject by means of a copulative verb. In other words, "love"
cannot exist apart from participants. One cannot say, therefore,
"God is love" but simply that "God loves. " This is, of course, essentially what the Biblical passage means, not that God is to be equated
with love, for the expression "God is love" can not be inverted into
"Love is God. "

Grammatical Categories

When a language possesses certain categories which are not
in Greek or Hebrew, the question arises as to whether the translation
should conform to the categories of the receptor language. If such
categories are obligatory there is really no alternative, unless one
wishes to produce a translation which is grammatically incorrect.
However, the problem is not quite so simple, for there are two types
of factors: (1) the nonexistent, ambiguous, obscure, implicit, or
explicit nature of the information in the source language, and (2) the
obligatory or optional character of the category in the receptor language.

The following outline indicates those types of situations in
the source and receptor languages which give rise to the most common
problems of equivalence:

A. Instances in which M_1 lacks information which is obligatory in M_x. For example, in Matthew 4:13 there is no information
available from the New Testament record as to whether Jesus had
ever visited Capernaum prior to his trip recorded at this point. When,
as in the Villa Alta dialect of Zapotec, spoken in southern Mexico, it

is obligatory to distinguish between actions which occur for the first
time with particular participants and those which are repetitious, one
must make a decision, despite the lack of data in the source language.
Since there is a greater likelihood that Jesus would have visited nearby Capernaum than that he would not have done so, the translation
into Villa Alta Zapotec reflects this probability, and there is accordingly a distinct increase in "information" in the translation. When,
however, such information is purely optional in a receptor language,
it is of course not introduced.

B. Instances in which information which is obligatory in M_x
is obscure in M_1. The status of Jesus as a rabbi was well recognized
by his friends and followers but was openly challenged by others. If,
accordingly, we must apply to the Gospel accounts the categories of
an honorific system (such as are common in the languages of Southeast
Asia), we cannot always be sure precisely what would be the relative
social position of Jesus and those who would speak to and of him.
Though considerable information is given, there is also real obscurity
at many points. If, however, the receptor language requires honorific
indicators, they must be added (with at least a partial increase in
information).

C. Instances in which information which is obligatory in M_x
is ambiguous in M_1. Though ambiguities also involve a degree of
obscurity, they are different from simple obscurities in that either
alternative seems to have almost equal validity. For example, in
John 4:12 the Samaritan woman speaks to Jesus of "our father Jacob,
who gave us the well." If we apply to this statement the inclusive-
exclusive first person plural dichotomy, which occurs in many languages, we can argue almost equally well for the inclusive form (assuming that the woman would be willing to admit that the Jews were
also descended from Jacob) or the exclusive form (reflecting something more of the traditional hostility between the Samaritans and the
Jews and the evident contrast mentioned in verse 20 of the same chapter). When the inclusive-exclusive distinction is obligatory in the
receptor language, the translator must make a decision, and regardless of the results there will be at least a partial increase in information. When, however, the receptor language allows such information to be optional, then the translator should retain the ambiguity
of the original.

   D. Instances in which information which must be made
explicit in M_x is only implicit in M_1. When information is implicit
in the source language context, but must be made explicit in the receptor language, there is actually no gain in information carried by the
message. It is merely carried in a different way—explicitly rather
than implicitly. For example, in John 4:20, when the Samaritan
woman is reported as saying, "Our fathers worshiped on this mountain; and you say that in Jerusalem is the place where men ought to
worship," there is no possible doubt as to the exclusive use of "our."
However, this fact is implicitly given, not explicitly so. In many
instances, however, what is quite implicitly understood in one language is not so understood in another, especially in those instances
where the cultural context is very different. For example, a literal
translation (one which translates only the strictly explicit features)
of Hebrews 7:3, "He is without father or mother or genealogy, and
has neither beginning of days nor end of life ..." is likely to be understood in many languages as implying that Melchizedek was a theophany,
rather than simply a person for whom there is no record of human
descent. Accordingly, to avoid serious misunderstanding it is often
necessary to make explicit in the receptor language (even on an optional and nonobligatory basis) what is only implicit in the source
language.

   E. Instances in which information which is explicit in M_1
must be differently treated in M_x. Explicit information in the source
language should be communicated in the receptor language. There
are, however, two exceptions to this general rule. In the first place,
the receptor language may not have a corresponding method of indicating such information. For example, in the Greek verb system
there are numerous subtle distinctions of aspect which cannot be translated into English without very heavy circumlocutions, which in the
end tend to make the aspectual distinctions far more explicit than they
were in the source language. Such translations involve a partial increase in information by virtue of their emphasis. In the second
place, when the indication of such information is optional in the receptor language, the frequency of occurrence of information of this
type may be quite different from what it is in the source language.
For example, in Greek and Hebrew number and tense are indicated
repeatedly, while in many languages number and tense may be indicated once within a context, but left implicit throughout the rest of
the passage in question. It is necessary that a translation indicate

such optional factors with a frequency which is comparable with what would normally occur, or the translation becomes unnatural, since the patterns of "redundancy" have been altered.

This outline of criteria for the addition or omission of information is applicable not only to the immediate problem of grammatical categories, but to any and all types of mensurability between the source and receptor languages.

Arrangements of Words

The same principles elaborated in the preceding section with regard to corresponding categories also apply in matters of arrangements of words, whether of order of words or of the number and types of dependencies. Of the numerous problems involved in grammatical arrangements of words, we can only touch briefly upon hypotactic and paratactic constructions. A language with a heavy hypotactic structure (e. g., Greek) simply makes explicit a number of relationships which are left implicit in a language which employs a paratactic type of structure (e. g., Hebrew). Unfortunately, there is a tendency to think that the hypotactic structure is fundamentally superior and that accordingly in translating into a language which has an essentially paratactic structure one should introduce (for example by overworking potential hypotactic patterns and by creating new grammatical forms or arrangements) the same number and types of hypotactic constructions as one finds in Greek. Such a procedure is quite unwarranted, for one should permit to be left implicit in the receptor language what is explicit in the source language if the receptor language in question would normally employ an implicit type of structure. The breaking up of long, involved sentences and the omission of corresponding conjunctions (provided such processes are carried out in conformity with the requirements of the receptor language) do not actually result in any loss of information. It simply means that the information is carried implicitly, rather than explicitly.

Hierarchy of Semantic Constituents

Despite our recognition of the fact that there are no complete synonyms, that is to say, words which may substitute for each other in all possible positions of occurrence, nevertheless, we do recognize that some words are substantially identical with others in the sense that they may be substituted for each other without any appreciable loss or change in meaning within a particular discourse. This is, of course, the experience of everyone who attempts to write without dull repetition of the same words. Not infrequently we need to mention the same referent, but stylistic considerations make it necessary for us to employ some other term which will serve the purpose. A brief examination of this process soon reveals that some words substitute for many words (words such as <u>thing</u>, <u>matter,</u> <u>object</u>, <u>feature</u>, <u>apparatus,</u> <u>this</u>, <u>he</u>, <u>they,</u> <u>go</u>, <u>come,</u> and <u>move</u> have a wide range of substitution), while other words may substitute for very few words (<u>raccoon</u>, <u>elephant</u>, <u>thimble,</u> <u>equator</u>, <u>seismograph,</u> <u>crawl</u>, <u>kiss,</u> and <u>assassinate</u>). If we group such words into related series and classify them on the basis of their range of substitution, we soon discover a series of hierarchies, ranging from the most concrete, "low-level" vocabulary at the base (with words having the greatest specificity), and the most generic, "high-level" vocabulary at the top (with words possessing the greatest degree of generality).

For the translator this factor of hierarchical series of concrete-generic vocabulary poses special problems, for though languages exhibit considerable agreement as to the segmentation of experience exhibited by the concrete vocabulary (for such segmentation is dependent largely upon "figure"-"ground" contrasts which are more or less well outlined, in terms of Gestalt psychology), the generic vocabulary, which is dependent upon the recognition of common features, is much more subject to differences of interpretation. Accordingly, it is much easier for the Bible translator to translate the Book of the Revelation, which is filled with symbols, of which the meaning is obscure though the language is specific and concrete, than the Gospel of John, of which the meaning is more evident but the language of a higher hierarchical level.

What makes such high-level generic vocabulary difficult to translate is not the fact that receptor languages lack such vocabulary, but that the generic vocabulary which does exist does not parallel the generic vocabulary of the Bible.

Unfortunately, there are two erroneous (and at the same time contradictory) impressions about so-called primitive languages. One

often hears, on the one hand, that a language exhibits a primitive
character since the language does not have any generic vocabulary,
but only specific terms. On the other hand, people not infrequently
lament the fact that a "primitive" language is inadequate as a means
of communication because the words in question cover too wide an
area of meaning, as for example in Anuak, a language of the Sudan,
in which the same word may designate anything made of metal, from
a needle to an airplane. The actual situation that one finds in languages is not the real absence of generic vocabulary, but its occurrence on different levels, and with difficult subpatterns of substitution.
For example, in Bulu, spoken in the Cameroun, there are at least
twenty-five terms for different kinds of baskets but no specific generic
term which includes just baskets and nothing else.[2] However, one can
refer to such objects by words which would have a higher-level value
than our word basket, namely, the Bulu equivalent of "thing," "object,"
or "it." On the other hand, there are not only many different specific
words for fruits, but a generic term for fruits as a whole, on a level
which more or less corresponds with our term. In Kaka, a related
language in the eastern part of the Cameroun, there are two generic
terms for fruits, one which includes bananas and pineapples, and
another which includes all other kinds of fruits (in terms of our meaning of fruit), plus testicles, glands, hearts, kidneys, eyeballs, soccer
balls, pills, and the seed of any fruit or plant.

Analytical studies of semantic problems in so-called primitive
languages reveal that the general proportion of specific to generic
vocabulary is not appreciably different from what it is in the languages
of so-called civilized societies. The reason for the false impressions
about specific and generic vocabulary is that people have wrongly expected generic vocabulary in various languages to exhibit the same
degree of correspondence which they have observed in the study of
specific vocabulary. Such is simply not the case, nor should one
expect this to be so, since specific objects provide a much surer
observable base of segmentation than the classification of objects,
events, abstracts, and relations, on the basis of shared or unshared
features. In other words, the more one depends upon the factors of
human "judgment" rather than responses to more or less immediate
perception, the greater will be the tendency to diversity.

Areas of Meaning and Amount of Information

The wider the area of meaning of a word (in terms of the wider segment of experience covered by a term) the greater is the likelihood of its statistical frequency of occurrence. This greater statistical frequency means that it tends to have a higher predictability of occurrence and hence greater redundancy. The greater the redundancy the less the information that is actually carried by the unit in question. This means that a translation made up primarily of words with wide areas of meaning does not carry the load of information which is often presumed.

There is, of course, another factor, namely, the transitional probabilities. If, for example, words with wide areas of meaning and hence greater frequency of occurrence in the language occur in unusual combinations and hence have low transitional probabilities in the particular context in question, the signal consisting of these words may still carry considerable information. Nevertheless, a translation made into any artificially restricted vocabulary will inevitably be one which carries less information than the original, unless extensive circumlocutions are employed and the meaning is thus "padded out."

There is a tendency for translators to overwork "good terms." They find certain expressions which may be used in a wide range of situations and hence employ them as frequently as possible. The result is often a marked rise of frequency, in contrast with normal usage, and the resultant loss in information because of their predictability within the Biblical context. In an analogous manner translators often feel compelled to translate everything in the source language, to the point of employing corresponding expressions in the receptor language with an unnatural frequency. For example in Greek almost all sentences begin with a connective, and the result is that the connectives have relatively less meaning than the corresponding connectives in English, which occur with much less frequency. If one translates all the Greek connectives, the result is actually over-translating, for the Greek words (with proportionately less meaning) are translated by corresponding English connectives (with proportionately more meaning). At the same time, while the occurrence of connectives with almost every sentence is a mark of good style in

Greek, this is certainly not the case in English. This problem becomes even more acute in a language which is predominantly paratactic in structure.

Endocentric and Exocentric Structures

In the same way that there are endocentric and exocentric constructions on a formal level, there are corresponding structures on a semantic level. For example, it is quite impossible to determine the meaning of "to heap coals of fire on one's head" by knowing the semantic distributions (types of discourse in which such words may be used) of all the component parts. The meaning of this idiom can be determined only by knowing the distribution of the unit as a whole. Accordingly, we regard it as a semantically exocentric expression. Since, however, the majority of expressions in any language are semantically endocentric, not exocentric, those who interpret the source language idioms as rendered in a receptor language are more likely than not to understand the expressions as endocentric rather than as exocentric (unless there are some special markers which provide the clues). That is the reason why, for example, in some of the languages of Congo this expression "heap coals of fire on one's head" was regarded as an excellent new means of torturing people to death, not a means of making them ashamed by being so good to them.

The problem of endocentric interpretation of exocentric expressions can, however, be overcome in part by certain markers. For example, many of the metaphors of the Scriptures—"I am the bread of life," "I am the door," "a camel through a needle's eye"— can be properly understood if they are made into similes—"I am like the bread which gives life," or "I am like a door." By the introduction of the equivalent of "like" the receptor is alerted to the fact that this is a kind of exocentric expression involving a "non-normal" extension of meaning.

Similarly the context may serve as a guide to interpretation. For example, idioms occurring in a poetical context will be more readily understood in their proper exocentric values, since the total context provides the clue to their correct interpretation.

Relationship of Linguistic Form to Semantic Function

In attempting to discover the closest natural equivalent, whether of meaning or style, one is always faced with the difficulty of finding corresponding forms with analogous semantic functions. On the level of the meaning of words in terms of their referents and their function in the cultural context (space does not permit us to deal with the parallel problems of corresponding styles), one is faced with the following types of situations:

1. <u>The nonexistence of a term (and its corresponding referent) in the receptor language, but with an equivalent function being performed by another referent.</u> For example, in some languages there is no word for "snow," for such a phenomenon is outside the realm of the people's experience. However, the widely used equivalent of the phrase "white as snow" is "white as egret feathers." Accordingly, in a translation this different referent with the corresponding function may be introduced. On the other hand, if "white as egret feathers" is not a regular expression for the meaning of very white, then the introduction of "egret feathers" is not an equivalent of "snow," and it would be more accurate to translate simply as "very, very white." The equivalence of the two expressions "white as snow" and "white as egret feathers" is not primarily a matter of the whiteness of the respective referents, but the recognition of this fact in the traditional use of referents in both the source and the receptor languages, respectively.

2. <u>The existence of the referent in the receptor language, but with a different function from what it has in the source language.</u> This means, for example, that "heart" in Greek must often be rendered by "liver," as in the Kabba-Laka language of French Equatorial Africa, by "abdomen," as in Conob, a Mayan language of Guatemala, and by "throat," as in some contexts in Marshallese, a language of the South Pacific. In languages in which "gall" stands for wisdom and a "hard heart" is a symbol of courage, the Bible translator is obliged to make certain adaptations or cause serious misunderstanding.

In some circumstances, however, the referent in the source language is such an integral part of the entire communication that it must be retained and the distinctive functions explained in footnotes.

This is true, for example, of such Biblical terms as "sheep," "sacrifices," and "temple."

3. The nonexistence of the referent in the receptor language and no other referent with a parallel function. In such circumstances the translator is obliged to borrow foreign words (with or without classifiers) or employ descriptive phrases. For example, he may borrow the names of precious stones, amethyst, ruby, pearl, or the names of classes of people, Pharisees and Sadducees. If he adds a classifier, with resultant expressions such as "valuable stone called amethyst" and "sect called Sadducees," he can do a good deal to compensate for the lack of correspondence between the receptor and the source language. By employing descriptive phrases, he may, for example, translate "phylacteries" as "little leather bundles having holy words written inside" (as has been done in the Navajo translation).

Within the brief scope of this essay it has been impossible to give adequate consideration to a number of significant matters: (1) stylistic parallels, a study for which certain special methods and techniques are required, (2) the influence of a translation of the Bible upon the meanings of words (that is, the important factor of the "Christianization of vocabulary," with a clear recognition of the limitations of such a process), and (3) the precise manner in which new developments in information theory, and in the broader field of cybernetics, are integrally related to Bible translating; though anyone in these fields of study will appreciate the degree to which the above analysis is dependent upon these relatively new disciplines.

In summary, however, it is essential that we point out that in Bible translating, as in almost all fields of translating, the most frequent mistakes result from a failure to make adequate syntactic adjustments in the transference of a message from one language to another. Quite satisfactory equivalents for all the words and even the idioms may have been found, but a person's oversight or inability to rearrange the semantic units in accordance with the different syntactic structure immediately stamps a translation as being "foreign" and unnatural. These most numerous errors are not, however, the most serious, for though they may be wearisome and frustrating, they do not usually result in the serious misunderstandings which arise because of a lack of cultural adjustments.

When there are inadequate equivalents in the formal patterning of sentences (i. e. , mistakes in syntax), we generally recognize such faults at once and either excuse them, or at least are able to discount them in trying to ascertain the meaning. Mistakes in cultural equivalence, however, do not carry with them such obvious clues, and hence the lack of agreement is not understood nor the source of the error detectable from the text itself.

Though it is fully recognized that absolute communication is quite impossible, nevertheless, very close approximations to the standard of natural equivalence may be obtained, but only if the translations reflect a high degree of sensitivity to different syntactic structures and result from clear insights into cultural diversities.

NOTES

[1] A person with ill-will toward an S will purposely not make such an adjustment and will attempt to lift words out of context or not make allowance for background. Similarly, an S may have a haughty disregard for R, or be more interested in leaving an impression of his erudition than in communicating any set of facts.

[2] The following data on Bulu and Kaka were supplied in private correspondence by William D. Reyburn.

3 | Linguistic and Semantic Structure

The principal reason why traditional treatments of meaning have not revealed the semantic structure of a language is that they are predominantly concerned with the referent. Such a preoccupation with the referent rather than the symbol is quite understandable, since the very symbolic character of language points away from itself and the linguistic form is treated as only a label for the "real thing." At this point, however, the analyst has usually run aground on the shoals of epistemology, for some persons have insisted that one cannot arrive at any valid observations about the meaning of a term when there is no positive evidence for a satisfactory linking of symbol and referent. If one takes seriously this type of objection, then the tendency is to become involved in philosophical speculations about "ideal objects." But such philosophically fascinating problems do not materially help in resolving such relatively simple problems as the semantic relationships between such words as chair, stool, bench, and pew. We become hopelessly lost if we attempt to treat the relationships between the components of such a series of words by setting out to describe and classify all the different types of chairs, stools, benches and pews.

There are several reasons why the approach to semantic structure through the classes of referents is not very rewarding. In the first place, the relationship between each referent and corresponding symbol is essentially arbitrary. Words such as horse, cow, fox, and whale do not suggest by their forms any means for classifying the differences between the referents, nor do the linguistic forms help us to know, for example, that these four referents contrast (1) with possum and kangaroo, which are mammals, but non-placental, and (2) with wasp and ant, which are arthropods, not vertebrates. Even the onomatopoetic vocabulary of any language is essentially arbitrary, for no two languages have the same types of sound mimicry.

In the second place, related "experience" is broken up by languages into arbitrary segments. The different ways in which the colors of the spectrum are grouped by series of color words is striking evidence of this arbitrary segmentation.

In the third place, there is a conspicuous lack of agreement between (1) word classes, as defined by structural form, and (2) referent classes, as defined in any number of ways, e. g., shape, position, animate-inanimate, object-event, and real-unreal. One distinction which apparently exists to some extent in all languages is a contrast between object words (usually called nouns) and event words (usually called verbs). But this very fundamental distinction is in no instance carried out systematically throughout a given language. In English, for example, there are thousands of words, e. g., inspection, avoidance, baptism, peace, faith, work, and growth, which are formally nouns, but which are semantically "event words," and hence to this extent more closely relatable to verbs. In Navajo there is also an important noun-verb formal dichotomy, but the verbs not only indicate events but some verbs identify the types of objects involved in the event, e. g., áál̜ ' to handle one round or bulky object'; gheel̜ 'to handle a load or pack'; leel̜ 'to handle a slender flexible object'; and jol̜ 'to handle non-compact matter (e. g., wool)'. However, the incorporation of the type of object involved in an event is not systematically indicated in all verbs, but only in a relatively small class. To find this extent, therefore, the parallelism between the noun-verb formal classes and the object-event semantic classes breaks down. In the Maya language of Yucatan there are some words which function syntactically as conjunctions and which must be formally classified as particles. On the other hand there are a number of other words having completely parallel conjunctive functions (i. e., with identical types of distributions) which are formally possessed nouns. For example, yetel 'and' is actually a possessed noun meaning 'its (his or her) withness' and is declinable like any other noun. This lack of complete parallelism between formal and semantic classes means that any attempt to discover the semantic structure of a language by basing the analysis upon a classification of the referents is doomed to failure.

The agreement between the linguistic and the practical-world categories has been sufficiently similar as to encourage attempts to relate the two into a single system. Perennial discussions about the fundamentally logical character of languages stem from just such circumstances. However, there has always been such an untidy residue of data which have not fit into such classifications that most analysts have become skeptical of obtaining valid results from further attempts along the same lines, since there is scarcely a single feature of a language which wholly confirms this much proclaimed "logic." For example, the category of number in a language such as English is full of forms which do not fit in any formal-semantic classification (i.e., one which attempts to combine form and meaning into one classificatory system), e.g., oats, wheat, people, salmon, and scissors. Similarly, a so-called present-tense form in English may be used not only for present events, but for tenseless events (e.g., he comes every day at ten o'clock), for future events (e.g., if he comes tomorrow, I will speak to him), and for past events (e.g., he comes and hits him right in the mouth before anyone could do anything).

Independence of Formal and Semantic Structure from Referent Classes

In order to understand what can and should be done to discover the semantic structure of a language we need to realize not only that formal and semantic structures are different from each other, but also that neither the formal nor the semantic structure can be determined or described if the referents are made the basis of classification. In the case of the formal structure of a language this should be perfectly evident, for as long as the "meaning" of words remained the determining factor in structural analysis the results were hopelessly confusing. For example, as long as a noun was defined as "a name of a person, place or thing," it was impossible to bring any order out of chaos. If masculine, feminine, and neuter genders are to be satisfactorily described for any Indo-European language, they cannot be based upon biological sex-distinctions or even upon any analogically derived extensions of these distinctions. Descriptive linguistic methodology became fully useful only when it repudiated all attempts to tie it to meaning in this sense.

As a result of this type of emancipation from so-called "meaning categories," descriptive linguistic procedures could describe units (from simple to complex) and their distribution. This distribution was in terms of (1) the range of such units and (2) the classes of substitutability, e.g., the relationships of such units to other units having different, similar, and overlapping ranges of distribution. This resulted in a series of classes and subclasses with definable relationships within the total hierarchy of the language structure.

The same type of procedure is necessary in the case of semantics. In order to discover the semantic structure of a language we must be concerned with the semantic units and their distribution within the linguistic discourse, not with the referents and their classification in the non-linguistic world. The distribution which concerns us is not describable in terms of the practical-world context (i.e., the when, where, and how of the use of the referents) but in terms of the linguistic context (i.e., the when, where, and how of the use of the semantic units). Of course, as we shall find, there will always be a relationship between these contexts, presuming, that is, that language has meaning for life in general, but the semantic structure is to be defined exclusively on the basis of semantic units and their distribution within languages, and practical-world contexts may be overlooked for the time being. Only after we have defined the semantic structure in terms of the linguistic context can we profitably proceed to make observations about the correspondence between the structures in question. This type of procedure may seem strange, but it is completely justified. It is precisely what has been done on a formal level. In formal analysis we exclude "meaning," in the sense that we describe the structure purely in terms of forms and distributions. Later, and on quite a different level of discourse, we may do anything we like about pointing out parallelisms between these formal linguistic classes and the classifications of referents (such as biologists, psychologists, or philosophers might make), but such observations are not a part of the formal structural analysis. Similarly, in order to determine the semantic structure, we should exclude a consideration of the referents themselves and attempt to describe the distributions of semantic units within the total discourse of a language in question. This may seem like determining the semantic structure without recourse to meaning. If by "meaning" one implies consideration of the nature of the referents, then this is what we are advocating.

The fundamental differences between the linguistic and the practical-world contexts and between the formal and semantic distributions may be illustrated by the distribution of chair in the following contexts in English:

1. sat in a chair
2. the baby's high-chair
3. the chair of philosophy
4. has accepted a university chair
5. chairman of the meeting
6. will chair the meeting
7. the electric chair
8. condemned to the chair

In describing the formal structures involved in the distribution of chair, we are concerned with (1) chair as a component in the morphological structures of the compounds high-chair and chairman, e.g., that chair is the head of an attributive endocentric adjective-noun construction in high-chair but is the attributive endocentric noun-noun construction in chairman, and (2) the distribution of chair (as a noun or verb) in the second member of an exocentric phrase; in 3, the head of a noun phrase with preposed articular determiner and postposed prepositional phrase; in 4, the head of a noun expression (functioning as object of the verb) with preposed determiner and noun attributive; in 6, the second member of a verb phrase, which in turn is the head of the predicate construction; in 7, the head of an attributive endocentric noun-noun construction; and in 8, head constituent of the second member of an exocentric phrase.

By comparing our descriptions we find that chair in items 2 and 5 is treated formally under word-forming construction (i.e., in the morphology), while the rest of the items come under syntax. (This distinction between morphology and syntax in English is based upon relative degrees of structural cohesion as indicated in the patterns of distribution.) From the standpoint of purely formal syntactic structure of the phrases containing chair, the following sets of items are parallel: 1 and 8, 4 and 7.

If, however, we examine these same sentences from the standpoint of the semantic structure we will discover quite different alignments, but it will not be so easy for us to point out the distinctions without appearing to bring in additional data. Actually, of course, in our descriptions of the formal structure we assigned names to structures, not solely upon the basis of the data before us but as the result of comparing by implication many other related formal structures. We shall have to do the same thing in connection with the semantic structure. However, the additional data are not what we know about the various kinds of <u>chairs</u> referred to in the eight expressions, but the kinds of discourses in which the word <u>chair</u> may occur. For example, we can cite a number of contexts in which <u>chair</u> can be used in different syntactic positions. For instance we may say:

> He sat in the chair.
> I saw the chair in Macy's window.
> I would like to buy the chair for Tom.
> The chair is so comfortable.
> How much does the chair cost?

There are any number of different kinds of chairs that we could speak about in just such a series of contexts (which for convenience we will label type A). From the standpoint of the formal syntactic distribution the word <u>chair</u> in these various sentences plays quite a different role, but from the standpoint of the semantic distribution it is essentially identical, for it may be said that all the sentences may be employed in speaking about one and the same object. However, for our purposes the important fact is that this word <u>chair</u> may be substituted for by <u>piece of furniture</u>. Such a substitution is quite possible in sentences of context type A without shifting the subject of discourse or changing the semantic relationships between the parts.

In the analysis of the formal structure we found that <u>chair</u> in items 1 and 8 had essentially the same distribution, but we cannot extend the use of <u>piece of furniture</u> in contexts illustrated by items 7 and 8. For example, such combinations as *<u>the electric piece of furniture</u> and *<u>condemned to the piece of furniture</u> indicate clearly that <u>chair</u> in phrases 7 and 8 has quite a different semantic distribution. The <u>con</u>-texts in which this second use of chair does fit include:

> the electric chair
> condemned to the chair

> awaited the chair in cell block 13
> deserves the chair because of his crime

We may speak of these phrases as being illustrative of a "second use" of chair; but in doing this, we are not simply trying to dodge the use of the word "meaning." We are trying to point out that there is a distributional, and hence structural, validity for the distinction. For example, we may readily substitute death for three of the four contexts of type B, while in many contexts death may substitute for the fuller phrase electric chair:

> condemned to death
> awaited death in cell block 13
> deserves death because of his crime

The details of the problems of range of distribution and substitution will be treated in later sections of this paper, but at present we are concerned with the problem of pointing out (1) the differences between the formal and semantic structures as revealed by the range of distributions of semantic units and (2) the ways in which different semantic units substitute for each other. Suffice it to say, however, that when we do substitute one word or unit for another, we must not violate the semantic relationships of the parts nor the semantic value of the whole. This is the same procedure which we employ in making substitutions on a formal level of analysis, for we must not change the structural relationships of the parts (i.e., the related series of immediate constituents) nor the structure of the whole.

A further glance at the original series of eight items containing chair shows us that though the uses of chair in 5 and 6 are formally very different, they are semantically very similar. The type of context 5 and 6 may be called type C, e.g.,

> chairman of the meeting
> will chair the conference
> chairman of the board
> would not chair the convention
> hates to be chairman of anything

In contexts of type C we may substitute preside over (or preside at), e.g.,

preside over the meeting
preside over the conference
preside over the board
would not preside over the convention
hates to preside over anything

There is still another type of context (type D) represented in items 3 and 4:

the chair of philosophy
has accepted a university chair

There are of course many additional contexts which parallel these two, e.g.,

He does not want to give up his chair in the humanities.
They are competing for the chair of ancient history.
Who wants a chair in that department anyway?

For chair in contexts of type D, we can usually substitute position or post, e.g.,[1]

his position in the university[2]
He has accepted a university position.
the post of philosophy
his post in the humanities
a post in that department

There are a number of implications in what we have done in tracing the distributions of chair in terms of formal and semantic distribution, but these will be explained more fully in later sections. What we have tried to do up to this point is simply to indicate that (1) the formal and semantic distributions of units such as chair may be quite different and (2) the range of distribution is determined not on the basis of the referents of chair in the practical-world situation, but on the basis of linguistic contexts in which chair occurs. Furthermore, the different types of contexts have not been determined by arbitrarily assigned distinctions in meaning but by processes of substitution, involving partial overlapping of distribution of terms having related semantic distributions.[3]

Semantic Units

The semantic units which we must recognize and the distribution we must describe include theoretically everything from the morpheme to the total discourse. Within this range, however, there are three principal levels which require consideration and on the basis of which the larger structures are generally describable: the morpheme, the derivative layer formation, and the semantically exocentric phrase.

The individual morpheme is the fundamental semantic unit, but it is not easy to describe the semantic distribution of some morphemes, e. g. , bound roots occurring with bound morphemes having limited distributions: -ceive (as in receive, deceive, perceive, etc.) and cran- (as in cranberry). Morphemes which have a wide range of distribution and especially those which substitute for many other morphemes have a distribution which is in a sense more easily described, even though the structure is far more complex.

In the description of the distribution of semantic units, it is useful to make a distinction between derivative and inflectional layer formations, for the relevant semantic context of inflectional morphemes is generally not the immediate words with which such sound morphemes occur, but the broader context of the complete sentence or larger unit of discourse. For example, if one is describing the semantic distribution of the Spanish first-person singular suffix -é, as in cantaré 'I will sing,' it really is not particularly pertinent that it is suffixed to future stem forms. What is more significant is that this is just one of several semantically related forms which identify the first-person singular participant in expressions which have very different formal structures, e. g. , para mí 'for me,' mi amigo 'my friend,' me pegó 'he hit me,' and Juan y yo 'John and I.' From the standpoint of the significant distribution of the semantic units we should not treat cantaré as a single unit, but as three separable units: the root cant-, the future formative -r, and the first-person suffix -é. The element cant- 'sing' should be described in terms of all the contexts in which it may occur and the situations in which similar words may substitute for it, e. g. , gorjear, trinar and arrullar. Likewise, we should treat the future formative -r not merely on the basis of its suffixation to verb stems such as canta-, but as a form paralleled by other means of expressing future tense, e. g. , the verb ir, as in voy a cantar 'I'm

going to sing,' a phrase which may substitute for cantaré in a number
of contexts. [4]

Another approach to this same problem of determining the
significant semantic units may be illustrated from Classical Greek.
For example, in analyzing the semantic distribution of the elements
in the Greek word pepoiēka 'I have done,' we distinguish between the
derivative layer poiē- 'to do' (in this case the stem) and the perfect
inflectional elements pē ... ka, indicating first singular perfect
active indicative. The pertinent semantic environment of the root
poi- or the stem poiē- (i.e., its semantically relevant distribution)
is not the inflectional affixes of the perfect tense but all the contexts
in which poi- (or poiē-), in whatever tense form, may occur.

Perhaps the relevance of this distinction between syntactic
and derivational layer formations may become more obvious by noting
certain problems involved in the verb structure of Congo Swahili. The
verb tutakamupika 'we will hit him' is made up of tu- 'we', taka- future
tense prefix, mu- 'him', pik 'to hit' and -a a modal suffix. In our
analysis of the semantic structure, our basic concern is not to describe where in the total discourse of the language this particular form
tutakamupika may occur, but all the semantic contexts in which each
of these elements including the root pik- may occur.

On the one hand, in the interests of relevant semantic distribution our procedure results in breaking up some types of morphological structures. On the other hand, we must frequently recognize
as semantic units certain formal structures consisting of several
words. For example, we must treat as a single unit a phrase such
as "heap coals of fire on his head." There is no way in which we can
"predict" the distribution of the whole from any analysis of the distribution of the parts. The fact that the semantic distribution of this
phrase is different from the total of the distributions of the parts leads
us to assign this an exocentric status, in contrast with most combinations of words, which are endocentric. For example, we may say
that the semantic distribution of he is in the house is predictable (or
describable) in terms of the range of distribution of the constitutent
parts. However, he is in the doghouse is not the same type of expression. If, as is not likely the case, he is actually in the doghouse,
then the phrase would be endocentric; but the far greater probability

is that this phrase means that the man is in trouble with his wife.
This quite different "meaning" (from our standpoint, a different range
in distribution) cannot be determined by knowing the range of the individual parts, but by ascertaining the distribution of the phrase as a
whole. While a phrase such as a pain in the neck may have either an
endocentric or an exocentric meaning, some expressions are only
exocentric in meaning, e.g., horsefeathers and hens' teeth.

Range of Distribution of Semantic Units

In most descriptive linguistic analyses, the principle of
distribution of semantic units has been recognized but only very indirectly. When, for example, it is stated that a particular class of
qualitative adjectives may precede a certain class of nouns, it is taken
for granted that not all of the adjectives necessarily occur with every
noun. For instance, big may be in a class of adjectives including
white, black, fine, good, and strong, which may be preposed to a
group of nouns including boy, girl, house, and wool. All the combinations are possible except *big wool. We simply assume that all the
combinations occur, "subject to the limits of semantic possibilities."
But it is just this description of the limits of semantic possibilities
which concerns us now. We are interested in precisely how many
words or phrases may be modified by (or occur with) big, for that is
the semantic distribution of big. In English we may use big with such
words as man, monkey, rock, cloud, and rain, but we do not say *big
atmosphere and *big buoyancy. This limitation is significant, for
such restrictions on distribution cannot be attributed to any derived
qualities of the word big. The essentially arbitrary character of such
distributional limitations may become clearer if we compare the distribution of English big with a corresponding word grande in Spanish.
The word grande, generally translatable as 'big,' has much the same
range of distribution as English big, in that it may occur with the
Spanish equivalents of 'man', 'monkey,' 'rock,' and 'cloud,' but it
cannot be used with lluvia 'rain.' In Spanish one may use a variety
of terms (varying considerably from one locality to another), including
aguacero, tempestad, and temporal, but not *lluvia grande.

While in this particular detail the distribution of the Spanish
term grande is more restricted than English big (though the former

may occur in a number of semantic contexts in Spanish from which in
corresponding English contexts <u>big</u> would be excluded), the Spanish
word <u>hacer</u> 'to do, to make' has an exceedingly wide distribution,
including <u>hace sol</u>, literally 'makes sun,' but meaning 'the sun is
shining.' But the corresponding English combination *<u>makes the sun</u>
is meaningless, or ridiculous. The point of these comparisons is
not, however, the fact that Spanish and English (or any two languages
for that matter) are different, but that the range of distribution of any
semantic unit is essentially arbitrary. For example, we may speak
of <u>whalebone</u>, but in French one must say <u>barbe de baleine,</u> literally
'whale's beard.' The range of distribution of English <u>bone</u> or French
<u>barbe</u> is not determined by the nature of the referent involved (it is
the same material in either case), but is an arbitrary "property" of
the respective words <u>bone</u> and <u>barbe</u>. By "property," however, we
mean only that it occurs with a particular distribution.

There is a sense in which we already recognize this principle
of range of distribution, namely, in describing meaning in terms of
so-called areas. For example, if we describe the meaning of such
Greek words as <u>agapaô</u> 'to love (appreciation),' <u>phileô</u> 'to love, to like
(friendship),' <u>eraô</u> 'to love (passion),' and <u>stergeô</u> 'to love (family
relationships)' in terms of the total number of situations in which such
words may be employed, we approximate the point of view indicated
here. However, for our purposes the distribution of these terms
should be on the basis of the range of linguistic discourses in which
they may occur, not on the basis of the practical-world circumstances.
Though the latter may be more easily summarized, they are not adequate in describing the complete range of distribution.

<u>Substitutability</u>

Substitutability is common enough to us on a formal level of
structural analysis, but in terms of semantic distribution it is known
for the most part only on the practical level of stylistic avoidance of
words. For example, stylistically acceptable writing frequently involves the substitution of words which are semantically equivalent in
order to avoid "unpleasant" repetition. Rather than use <u>finished</u> three
or four times in close succession we may in many contexts use <u>com-
pleted</u>, <u>accomplished</u>, or <u>done</u> to substitute for <u>finished</u>. It is quite

true that there is a slight difference in meaning, but the "native speaker" will often insist that such words mean the same. Not infrequently one hears such statements as, "It's the same thing in different words." That is to say, within the limits of the particular contexts two different words (or semantic units) may be recognized as completely equivalent, and thus freely substitutable, one for the other.

The extent to which words are freely substitutable for each other defines the degree of synonymity between them. This may vary from substitutability in a single context to almost complete substitutability. However, it is doubtful if one can find in any language any two (or more) words which are completely substitutable in all contexts.[5] It often happens that corresponding longer and shorter forms exhibit a high degree of substitutability. For example, one may employ phone in numerous contexts in which telephone is also used, e.g., he telephoned, he phoned; we have a telephone, we have a phone; a telephone booth, a phone booth; a telephone call, a phone call; but only telephone operator, telephone pole, and telephone line.

By stating that two forms are freely substitutable we do not wish to imply that they are exactly equivalent and that there are no perceptible differences in the meanings of the respective expressions. There are recognizable differences, and these bear an interesting analogy to distinctions on the allophonic level. For instance, we claim that two allophonically different sounds may vary freely in a particular word; but nevertheless, these distinctions may signal some important facts about (1) the background of the speaker (e.g., his dialect and education) and (2) his emotional state. Similarly, the selection of one or another alternate of two substitutable words may tell us a good deal about the speaker's home background, education, and circumstances of speaking (including such matters as emotional tensions and accomodations of his dialect to the audience in question).

Hierarchical Structure

The study of substitutability within semantic contexts reveals certain very important differences between words. Some words substitute for many words, others for very few, and still others for none at all. This gives us a clue as to a hierarchical system, which though exceedingly complex is the framework of the semantic structure. In English, words which have a very wide domain of substitution include the pronouns he, she, it, and they. Of these words they has the widest domain (if singular and plural are equated), and the pronominal sets (1) he, she, it, (2) who, which, and (3) that and this follow in the next hierarchical level. These last three sets criss-cross each other's substitution domain. On lower substitutional levels one encounters a host of classes and sub-classes. A word such as animal may substitute for numerous other words such as dog, rat, beaver, and in some contexts even for man. But in popular usage animal is not a substitute for sparrow, robin, or hawk, except in the trichotomous classification of vegetable, animal, or mineral. For most people animal does not substitute for fish, e.g., trout, barracuda, or shark, except in a rather technical kind of context, but for many of these same people animal may freely substitute for whale, porpoise, or seal. However, for others fish rather than animal is the proper substitute for such sea mammals. The word whale itself is a type of generic substitute for words denoting various types of whales as well as for one individual whale, Moby Dick. [6]

In German the word Walfisch 'whale' gives a clue to its traditional substitute, namely Fisch, further evidenced in the term Fisch bein 'whalebone.' We are, however, concerned only with the patterns of substitution, not with the validity of the implied zoological classification of the referents.

In Miskito, an Indian language of Honduras and Nicaragua, some important substitutions which may be diagrammed as follows: [7]

Diagram 1

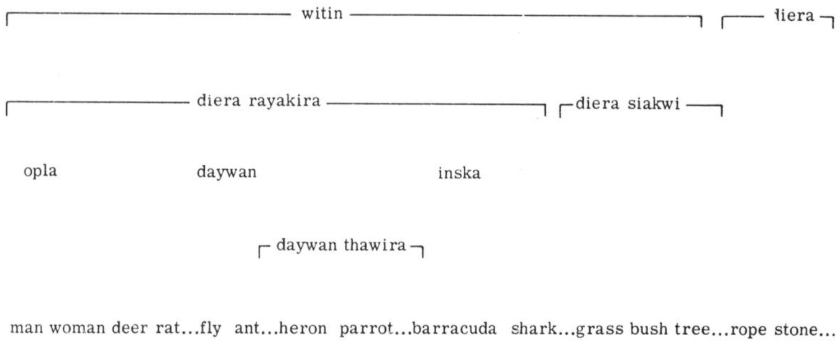

```
┌──────────────────── witin ─────────────────────┐   ┌── tiera ─┐


┌──────────── diera rayakira ──────────────┐ ┌─diera siakwi ──┐

  opla              daywan                  inska


                ┌─ daywan thawira ─┐

man woman deer rat...fly ant...heron parrot...barracuda shark...grass bush tree...rope stone...
```

On the bottom line we have listed the English equivalents, so that the semantic structure of the Miskito substitution patterns might be more evident. However, the Miskito words which would normally occupy the bottom line are by no means the lowest level in the system of substitution, for they are themselves generic terms. For example, 'man' and 'woman' are substitutes for numerous proper names of people, and the terms for 'deer' and 'rat' include several sub-classes.

The generic terms in the ascending ranks of substitution include not only such single words as opla 'people' and inska 'fish' and diera 'things' but the phrases daywan thawira 'animals with wings,' diera rayakira 'things with life,' and diera siakwi 'green things.' It may be argued that such phrases are only descriptive phrases such as anyone might make up to identify any class of objects. However, these phrases are conventional designates for the classes in question and within the system of substitution function the same as any single term. Note that rayakira 'with life' and siakwi 'green' do not sub-divide a class of diera 'things.' That is to say diera is not a substitute for diera rayakira and diera siakwi. This means that these phrases are semantically exocentric and as such must be treated as semantic units. For such phrases one must employ the substitute witin, which in English would be translated variously as he, she, or it, but would not be equivalent in substitution domain to such English pronouns.

In English the patterns of substitution are somewhat different. If we take this same series of terms and analyze the patterns of substitution on the basis of non-scientific popular usage, we may find in the speech of many, but by no means all speakers of English, the following type of structure:

Diagram 2

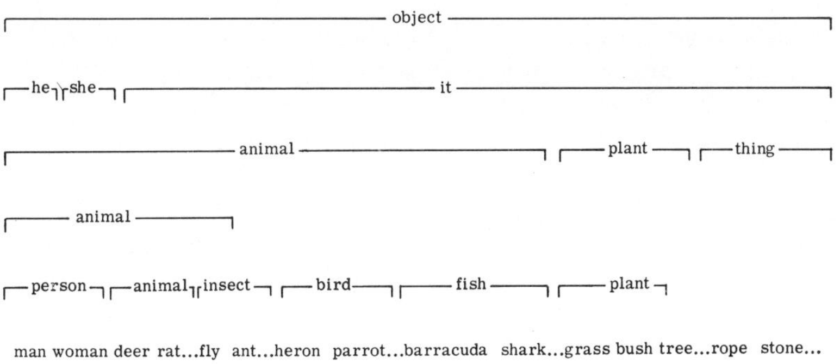
object
he
she
it
animal
plant
thing
animal
person
animal
insect
bird
fish
plant
man woman deer rat...fly ant...heron parrot...barracuda shark...grass bush tree...rope stone...

This type of diagram suggests several problems:

1. The same word may occur as a substitute on different levels. For example, <u>animal</u> contrasts with <u>person</u> on one level but includes human beings on another. Similarly, <u>animal</u> as a substitute on the second level may stand in contrast with <u>insect</u>, <u>bird</u>, and <u>fish</u>, but on the third level, when it is in contrast with <u>plant</u>, it includes <u>insect</u>, <u>bird</u>, and <u>fish</u>.

2. There are differences of usage. Some persons insist that they would never call a tree a plant, regardless of the hierarchical level, but others do so freely.

3. Substitutes cannot be so neatly pyramided as the above diagram presupposes. For instance, <u>she</u> is not only an obligatory substitute for <u>woman</u>, but an optional substitute for such other objects as large sex-distinctive animals, birds, ships, and institutions.

4. There is a considerable degree of overlapping of parts of classes, especially in limited contexts. For example the word <u>thing</u> has a very wide substitution domain in the negative, where it may substitute for animals (<u>we didn't shoot a thing</u>), for fish (<u>we didn't catch a thing</u>), and for almost any object, including persons (<u>we didn't see a thing</u>).

5. To say that one term may substitute for another does not mean that the two terms are completely synonymous. Synonymity depends upon the percentage and types of contexts in which the terms in question may substitute for each other. For two or more terms to be highly synonymous, they should not only occur in many similar contexts but should be substantially on the same hierarchical level. Actually, if two words are not on the same hierarchical level, the percentage of similar contexts is not likely to be very large. For example, <u>sorcery</u> and <u>witchcraft</u> may be regarded as highly synonymous because they are freely substitutable in a high percentage of their mutual contexts. However, <u>magic</u>, though it may substitute for <u>sorcery</u> and <u>witchcraft</u> in a number of contexts, also substitutes for <u>necromancy</u> and <u>legerdemain</u>, as well as for such phrases as <u>mysterious enchantment</u>, <u>the use of occult powers</u>, and <u>the manipulation of supernatural influences</u>. This means that <u>magic</u> by virtue of its higher

hierarchical status does not share with <u>witchcraft</u> or <u>sorcery</u> the same percentage of substitutable contexts that <u>witchcraft</u> and <u>sorcery</u> share with each other. Accordingly, it is less synonymous with <u>witchcraft</u> and <u>sorcery</u> than the latter two are with each other.

Some very significant features of hierarchical systems may be indicated in the following diagram based on data from Khmu', a Mon-Khmer language of Indochina. [8]

Diagram 3

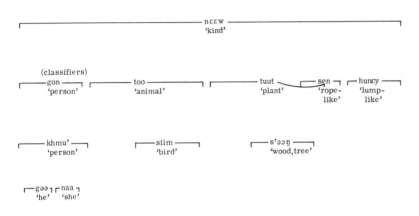

man woman spirit deer rat...fly crow parrot...grass bamboo...brush tree vine rope stone...

Several features of the diagram should be specially noted:

1. The items occurring in the second hierarchical level (counting from the top) are classifiers, used as substitutes for more specific terms, especially in the numerical system.

2. The distributions of the classifiers <u>tuut</u> and <u>sen</u> overlap. That is to say, a 'vine' may be substituted for by a term which identifies it as a member of the plant class, or by one which designates it as belonging to the 'rope-like' class. This is not appreciably different from what occurs in English, in which the word <u>spirit</u> may be substituted for by <u>it</u> or by <u>he</u>, depending upon the context.

3. Classifications may be exhaustive (even to the extent of being overlapping) as in the second hierarchical order or they may be "spotty" and incomplete, as in the third order.

4. There are two important types of divisions: (1) high-level ones and (2) multi-level ones, a series of substitutes with coterminous domains. The high-level divisions reflect the terms with the greatest generic values, and the multi-level divisions (in the Khmu' diagram between 'woman' and 'spirit') are likely to point to major class divisions which are significant on a cultural level.

In most of our illustrative data we have employed nouns and pronouns, not because they are the only types of words which exhibit a hierarchical structure of substitutability, but because such relationships are more obvious and easier to describe. However, all parts of speech in whatever language exhibit to a greater or lesser extent this same tendency toward hierarchical structure. English verbs such as do and make may be substitutes for a vast number of other semantic units; and good and bad may be regarded as kinds of generic adjectives, since their domain of semantic substitution coincides partially with so many other similar terms.

So-called "numerical classifiers" (whether single words or affixes) function as generic substitutes with relatively wide domains. In the Machiguenga language of Peru there are about fifty such classifiers, which by means of their respective substitution domains serve to subdivide almost all objects into such classes as (1) long rigid objects (stick, pencil, gun-barrel), (2) long, narrow, flexible cylindrical objects (rope, hose, snake), (3) long, thick, non-flexible cylindrical objects (tree-trunk, canoe, alligator), (4) objects enclosed in pod-like coverings (bananas, peas, beans), (5) objects made of bark-like material (cardboard, shell of turtle, certain types of containers), and (6) pulpy, fleshy objects (the fleshy part of any fruit, vegetable, or animal).

Analytical Procedures

The semantic structure cannot be so easily analyzed as the formal structure, for the patterns of semantic relationships are not

arranged in paradigmatic series nor in any substitution frames. It
is, of course, not too difficult to elicit "specific" vocabulary (semantically low-order terms) either by direct questioning or pointing, but
to obtain highly generic vocabulary (semantically high-order terms)
is often quite difficult because (1) there are frequently no corresponding terms in the language used by the investigator or (2) if generic
terms occur in native-language texts, they often appear in contexts
referring to specific objects and their generic significance is not
recognized. Only by comparing occurrences in a considerable volume
of text can one ascertain the degree of generic usage of any word.
Because of these difficulties in analysis there has been a tendency on
the part of investigators (especially amateur linguists) to deny the
existence of generic vocabulary in many languages.

    The only two sources of data on the semantic structure are
a very extensive corpus of data (much greater than would be required
for a comprehensive analysis of the formal structure) and an informant
of unusual ability to reply to questions about semantic domains without
being unduly influenced by the nature of the inquiries. In dealing with
a written corpus one would have to determine the range of distribution
and the substitution domains for each term (a process which could
never be exhaustive in any living language). In eliciting data from an
informant one could test range of distribution by asking whether various combinations "make sense" and explore the substitution domain
by taking every apparent substitution of a generic for a specific term
and probing the limits of the pattern in question. For example, if in
a story about a raccoon the informant uses a term which refers to the
raccoon but is not the specific name of the animal, this would constitute a starting place for asking if one can use the same term in speaking about a 'bear,' 'dog,' 'turtle,' 'fish,' 'snake,' 'bee,' etc. By
cross-checking such responses with other informants a relatively
accurate picture of substitution domains can be obtained. In general,
there is no easy and safe way of speeding up this process by so-called
definitions, for there are almost always peripheral features which are
quite arbitrarily determined.

    It is also possible for one to ascertain a good deal about the
semantic structure of a language from the ways in which bilingual
persons translate from one language to another. This type of analysis, however, is subject to severe misinterpretations unless it is

used as supplementary to the study of distributional range and substitution domain within the language in question.

Implications Derived from a Study of Semantic Structure

Even on the basis of very preliminary investigations of semantic structure along lines proposed in this paper, one may make certain significant inferences as to the relationship of semantic structure to culture, complexity of the hierarchical structure, comparison of structures, and changes within structures.

1. Hierarchical structures of semantic substitution are very often more subdivided and complex for that portion of the vocabulary which is related to the foci of the culture or subcultures. Not only is the vocabulary more extensive for a cultural focus (or foci), but it is frequently, but not always, more graded in hierarchical structure. For example, one may compare English terms for tools and sweet potatoes with Ponapean words for these types of objects, or the average person's names for different insects with entomologists' elaborate classification.

2. The more complex, elaborate series of grading are those which in general involve the greatest self-consciousness or awareness on the part of the speakers. The factor of awareness is, of course, related to a great extent to the fact that such complex series tend to occur in the areas of cultural focus. Greater awareness means that it is considerably easier to elicit patterns of substitution in the areas of cultural focus than in other phases of the culture. Similarly, those who are specialists in some field or leaders in a subculture are able to respond more readily to questions concerning their area of specialization than to those concerning general experience or behavior outside the cultural foci.

3. The semantic structures of languages differ more conspicuously in the hierarchical structure than in the segmentation of phenomena on the level of specific vocabulary. That is to say, the classifications of experience are more diverse than the identification of varieties. Translators consistently find it much easier to translate texts dealing with specific details than those involving generalizations.

4. As one ascends the scale of hierarchical structure differences between languages become proportionately greater. Not only are hierarchical structures different, but also they become increasingly incommensurable as one goes up the series. Slight differences on lower levels tend to multiply themselves as substitution domains increase. For example, equivalents for 'sly,' 'dirty,' 'gossipy,' 'insane,' and 'helpful' are decidedly much easier to find than adequate correspondences for 'good' and 'bad.'

5. The widest divergencies between languages occur in the area of exocentric units. Not only are such units "unpredictable" from the standpoint of the language in question, but there are no universally valid factors which prescribe the limits for the range of distribution of such combinations. Love is a sentiment of the 'heart' in English, but of the 'liver' in Karre (a language of French Equatorial Africa), of the 'abdomen' in Conob (a Mayan language of Guatemala), and of the 'throat' in Marshallese, spoken in the South Pacific. Such exocentric expressions have their "grounding" in the cultural behavior (i. e. , practices or beliefs, whether contemporary or historical), e. g. , he went like sixty, he's on the beam, and her sugar-daddy; but neither the form nor the distribution can be predicted from a knowledge of the range or substitution domain of the constitutent parts.

6. The semantic structure, especially in its upper hierarchical levels, is subject to change. It is, of course, a truism that living languages change, and certainly the meanings of words are no exception. However, whereas for the most part the morphological and syntactic structures tend to change very slowly, the semantic structure may undergo significant changes in a relatively short time, especially within the area of the cultural focus (or foci). New knowledge about the universe made it possible for people to speak of the sun as a star and the stars as distant suns, statements which previous generations would have regarded as utterly ridiculous. Astronomical knowledge has also raised the word moon from its status as a purely specific term to a generic one, e. g. , the moons of Jupiter. Scientific investigations are resulting in widespread readjustments in the semantic structure of English, changes which begin within the scholarly subculture, but which spread rapidly in our "science-worshipping age." But science is not the only factor which causes shifts within

the semantic structure. Any ideological system may transform a word
so that it is almost unrecognizable, e. g. , the change of meaning of
Greek daimôn from its classical substitution domain of 'a god, fate,
fortune' to its Christian usage as a substitute for 'evil spirit. ' Words
such as democracy, colonialism, curtain (e. g. , iron curtain and bamboo curtain), co-existence, and propaganda have undergone drastic
changes in their domains and substitution capacities.

      7. The semantic structure reveals more clearly than any
other part of language a people's world view. This does not mean that
by merely examining the semantic structure one may discover the
entirety of a people's world view, for the structural patterns always
tend to lag behind formative thinking. Furthermore, in stating that
the semantic structure gives some indication of a people's world view
we mean something rather different from what Whorf claimed, namely,
that one may discover in the purely formal structure the significant
elements of a people's world view. What we are saying here is that
in the semantic structure one finds the manner in which experience
tends to be classified (by successive orders of increasingly more
generic terms) and that this classification is indicative of the way in
which people view experience, i. e. , their world. For example, a
description of the range and substitution of terms such as good and
bad indicate a great deal as to the popular ethical judgments of English speakers. Compare these with the nearest Zulu equivalents:
-hle (defined as 'good, nice, beautiful, handsome, pretty, pleasant,
enjoyable, moral, right, and orderly') and -bi (defined as 'bad,
wicked, evil, inferior, useless, base, dirty, untidy, ugly, deformed,
nasty, distasteful, dangerous, serious, grievous, and grave'). A
further comparison may be made by noting the corresponding differences between the Greek terms kalos and agathos, corresponding
somewhat to Zulu -hle, and kakos and ponêros, corresponding more
or less to Zulu -bi.

      Anyone attempting to make studies of value judgments by
means of any set (or sets) of contrasting terms has employed (though
usually unconsciously so) the principle of semantic range. Corroborating evidence for such native-speaker responses may be obtained by
testing the substitution domains of semantically related words.

      It would be quite wrong to think that the semantic structure
is a perfect mirror of a people's world view. It is not. However,

since the structural relationships of semantic units (1) reflect a classification of experience, and (2) are subject to change as beliefs and attitudes toward the symbols and the corresponding referents change, one should reckon with the semantic structure as providing significant clues to a people's orientation toward life.

Studies of national types, even though not based on verbal behavior, are often influenced, consciously or unconsciously, by the semantic structure of the language of the people studied. But whether or not the analyst is influenced by the language in question, it is certain that he can and does obtain from the semantic structure many significant hints as to basic attitudes, beliefs, and orientation.

The study of semantic structure, though admittedly fraught with numerous difficulties and involving incredibly detailed analyses, nevertheless provides the promise of being one of the most fruitful and stimulating areas for future interdisciplinary investigation in the fields of linguistics, cultural anthropology, and psychology.

NOTES

[1] In some contexts it may be necessary to employ a somewhat more expanded substitute, e.g. position as full professor, depending upon the special semantic values of the unit chair.

[2] There is one interesting problem posed by the phrase his chair in the university. If this phrase belongs to context Type A, then piece of furniture is substitutable for chair, but if the phrase belongs to Type D, then post, position, or some other semantically related equivalent is the proper substitute. There are many instances in which semantic contexts may be ambiguous, e.g., he has four degrees. If the context is academic, the man is well off, but if the context is state of health, the man is very badly off. However, in most discourses the semantic contexts are more or less clearly identified. Otherwise, communication would be extremely difficult.

[3] In a sense this procedure is not very different from what Joos has done in his article on "Semology: A Linguistic Theory of Meaning" (Studies in Linguistics, 13.53-72, 1958), though he has set up his classes, not on the basis of substitution but on the basis of types of meaning which are distributed according to patterns of

contextual overlapping by various co-occurring lexical items. How-
ever, the use of substitutional patterns to determine the classes of
meanings of a term and the relationships between such classes seems
to provide not only a much simpler technique, but one which is even
more justifiable from a structural standpoint since it depends on no
extra-systemic data or procedures. The ultimate results are, of
course, substantially the same, for in Joos' method one can usually
substitute the "definitions" in the different meaning classes, thus
ending up with essentially the same kind of structural configuration.

[4] Methodologically, we are in no way concerned with the fact
that the future formative -r is historically related to the verb haber.

[5] Perhaps the closest approximation to complete substitutability exists when a language employs two sets of numerals, a traditional set and one newly borrowed from a trade or national language.
But even in these circumstances there are almost always some contexts in which one may not freely substitute forms without such appreciable differences in meaning that the "native speaker" reacts to such
collocations as not being natural or appropriate.

[6] The word whale also occurs in the exocentric phrase a
whale of a ..., e.g., a whale of a job, a whale of a time.

[7] The following data have been supplied by Rev. Werner B.
Marx of the Moravian Mission, Brus Laguna, Honduras.

[8] The data of Diagram 3 have been supplied by my associate
Dr. William A. Smalley.

4 | Difficulties of Translating Hebrews 1 into Southern Lengua

The first chapter of Hebrews has always posed a number of problems for translators. There are, for example, a number of interesting textual alternatives, difficulties of Old Testament quotations in the New, and uncertainties as to the precise exegesis of certain expressions. However, in addition to those complications of text exegesis, there are also a number of translational problems arising from the transfer of the message from the source to a receptor language.

Rather, however, than discuss the translational difficulties of this chapter in general or by types, it would seem that a very useful purpose might be served in analyzing a number of the typical translational difficulties which have occurred in the translation of Hebrews 1 into the Southern dialect of Lengua, an Indian language spoken by some three thousand persons in the central part of Paraguay. Not only are the difficulties encountered in this translation illustrative and typical of what occurs in many other languages, but it is helpful to analyze these difficulties verse by verse in order to appreciate something of their number, significance, and interrelationships.

As will be readily noted, the principal problems in translation involve (1) secondary agency, i.e. a first agent causing another to perform some action, e.g. 'God spoke through the prophets'; (2) direct quotations, particularly when the personal reference is obscured by shifts from first to third person; (3) rhetorical questions, which must frequently be altered into emphatic statements; (4) lack of cultural correspondences, e.g. the Lengua do not anoint with oil; and (5) incommensurate logotactic patterns, that is to say, words cannot be used in Lengua in the same kinds of combinations as the corresponding lexical units occur in Greek. However, rather than discuss these various problems by classes or types, it has seemed more relevant to examine them in their contextual order.

The following discussions are based on the careful observations and work of Mr. Derek Hawksbee and Miss Elizabeth Richards, both members of the South American Missionary Society of the Anglican Church and for a number of years associated with the work among the Lengua-speaking Indians of Paraguay. In citing the various phrases which provide translational difficulties, the wording of the R.S.V.* has been employed.

Hebrews 1:1

The rendering of 'in many and various ways' is difficult in Lengua, for 'ways' cannot be modified by both 'many' (or 'fragmentary', cf. N.E.B.*) and 'various'. Moreover the translators felt that the N.E.B. use of 'fragmentary' was distinctively preferable and, therefore, have employed an expression in Lengua meaning 'by means of little bits and in various ways'.

Hebrews 1:2

Since there is no pattern of inheritance among the Lengua people, there is no way in which one can speak of 'the heir of all things' in a technical sense. However, essentially the same kind of meaning can be communicated by a phrase meaning 'God gave all things to him'.

A further problem is encountered in verse 2 because the linguistic order and the temporal order in the source-language text are not parallel, for presumably the creation of all things would have to take place before they could be given to the Son. Therefore, the order is reversed, but the essential connections are preserved.

A still further problem in verse 2 is involved in the difficulty of primary and secondary agency, for the text says that God

---

Bible). *R.S.V. (Revised Standard Version), N.E.B. (New English

created the world through the Son. In general, secondary agency can
be readily expressed by restructuring the sentence in some such form
as 'God caused His Son to make the world'. However, the Lengua
verb 'make' has a special meaning of doing something on behalf of
oneself, and therefore this passage must be altered so as to read
'Jesus is together with God in making the universe'. Only in this way
can Lengua accurately reproduce the meaning of the Greek text.

In the phrase 'in these last days' (R. S. V.) (or 'in this the
final age', N. E. B.) there are certain problems, for one does not wish
to say 'at the end time', for this would imply simply the final judgment.
Since there is no good word for 'age', the semantic elements need to
be rather completely restructured, with the resulting phrase 'now is
about to become the end'. The element 'become' makes it possible to
conceive of a period of time rather than merely some abrupt termi-
nation.

Hebrews 1: 3

For a language which has no ready equivalent of either 'stamp'
or 'nature' the closest equivalent of 'the very stamp of his nature' is
'was exactly like God'.

'His word of power' becomes in Southern Lengua 'his powerful (or strong) word'.

'When he had made purification for sin' (note N. E. B. , 'pur-
gation') is rendered as 'when he had taken away our sin'. One does
not speak directly of purifying sins, for they cannot be 'cleaned up';
they can only be 'eliminated'. Moreover, one cannot speak of sins
apart from people performing sins, and therefore, the expression
'our' identifies the most general way of speaking about people
sinning.

'The glory of God' causes some difficulty for the translator
since 'glory' cannot be translated, as it so often is, by a word meaning
'to shine' or 'to be brilliant'. Such concepts are simply not related to
the idea of distinction or eminence. For the Lengua, the closest
equivalent of Biblical glory is 'greatness'.

Hebrews 1: 4

The phrase 'superior to angels' (compare N. E. B. 'above the angels') is translated literally as 'before the angels', for in this language 'before' is equivalent to 'greater' in such a context of comparison.

Hebrews 1: 5

The rhetorical question in Heb. 1: 5 is particularly difficult since the question applies to the introductory portion, which is then followed by a direct quotation not in the form of a question. Moreover, there is no practical context in which anyone is likely to answer such a rhetorical question. Therefore, this has been changed into an emphatic negative, e. g. 'for God never said to any angel' (compare N. E. B.).

A literal translation of the expression 'begotten thee' is awkward, for it would either refer to certain sex relationships or be largely incomprehensible. Therefore, the equivalent rendering is 'this day I make you my Son'.

The connective phrase 'or again' poses a number of problems, for it appears as though God is simply repeating himself in the same passage. Furthermore, before the direct quotation can be introduced some emphatic negative expression must be included so that the second part of verse 5 may carry forward the meaning introduced in the first portion. Therefore the corresponding transition would be 'or similarly, he never said to angels ... I will be to him a Father'.

Hebrews 1: 6

The first equivalent which a Southern Lengua speaker would give to the word 'firstborn' would be the word 'eldest'. However, this always implies that there are other children of the same father. Therefore, one must use 'the first and only Son'.

The direct discourse in verse 6 provides certain difficulties, for the introductory expression points clearly to God as the speaker.

However, the direct quotation speaks of God in the third person, and therefore the Lengua reader is immediately confused, for in Lengua one must clearly and consistently mark direct discourse by appropriate shifts in person. Therefore, this passage must be changed to read, 'You, my angels, shall worship him'.

The Lengua language has borrowed the Spanish word <u>Dios</u> for 'God'. However, the Lengua people themselves consistently combine <u>Dios</u> with their own word 'father', so that consistently and throughout this type of passage 'God' is really 'God Father'. This type of rendering is particularly important for Lengua speakers who are outside of the Christian community.

Hebrews 1:7

The metaphor contained in the two phrases 'makes his angels wind and his servants flames of fire' is scarcely intelligible in Lengua for 'to make' would mean simply to transform angels into winds and servants into fire. Therefore, this passage should be altered to read 'make my angels like winds and my servants like flames of fire'.

In this passage it is also necessary to make certain changes in the personal reference since God is speaking. Therefore 'his angels' becomes 'my angels' and the subject is no longer 'who' but 'I'.

Hebrews 1:8

In the loosely structured Lengua society there is no strong chieftainship, and much less a concept of kings, kingdoms, and thrones. Hence, the clause 'thy throne ... is forever and ever' poses certain semantic difficulties. To say that the king's chair lasts forever does real violence to the meaning of this passage. Therefore, the translators have chosen to render the meaning at this point by the phrase 'you are the chief unceasingly (or unendingly)'.

Similarly, a 'sceptre' has no equivalence in Lengua society. It could be explained by means of a footnote, but it seems more relevant to restructure this passage semantically so as to read 'your commanding of your servants is right'. In this translation 'kingdom' is taken not as territory, but as 'rule', and therefore is rendered literally as 'commanding'.

The expression 'your servants' is a way in which the Lengua identify all of those persons who are under the command or control of anyone else. In other words, 'you rule your servants (or people) in a righteous manner'.

Hebrews 1: 9

A literal translation of 'thou hast loved righteousness' could be quite misleading. For example, it could mean that the individual loved the benefits of other people's being good to him. It could also mean that he loved 'our right deeds', and therefore honored us accordingly. However, in keeping with the meaning of the Biblical context it has been rendered 'love to do what is right'.

The expression 'has anointed thee ... beyond thy comrades' involves certain problems since anointing is completely foreign to Lengua culture. The closest equivalent is 'to select and place'. This corresponds to commissioning and appointing or designating.

Following the N. E. B. the Lengua translators have divided this passage between the phrase of 'setting thee above thy fellows' and 'anointing with the oil of exultation', so that in Lengua God first 'puts you above your companions' and then 'gives you your work which will cause you great joy'. The phrase 'gives you your work' is a further amplification of the concept of commissioning and appointing.

Hebrews 1: 10

In the phrase 'found the earth in the beginning' the term 'found' must be understood in the sense of 'making' or 'creating', and 'in the beginning' can also be translated as 'of old' (see N. E. B.). Since Lengua does not readily speak of beginning without saying what begins, it is much more satisfactory to translate this passage as 'a long time ago you, the Lord, created the world'. The time factor here is emphasized by a particular form of the verb which identifies 'legendary times'.

It is not appropriate to speak of 'the heavens are the work of thy hands', for this seems to be too anthropomorphic in Lengua, especially since one does not say in Lengua 'to work with the hands'. Therefore, the translators have employed the phrase 'the heavens are your work'.

Hebrews 1: 11

Since one is here speaking of the earth and the heavens, Lengua requires as a translation of 'perish' a term such as 'disappear', for though works of man and people may 'perish', it is only appropriate to speak of the universe as 'disappearing'.

Similarly, in the phrase 'grow old like a garment' it is necessary to make a semantic judgment, so as to read 'like clothing they will rot away'. People may grow old; similarly, animals may age, but clothing can only 'rot'.

Hebrews 1: 12

In many languages, years can 'end', but in others, only objects or people can 'come to the end of their years'. Therefore, in Southern Lengua the clause 'thy years will never end' is restructured to read 'you will never come to the end of your years'.

Hebrews 1: 13

The rhetorical question 'but to what angel has he ever said ...' must be translated as an emphatic negative expression, 'God never said to an angel ...' (compare verse 5).

'Sit at my right hand' can be translated literally, but it will have relatively no sense since there is no protocol in Lengua society which distinguishes between the relative values attached to right and

left placement. Since, however, this concept of being on the right or
the left is widely employed in the Scriptures, it is important to preserve it. Some kind of marginal note therefore is necessary if the
significance of such an expression is to be properly comprehended.
Accordingly, a note should be introduced so as to identify the use of
this particular expression both in verses 3 and 13.

The clause 'till I make thy enemies a stool for thy feet' must
be broken into two parts in Lengua, for there are really two aspects
of this event, (1) the defeat of the enemies and (2) their placement
beneath the feet of the conqueror. Accordingly, this passage is translated to read 'until I beat down to the ground your enemies and put
them underneath your feet like grass'. The phrase 'like grass' is the
exact Lengua functional equivalent of 'footstool', for a Lengua rests
his feet on a small clump of dried grass rather than have them exposed
to the cold dirt floor.

Hebrews 1: 14

This final rhetorical question should likewise be changed into
a positive statement referring to the angels, 'these are certainly the
sent-ones of God to help ...'. It is impossible to use the generic
term for 'spirits' in this passage since Lengua terms for 'spirits'
normally identify demons. The Spanish word espíritu has been borrowed in the meaning of 'Holy Spirit', but this would not be appropriate
in this type of context. The meaning of 'ministering' and 'serving'
have both been combined in the concept of 'helping'.

In the problems which have just been discussed, difficulties
of text and exegesis have purposely been avoided for the most part
since we are concerned here primarily with the problems of transfer
from the source to the receptor language. Quite obviously, any translation involves a certain loss of meaning, for it is impossible to restructure any message with the total content and explicit and implicit
semantic relationships which are found in the original message. Nevertheless, as can be readily noted, the essential elements of the source
language message can be communicated in a receptor language, even
one spoken by such presumably primitive people as the Lengua, who
have been traditionally one of the semi-nomadic groups in the Chaco
of South America.

5 | Science of Translation

1. The Nature of Translating

In view of the fact that one can translate without knowing anything about linguistics, even as one can speak a language without being a student of the science of language, many persons have concluded that translation is scarcely even an aspect of applied linguistics.[1] Rather, it has often been regarded only as a more complicated form of talking or writing, in which one decodes from one language and encodes into another. Those who have seen in translation something which merits scientific description have been inclined, however, to think of translating merely in terms of certain more or less complex techniques of comparative linguistics (Jumpelt 1961, Cary and Jumpelt 1963). This has led to attempts to set up series of ordered rules, which could be more or less mechanically applied, bearing in mind at least two conditioning elements: the context and the literary level. Such a description of linguistic procedures has led to the establishment of techniques for moving from one set of surface structures to another, with the least possible interference or distortion.[2] Most programs for machine translation are based on essentially the same principles (Oettinger 1959, 1961).

However, a careful analysis of exactly what goes on in the process of translating, especially in the case of source and receptor languages having quite different grammatical and semantic structures, has shown that, instead of going directly from one set of surface structures to another, the competent translator actually goes through a seemingly roundabout process of analysis, transfer, and restructuring. That is to say, the translator first analyzes the message of the SOURCE language into its simplest and structurally clearest forms,

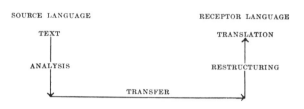

Figure 1

transfers it at this level, and then restructures it to the level in the
RECEPTOR language which is most appropriate for the audience
which he intends to reach.[3] Such a set of related procedures may be
represented diagrammatically as in Figure 1. This roundabout procedure may be compared to the experience of the hiker who finds a
stream he must cross is so deep and the current so swift that he cannot risk crossing over directly from one point to another. Therefore,
he goes downstream to a ford, at which point the transfer from one
side to another can be made with the least possible danger to himself
and his equipment. He can then go back upstream to the point which
best suits him. The processes of analysis are, however, relatively
complex, for they involve at least three different sets of features:
(1) the grammatical relationships between constituent parts, (2) the
referential meanings of the semantic units, and (3) the connotative
values of the grammatical structures and the semantic units.[4]

2. Processes of Grammatical Analysis

        In order to appreciate more fully the nature and significance
of grammatical analysis as the first step in translating, it may be
useful to describe briefly the ways in which we discovered grammatical analysis is carried out. For example, when event nouns (i. e. ,
nouns which refer to events rather than objects) are transferred from
one language to another, they are quite generally back-transformed
into verb expressions. A biblical phrase such as Holy Spirit of
promise (Ephesians 1.13) becomes '(God) promised the Holy Spirit, '
while creation of the world (Ephesians 1. 4) becomes '(God) created
the world'. Note that the position of the goals in these two English
expressions is entirely different in the two nominal expressions. In

a more complex expression, e. g. perfect love casts out fear (1 John 4. 18), it is often necessary to make certain radical adjustments, e. g. 'when people completely love as they should, they no longer fear'. In the same way, abstracts are usually transformed into adjectives or adverbs, so that the riches of his grace (Ephesians 1.7) becomes 'he showed grace richly' (or 'abundantly'), and the beauty of holiness (2 Chronicles 20. 21) becomes 'being holy is beautiful'. These back-transforms are not, of course, to be rendered literally into the receptor language, for they do not represent the appropriate focus. They are simply the basis for transfer into the receptor language, on a level at which the relationship between the constituent parts is expressed in the clearest and least ambiguous manner.

In the process of back-transforming expressions from the surface structure to the underlying kernel or core structures,[5] four basic structural classes emerge, which may be described as objects, events (including actions), abstracts (as features of objects, events, and other abstracts), and relationals. (These units are not to be equated with words, which are morphological units.) Basically, the objects are those elements—e. g. man, dog, horse, tree, sun, river oil—which participate in events. Events are expressed primarily as verb-like terms, e. g. run, walk, see, think, fall, make. Abstracts may be qualitative (red, big, fast), quantitative (much, many, twice), intensive (too, very), or spatio-temporal (here, now, that, this). Relationals are any units which function primarily as markers of relationships between other terms, e. g. at, by, because, and, or. The classification of any linguistic unit as object, event, abstract, or relational depends entirely upon the way in which the unit functions within a particular context. For example, stone is an object in Bill threw a stone at him, an event in They will stone him, and an abstract in the expression He is stone deaf.

The same word may, of course, simultaneously contain more than one semantic element. For example, dancer may be described as both object and event—i. e., 'one who dances', in which the object participates as the actor of the event. The term apostle, in the New Testament usage, also has two elements, object (the person) and an event ('being sent'); but the relationship is of goal to action, i. e. 'one who is sent'. In many languages it is important to distinguish clearly between such related structural elements within a single obligatory. In English the expression <u>She is a good dancer</u> refers to the quality of her dancing and not to her character. Hence the back-transform of <u>good dancer</u> is '(she/he) dances well'; but in some languages such an adjective attributive to a noun might be attributive to the object component, not the event component, of the semantically complex substantive.

One may argue that setting up complex structures for words such as <u>dancer</u> and <u>apostle</u> is merely a kind of morphological conven-ience, whether on a synchronic level (as in the case of <u>dancer</u>) or on a diachronic level (as in the case of <u>apostle</u>). This, however, is by no means the case. In the two expressions <u>owner of the property</u> and <u>heir to the property</u>, the unit <u>property</u> stands in essentially the same relationship to <u>heir</u> as it does to <u>owner</u>. One cannot, to be sure, regard <u>heir</u> as morphologically complex; but it does have a complex transformational structure, and this needs to be recognized if one is to analyse structures in such a way as to prepare them most accept-ably for transfer from one language to another.

The implications of this type of analysis may be well illus-trated by a relatively simple expression occurring in Mark 1.4: <u>John . . . preached the baptism of repentance unto the forgiveness of sins</u>. Such a sentence becomes especially difficult to translate in a language which does not have nouns for terms such as <u>baptism</u>, <u>repentance</u>, <u>forgiveness</u> or <u>sins</u>. In fact, in a high percentage of languages these words correspond regularly to verbs, not to nouns, for they represent events, not objects. A series of kernels or core sentences for this structure could consist of the following: (1) <u>John preached</u> (the message) (to the people), (2) <u>John baptized</u> (the people), (3) (the people) <u>repented of</u> (their) <u>sins</u>. (4) (God) <u>forgave</u> (the people) (their) <u>sins</u>, and (5) (the people) <u>sinned</u>.

Certain features of this series should be noted. First, there are two implied elements which need to be made explicit, e.g. <u>the people</u> and <u>God</u>. Second, some of the implied elements in these near-kernel structures include embedded kernels, e.g. <u>their sins</u> may be further back-transformed to <u>they sin</u>. Third, an element such as <u>message</u> is a substitute for the series of kernels 2 through 5.

A translator, however, cannot employ a mere string of kernels or core sentences as a basis for transfer into a receptor language. He must have these kernels related meaningfully to one another. This means that he must back up from a strictly kernel level and analyse the relationships between the kernels. A careful analysis of the Greek text underlying this sentence in Mark 1.4 clearly shows the following sets of relationships: (1) the goal of preached is the series of kernels 2-5; (2) kernels 2 and 3 are merely coördinate events which occur in an historical order in which 3 precedes 2, i.e., baptism of repentance is a nominal transform of the verb expression repent and be baptized; (3) kernel 5 is the goal of the event of kernel 4; and (4) kernels 4 and 5 are the purpose (or result) of the combined events of kernels 2 and 3. A possible combination of kernels which might be adequate for transfer to some receptor languages could be formulated as: John preached that the people should repent and be baptized so that God would forgive the evil they had done. In instances in which a form of direct address is a preferred base for transfer, one might have: John preached, Repent and be baptized so that God will forgive the evil you have done.

In describing, within the core or kernel, the relations between the event and the participants in the event, it is important to use a more sophisticated instrument than is implied in the use of such terms as subjects, objects, goals, and actors. Most of these grammatical terms tend to represent primarily the surface structure, rather than the underlying relations. For this type of analysis, the works of Fillmore (1965, 1966, 1968), Halliday (1968), and Langendoen (1968) are most helpful, since their models, based upon the roles of the participants, as stated in terms of 'cases', constitute effective instruments for describing the relations between the major semantic carriers of the message.

2.1. The problem of deep structure. At this point in the description of the analytical procedures in translating, it is quite natural to question the reasons for stopping at the kernel level. Why not proceed to the level of the deep structures? There is, of course, one very important practical reason for not doing so—namely, the fact that these can only be dealt with on paper, and the translator needs a level of structural correspondence which he can readily manipulate in his mind. Back-transforming to the deep level would generally be unnecessarily complex and time-consuming, and would not provide any significant advantage which is not already to be found on the level of the near-kernel structures.

There is also another practical consideration: namely, the
resistance of so many native speakers to the concept of the deep
structures. Most people recognize quite readily the validity of the
kernel level as related to the surface structures. Moreover, they
readily grasp the concepts of forward-transformations and back-
transformations. However, when they are encouraged to analyse
below the level of the kernels, there are often real difficulties and
serious objections. For one thing, the results of such analyses do
not seem to be especially revealing or rewarding, since there is very
little about the relationships of the parts which is not already generally evident at the kernel level.

In addition to the practical difficulties in going to the deep
level of structure, there are also certain theoretical considerations
which should be carefully weighed. In the first place, an analysis of
the deep structures of different languages shows rather startling
similarities. In fact, the deeper the analysis, the more alike, or
even identical, the structures appear to be. It would seem that
ultimately the deepest structural level involves simply a pool of
semantic universals—what any language can say. Rather than go
through the complex procedures involved in back-transforming in
the source language to this lowest level of universals, and then for-
ward-transforming the results again to the level of the kernels in the
receptor language, the translator instinctively concludes that it is
best to transfer directly from the kernel level in one language to the
corresponding kernel level in the receptor language. In this way he
can deal directly with the minimally contrasting manipulable structures. In reality the transfer at the kernel level can generally be
made with far less danger of skewing than if one follows the highly
involved processes of going to the level of semantic universals and
returning again to the kernel level.

This objection to the procedures involved in back-transforma-
tion to and forward-transformation from this deepest structure should
not be interpreted as implying that an analysis of semantic universals
is not valid; quite the contrary. There are fascinating implications
in recognizing such a pool of semantic universals. However, one
must make certain that such features are treated with sufficient pre-
cision and rigor so as to keep such a pool from becoming a bottom-
less pit, into which all sorts of meaningful features can be dumped
as a means of explaining later transformational developments. What

is theoretically and practically objectionable in the concept of the deep
structure, as employed by some persons, is the notion that one can
simply bury the semantics in the base, and then operate as though
the transforms are all devoid of meaning, or are merely some automatic outworking of certain residual meanings in the deep structure.
It seems equally objectionable to consider semantics as a kind of
capstone to the structure, as in the case of stratificational linguistics,
as though all the meaning in the total structure is derived from this
highest level.

Rather than consider semantics as an extreme, either on
top or at the bottom, it would appear much more in keeping with the
reality of language to regard meaning as something which is relevant
from the discourse to the sounds (i. e. in the area of sound symbolism).
There is obviously a declining influence of the semantic structure as
one proceeds from discourse to sounds, but the continuing relevance
of the semantic structure must be recognized, even though it is increasingly less determinative. At the same time, one must recognize that creativity in the communication process begins with the
discourse, where the semantic component is most involved. [6]

2. 2. The Problem of Models. Perhaps part of the difficulty
in linguistics, as in all branches of science, is not having fully recognized certain inadequacies in our models. Turbayne 1962 has clearly
pointed out the metaphorical nature of so-called scientific models.
They are essential aids to comprehension, but they must not be permitted to dictate the nature of what they are supposed to explicate. It
is particularly dangerous to employ mechanical models as ways of
describing the nature of language and the presumed manner in which
the human brain functions in encoding or decoding messages. Elaborate networks with and-or nodes are fascinating devices for suggesting certain logical relationships, but they should certainly not be
regarded as having any direct bearing on the way in which the brain
actually functions in encoding or decoding. Similarly, to declare that
one must not formulate a rule in a particular way since it cannot be
computerized in such a form really does not make much sense. The
description of linguistic relationships should never be determined by
procedures in computerization, if one is really concerned with any
kind of functional reality in one's descriptions of language performance
or competence. In both performance and competence, computers
have been correctly regarded as mathematical geniuses but judicial

morons. The human brain operates in a much more complex manner than any computer program, and is capable of many more intricate and interrelated analogies and comparisons.

Descriptions of language structure will always be more significant if one bears constantly in mind the limitations of the model being employed—even such a well-established model as the componential analysis of meaning by means of plus-minus matrices. Sanday 1968 has shown clearly that componential analysis is by no means the whole story in such relatively well-structured sets of words as kinship terms. There are always a number of different ways to describe the proverbial elephant. Nevertheless, despite the limitations of models, their use is obligatory if we are to comprehend something of the complex interrelationships of such a multidimensional structure as language. Our choice of models, however, must be dictated essentially by their practical usefulness and their explanatory power. For these ends, transformational techniques (both backward and forward) seem to be more satisfactory than any other existing system, provided we combine adequate treatments of case relations and of discourse units and structures. First, the procedures are intuitively comprehensible to most speakers, and the various stages are readily manipulable. Second, within the kernel structures the relationships between the component parts are more clearly marked. Third, the kernel structures of different languages are surprisingly similar, so that transfer may be effected with the least skewing of the content.

In a sense, the basic diagram of Figure 1 is misleading, for it seems to imply that the kernel structures of the source and receptor languages are as distant as their surface structures. In reality, the kernel structures are very much closer together, so that the distance which must be traversed in the process of transfer is much less when one goes from kernal structure to kernel structure. If one were concerned only with the formal rather than the semantic structures of different languages, one could conceive of languages as having widely differing surface structures, but with kernel structures converging toward a center. However, though the formal structures do converge significantly, the semantic content of the linguistic units may represent wide discrepancies, and we could be guilty of severe oversimplification of the transfer process if we placed the respective kernel structures too close together.

3. <u>Processes of Semantic Analysis of Referential Meaning</u>

      The semantic analysis of referential meaning applies to all types of linguistic units, from morphemes to idioms. In the past, certain formulations of this aspect of semantics have been too much concerned with the resolving of ambiguities (Katz & Fodor 1963). Such a procedure is entirely too much like trying to determine the phonemic structure of a language merely on the basis of minimal pairs. Only as one analyses how the language functions in its broader patterns can one determine properly how the minimal contrasts fit into these larger and more general structures.

      Rather than being impressed with the ambiguity in language, one ought to be much more impressed with the relatively small amount of it that exists, especially on the discourse level. Whenever one tries to describe language in terms of units, whether words or sentences, isolated from discourse, serious difficulties inevitably arise, for it is only in the context of the discourse that many potential ambiguities are actually resolved. What is impressive about language is the fact that, with a mere 25,000 or so lexical units, people can communicate with one another about literally millions of different objects, events, and features of such objects and events. This means that these lexical units must have relatively large potential domains, which can be neatly and efficiently delimited so that the precise meaning may be satisfactorily signaled by the context.

      Delimitation of meaning is accomplished in two different ways, but without either means having any structural priority over the other. On the one hand, the syntactic structure may clearly mark the differences of meaning, e.g. <u>She drank the water</u> vs. <u>She will water the plants</u>, where the contrast in noun and verb usage clearly determines which meaning is to be understood. On the other hand, the marking of meaning may be accomplished by the semotactic structure; i.e., the classes of markers may be determined not grammatically but semantically. For example, the verb <u>run</u> in its intransitive usage may be described as having some five different meanings (1) pedal action of an animate being, involving relatively fast movement in space, e.g. <u>The man ran</u>; (2) movement of a mass, e.g. <u>The water ran into the tub</u>; (3) internal action of a mechanism, e.g. <u>The watch runs</u>; (4) action or position of something capable of exten-

sion, e.g. The vine runs over the door; and (5) habitual movement
in space of a conveyance, e.g. The bus runs between New York and
Albany. These five different meanings are marked by certain semantically definable classes of co-occurring words. Meaning 1 is signaled by terms such as man, woman, dog, horse—a class of animate
beings, capable of a particular kind of rapid pedal movement. Meaning 2 is marked by a class of words identifying masses—water, oil,
flour—or objects associated with such masses—faucet, spigot, nose.
Meaning 3 is marked by such terms as motor, heart, watch, clock;
meaning 4 by anything capable of extension—vine, line, time (e.g.
time ran out); and meaning 5 by such terms as train, bus, ferry,
coach, subway.

The marking of different meanings of the same term (though
differently organized in each language) is not, however, so great a
problem for the translator as is the selection of different words which
have related or competing meanings. The reason is that the different
meanings of single terms are actually further apart in semantic space,
i.e. they share many fewer components than do related meanings of
different words. The translator must be able to distinguish between
such sets as walk and run (the technical difference being not one of
speed, but whether or not there is at least one foot on the surface at
all times), walk and stroll, and stroll and amble. These terms
which, in at least certain of their meanings, may be described as
competing with each other for semantic space are describable as
having three different types of meaningful relationships: (1) contiguous, e.g. walk and run; (2) included, walk and stroll; and (3) overlapping, stroll and amble. A fourth structure, namely polar opposition, describes such series as good/ bad , tall/ short, and generous/
stingy.

The fact that different languages segment experience in different ways is well known. What is less well recognized is the fact
that on the lower levels of the hierarchical structuring, where distinctions depend much more on perceptual differences than on conceptual classifications, divergences between languages are not too great,
even though the diagnostic features which tend to separate the different objects or events may be quite distinct. When, however, one
reaches the higher levels of the hierarchical structures, where distinctions depend primarily on conceptual classifications, not only are
the differences between languages much greater, but the distinctive

features which provide the basis for such classifications are generally quite diverse.

The area of cultural specialization, however, is likely to provide the greatest difficulties for the translator. In translating a text which represents an area of cultural specialization in the source language but not in the receptor language, the translator must frequently construct all sorts of descriptive equivalents so as to make intelligible something which is quite foreign to the receptor. On the other hand, when one is translating a document which represents a cultural specialization in the receptor language but not in the source language, the translator is forced to make decisions about the original account which may be only faintly implied.

4. Connotative Meaning of Syntactic and Semotactic Structures

The analysis of a text in the source language must not be limited to a study of the syntactic relationships between linguistic units or to the denotative (or referential) meanings of these same units. Analysis must also treat the emotive (or connotative) values of the formal structure of the communication. At this point, however, we specifically exclude the emotive response to the thematic content of the communication. This is something outside the realm of linguistics, though quite naturally one's enthusiasm for or dissatisfaction with the theme of a communication tends to color the emotive reactions to the syntactic and semantic structures of the message.

The connotative evaluation of the formal structures of the message is essentially an analysis of the style of the communication. But to accomplish this, one must obviously not be restricted to the sentence as the upper level of linguistic relevance. Stylistic factors affect the total form of any message, from the level of sound symbolism to the limits of the discourse. However, the principal area of stylistic concern is the discourse, not primarily the pleasing sound patterns or the juxtaposition of semotactically felicitous phrases. The analysis and evaluation of the stylistic features of a message involve a number of highly complex techniques, which cannot be treated within the scope of this paper. What is, however, perhaps even more important is a delineation of the essential elements involved in such an analysis. This will help materially in pointing out

the essential parallelism between the two sets of formal features:
the syntactic and the semotactic.

In evaluating the syntactic features of style for each language
level and for each literary genre, one must pose the following three
questions: (1) Do the grammatical forms of this message correspond
with the inventory of structures normally occurring on such a level
of language or in this type of literary genre (essentially a question of
syntactic well-formedness)? (2) Are the sequences of grammatical
structures mutually coherent? That is, is there proper motivation
for the sequencing of the series of structures, e.g. shifts from active
to passive, sequences of tenses, modifications in the historical order
of events (i.e. flashbacks and flashforwards)? (3) Is there sufficient
variety in the sequencing to sustain interest and provide impact
appropriate to the content?

An examination of the semantic structure must be made
along parallel lines, with essentially the same types of questions:
(1) Do the lexical units of this message correspond with the inventory
of forms normally used to designate the presumed referents? This
is essentially a question as to the fit between the linguistic world of
lexical items and the non-linguistic world of referents. (2) Are the
sequences of lexical units mutually coherent? Some of these sequences are strictly conventional, e.g. baked ham and roast beef;
others depend upon relatable components, which become conspicuous
by their absence, e.g. in cast-iron featherbed. (3) Is there sufficient
variety in the sequencing of lexical units to sustain interest and provide impact appropriate to the content? Different genres of literature
quite naturally differ radically in the extent to which novelty in wording is either desirable or obligatory, but in all communication a certain amount of lexical freshness is important in overcoming the
psychological noise of inattention.

The principal difficulty in the analysis of the connotative
values of syntactic and semantic structures is that we cannot employ
judgments based on binary contrasts of a positive or negative character. Rather, one must set up graded series which depend upon judgments of degrees of quantity and quality. In such cases the extent of
difference in individual evaluation becomes much greater, but this
should not be surprising or alarming. This is the very nature of
stylistic analysis, namely, the wide differences of judgment by different persons, even trained professional critics.

5. Transfer
        The process of transfer takes place on a near-kernel level
for two essential reasons. First, the relations between the linguistic
units of a message are most clearly marked at the kernel or near-
kernel level; second, languages exhibit far greater similarity of
structure at the near-kernel level than they do on the level of the
surface structures. By transferring on this near-kernel level, one
is least likely to distort the message.

        One must recognize, of course, that in any transfer there
is an inevitable modification in the meaning, generally associated
with some degree of loss, especially in the degree of impact of the
original communication. In fact, the greater the literary quality of
the original message, the greater the extent of distortion and loss,
for literary quality normally implies the fullest possible exploitation
of the genius of the source-language structure. To be able to exploit
the genius of the receptor language to a comparable degree requires
quite exceptional skill.

        Modifications of the syntactic structure in the process of
transfer are dictated primarily by the obligatory contrasts in the
respective near-kernel structures. The optional modifications
figure at a later stage as one undertakes to restructure the message
by forward-transformation to the appropriate level.

        In transferring the referential content of the message, one
is not concerned primarily with the precise words or exocentric
units (i.e. the idioms), but with the sets of components. In fact, one
does not really translate words but bundles of componential features.
The words may be regarded essentially as vehicles for carrying the
components of meaning. In fact the words may be likened to suit-
cases used for carrying various articles of clothing. It really does
not make much difference which articles are packed in which suitcase.
What counts is that the clothes arrive at the destination in the best
possible condition, i.e. with the least damage. The same is true in
the communication of referential structures. What counts is not the
particular words which carry the componential features, but the fact
that the correct componential features are lexically transported.

        In the process of transferring the referential content of the
message, there are three different types of redistribution of the

componential structures. First, there may be a complete redistribution. This is especially true in the transfer of idioms; for example,
a literal transfer of the biblical idiom <u>heap coals of fire on his head</u>
normally involves considerable distortion of meaning. One Congolese
tribe considered that this was a reference to some new method for
torturing enemies to death; they had not thought of such a technique
before. The meaning of this idiom—that is, its componential structure—must be completely redistributed, so that it can be transferred
in a form such as 'to be so good to one's antagonist as to make him
ashamed'. Second, the process of transfer may involve an analytical
redistribution of the components. This means that what is carried
by one lexical unit in the source language is distributed over several
terms in the receptor language. For example, <u>disciples</u> may be
transferred as 'those who followed him', <u>saints</u> may be 'the people of
God', and <u>phylacteries</u> may be rendered as 'little leather bundles
with holy words in them'. Third, the process of transfer may involve a synthesis of components. An expression such as <u>brothers
and sisters</u> may be transferred as <u>siblings</u>; and in the Moré language
of the Haute Volta, what is sixteen words in English—<u>in the morning,
a great while before day, (he) rose and went out to an uninhabited
place</u> (Mark 1.35)—becomes only one word for all the componential
features of meaning are included in the single Moré term.

6. <u>Restructuring</u>

        Describing the processes of analysis and transfer is much
easier than dealing with the processes of restructuring, for the
latter depend so much upon the structures of each individual receptor
language. Moreover, there are two principal dimensions of such
restructuring (formal and functional) which must be fully considered
if one is to understand something of the implications of this essential
procedure.

        The first formal dimension requires one to determine the
stylistic level at which one should aim in the process of restructuring.
In general there are three principal alternatives: technical, formal,
and informal (for some literary genres, there are also casual and
intimate levels of language). Perhaps the greatest mistake is to
reproduce formal or informal levels in the source language by something which is technical in the receptor language. This is what has

happened consistently in the translation of Paul's letters to the early churches. Rather than sounding like pastoral letters, they have turned out to be highly technical treatises. Such a shifting of levels is an almost inevitable consequence of not having thoroughly understood the original intent of a message, for when there is any appreciable doubt as to the meaning of any message, we almost instinctively react by raising its literary language level.

The second formal dimension involves the literary genre, e.g. epic poetry, proverbs, parables, historical narrative, personal letters, and ritual hymns. Though languages with long literary traditions have much more highly standardized literary genres, even some of the seemingly most primitive peoples have quite elaborate forms of oral literature, involving a number of distinct types; hence there is much more likelihood of formal correspondence than most people imagine. However, the real problems are not in the existence of the corresponding literary genres, but in the manner in which such diverse forms are regarded by the people in question. For example, epic and didactic poetry are very little used in the Western world, but in many parts of Asia they are very popular and have much of the same value that they possessed in biblical times. But for most persons in the Western world, presenting the prophetic utterances of the Old Testament in poetic form, as the closest formal equivalence, often results in serious lack of appreciation for the urgency of the prophet's message, which was put into poetic form in order to enhance its impact and to make the form more readily remembered. Such poetic forms are often interpreted by persons in the Western world as implying a lack of urgency, because poetic forms have become associated with communications which are over-estheticized and hence not relevant to the practical events of men's daily lives.

In addition to two formal dimensions in restructuring, one must also reckon with a functional, or dynamic dimension, related in many respects to impact. At this point especially, the role of the receptor is crucial, for a translation can be judged as adequate only if the response of the intended receptor is satisfactory. In order to understand the precise role of the receptor, it may be important to restate the basic elements in the translation procedure and to describe the role of the critic of a translation. Essentially the translation process is one in which a person who knows both the source and the receptor language decodes the message of the source language and encodes it into an appropriate equivalent form of the receptor language. This procedure may be diagrammatically described as in Figure 2. Here S_1, M_1, and R_1 stand for the source, the message, and the receptor(s), the original components in the communication event. The squares are designed to reflect the linguistic and cultural context of the original communication, in contrast with the circles, which represent the different structure of the receptor language into which the translation has been made. R_2-S_2 is the translator, half square and half circle, as the bilingual intermediary of the translation process. M_2 is the resulting message, and R_2 represents the receptors for whom the translation is designed.

In the past, a critic of any translation, R_3-S_3, was supposed to make a comparison of the forms of M_1 and M_2, and on the basis of such a formal comparison, he was supposed to be able to determine the validity of M_2 as a faithful translation of M_1. (This process of comparison is represented in Figure 2 by the dotted lines joining R_3-S_3 to the two messages.) One of the serious difficulties in this procedure has been the tendency for the critic to know the content of M_1 too well. Accordingly, he had little or no difficulty in understanding M_2, for his familiarity with M_1 provided him with the correct answers in any case of doubt. As a result, much that was judged to be a satisfactory translation often did not make sense to R_2, who had no such access to the original message. At present, those engaged in the analysis of the adequacy of translations have had to shift their viewpoints. No longer is it sufficient merely to compare the two forms M_1 and M_2. Rather, one must determine the extent to which the typical receptors of M_2 really understand the message in a man-

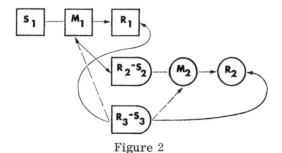

Figure 2

ner substantially equivalent, though never identical, with the manner in which the original receptors comprehended the first message (M_1). This new approach is symbolized diagrammatically by the solid lines leading from the critic R_3-S_3 to the respective sets of receptors.

By focusing proper attention upon the role of the receptors of any translation, one is inevitably led to a somewhat different definition of translation than has been customarily employed. This means that one may now define translating as 'reproducing in the receptor language the closest natural equivalent of the message of the source language, first in terms of meaning and second in terms of style.'

7. The Relation of Translating to Linguistics

The actual process of translating can be described as a complex use of language; but the scientific study of translating can and should be regarded as a branch of comparative linguistics, with a dynamic dimension and a focus upon semantics. If the scientific study of translation is understood in this light, it is possible that translation could serve as one of the best places to test some present-day theories about language structure. It is all too easy to spin out theories about language when one remains essentially within the realm of a single language (cf. Weisgerber 1962). Our theories need a kind of constant check, which will consist of more than a comparison of certain isolated formal or semantic features. We need a thoroughgoing comparison on a level of dynamic equivalence. This will test the potentialities of the compared structures and will not be merely a parallel description of two fixed corpora.

Perhaps translation can also provide a kind of dynamic typology of languages, with certain interesting theoretical implications and a number of practical insights. Let us assume, for example, that we could rank all languages in a series, beginning with those formally closest to a particular source language and then proceeding, language by language, to those structurally most distant from the source language. Such a rank-order of languages would depend upon both grammatical and semantic factors. Practically, it would be immensely difficult to undertake any such ranking of languages, but

one might be able to determine certain diagnostic features which
would provide a reasonable basis for setting up such an ordering.

The other dimension of our model would be the extent of formal
correspondence between the languages as revealed in actual translations. For languages which are close in rank to the source language,
there would be considerable formal correspondence. At the opposite
extreme, translations would exhibit relatively little formal correspondence, but a great deal of functional equivalence. It is interesting
to speculate upon the nature of the curve which would describe the
relative amount of formal correspondence at the intermediate position.
One's impression is that the amount of formal correspondence falls
off quite rapidly as one moves away from the languages closest to
the source language. On the other hand, a number of languages
seem to have about the same degree of formal correspondence, though
of course the nature of this formal correspondence is radically diverse. All this means that probably there is some type of componential curve which would describe the amount of formal correspondence
between the source language and those ranked in order from it.

If this type of projection is true, then one might be able to
determine the relative rank-order of languages from any source language by determining the extent of formal correspondence in translation. Similarly, if one could set up a reasonable rank-order, one
could predict something about the extent of optimal formal correspondence in translation. But such an optimal position, marking the
proportion between formal correspondence and functional equivalence
in a translation made from a particular source language, is rarely
realized in actual practice. There are several reasons for this. In
the first place, a totally inadequate control of the receptor language
by translators who are foreigners almost always results in a translator employing too high a degree of formal correspondence with the
source language. That is, in his ignorance of the receptor-language
patterns, he inevitably carries across the structures which are familiar to him in the source language. On the other hand, if this same
type of translator has some control of the receptor language but not
full mastery of it, he is very likely to go to the opposite extreme and
introduce too little formal correspondence. Not knowing precisely
how the receptor language would express a particular concept, he
tends to be entirely too periphrastic.

A second factor which keeps translators from realizing the optimum degree of formal correspondence is their linguistic bias. On the one hand, a translator may have such an exaggerated respect for the source language (especially if he regards it as in some measure divinely inspired) that he tends to force the receptor language toward too great a degree of formal correspondence. The result is a kind of translationese. On the other hand, translators may also have a bias in favor of the exotic. Having become enamored with the differences of the receptor language, especially if they seem to mirror a radically different world view, the translator may wish to employ far less formal correspondence than he should. It is interest ing to note in this connection that national translators (i.e., those who are translating into their own mother tongue) tend to have a bias in favor of the source language which they have mastered, often with great effort. Moreover, the prestige of such translators in their community may depend upon other people's recognizing their knowledge of the source language. Foreign translators, those who are translating into a language which is not their own mother tongue, often have a bias in favor of the receptor language and may overdo the extent of functional equivalence, sometimes as a result of linguistic fervor and other times as the result of unconscious paternalizing.

8. Conclusion

As has been clearly noted in the introductory sections, this paper does not presume to delineate all the principles and procedures of translation. It has been highly selective. But in presenting certain aspects of translation, the attempt has been made to include those elements which might have the greatest interest for and relevance to linguistic analysis in the more general sense. It is obvious that insights from linguistic theory have provided important help for those interested in the scientific analysis of translation. It would seem equally evident that the scientific analysis of translation can provide important insights, and even correctives, for various theories of linguistics. Eventually, the scientific study of translation may be recognized as a significant branch of comparative linguistics, providing a dynamic dimension with a focus upon semantics, a combination often lacking in past comparisons of languages.

NOTES

[1]This paper represents the author's Presidential Address to
the Annual Meeting of the Linguistic Society of America, in December 1968.
     Anyone attempting to discuss the science of translation (or,
perhaps more accurately stated, the scientific description of the
processes involved in translating) is almost inevitably confronted
with two questions. The first concerns translation as an art rather than
a science, and the second raises the issue as to whether translation
is even possible (see Güttinger 1963: 7-48, for a summary of opinions
on this issue). In reply to those who insist that translation is, at
least in some senses, an art, one can only heartily agree, but with
the proviso that speaking a language effectively and esthetically is
also an art. Translation is actually describable in terms of three
functional levels: as a science, a skill, and an art. In response to
those who insist that translation is impossible, one can only say that
from time to time it is very tempting to take such a position seriously.
One must, of course, recognize the incommensurability of languages,
in the absolute sense. This means that absolute communication is
impossible, but that is true not only between languages but also within
a language. Rather than being impressed by the impossibilities of
translation, anyone who is involved in the realities of translation in
a broad range of languages is impressed that effective interlingual
communication is always possible, despite seemingly enormous differences in linguistic structures and cultural features. These impressions as to the relative adequacy of interlingual communication
are based on two fundamental factors: (1) semantic similarities between languages, due no doubt in large measure to the common core
of human experience; and (2) fundamental similarities in the syntactic structures of languages, especially at the so-called kernel, or
core, level.
     [2]Vinay and Darbelnet (1958) have produced an excellent com-
parison of English and French, based essentially on the analysis of
the surface structures. Nida 1947 follows this same type of procedure, but in a much more elementary form.
     [3]The language into which one translates is here designated
as receptor language, rather than target language. The use of the
term 'receptor' is designed to emphasize the fact that the message
must be decoded by those who receive it. One does not merely shoot

the communication at a target. Rather, the communication must be received, and this process is crucial in evaluating the adequacy of a translation.

[4] It should be quite evident that the following description of translation procedures can only be sketchy at best. Further treatments of these problems are found in Nida 1964, in Nida & Taber 1969, and in Componential Analysis of Meaning by Nida (in preparation). Attention should also be called to Joos 1962; Mounin 1963; Weinreich 1963, 1966; Andreyev 1964; Catford 1965; Bolinger 1965, 1966; Colby 1966; Lyons 1968; and Wonderly 1968.

[5] No attempt is made here to define or to employ kernel or core structures in a strictly technical sense. Linguists differ as to the precise formulation of these structures, but most recognize the structural relevance of such sets of near-minimal structures at some point between the deep structure and the surface structure.

[6] Compare the treatment of semantic structure in stratificational grammar by Chafe 1968.

REFERENCES

Andreyev, N. D. 1964. Linguistic aspects of translation. Proceedings of the Ninth International Congress of Linguists, ed. by H. G. Lunt, 625-37. The Hague: Mouton.

Bolinger, Dwight. 1965. The atomization of meaning. Lg. 41.555-73.

_____. 1966. Transformulation: structural translation. Acta Linguistica Hafniensa 9.130-44.

Cary, E. , and R. W. Jumpelt (eds.) 1963. Quality in translation. New York: Macmillan.

Catford, J. C. 1965. A linguistic theory of translation. London: Oxford.

Chafe, Wallace L. 1968. Review of Outline of stratificational grammar, by Sydney M. Lamb. Lg. 44.593-603.

Colby, B. N. 1966. Ethnographic semantics: a preliminary survey. Current Anthropology 7.3-32.

Fillmore, Charles J. 1965. Entailment rules in semantic theory. Project on Linguistic Analysis, Report no. 10.60-82. Columbus, Ohio: Ohio State University Research Foundation.

Fillmore, Charles J. 1966. Toward a modern theory of case.
    Project on Linguistic Analysis, Report no. 15.1-24. Co-
    lumbus, Ohio: Ohio State University Research Foundation.
    _____. 1968. The case for case. Universals in linguistic theory,
    ed. by E. Bach and R. Harms, 1-90. New York: Holt,
    Rinehart, & Winston.
Güttinger, Fritz. 1963. Zielsprache. Zürich: Manesse Verlag.
Halliday, M. A. K. 1968. Notes on transitivity and theme in Eng-
    lish, 3. Journal of Linguistics 4.179-215.
Joos, Martin. 1962. The five clocks. (Indiana University Research
    Center in Anthropology, Folklore, and Linguistics, publ. 22.)
    Bloomington.
Jumpelt, R. W. 1961. Die Üversetzung naturwissenschaftlicher und
    technischer Literatur. Berlin-Schöneberg: Langenscheidt.
Katz, Jerrold J., and Jerry Fodor. 1963. The structure of a seman-
    tic theory. Lg. 39.170-210.
Langendoen, D. Terence. 1968. On selection, projection, meaning,
    and semantic content. To appear in Semantics: an inter-
    disciplinary reader in philosophy, linguistics, psychology,
    and anthropology, ed. by Leon Jakobovits and Danny Stein-
    berg.
Lyons, John. 1966. Toward a 'notional' theory of the 'parts of
    speech'. Journal of Linguistics 2.209-36.
Mounin, Georges. 1963. Les problèmes théoriques de la traduction.
    Paris: Gallimard.
Nida, Eugene A. 1947. Bible translating. New York: American
    Bible Society.
    _____. 1964. Toward a science of translating. Leiden: E. J.
    Brill.
    _____, and Charles R. Taber. 1969. The theory and practice of
    translating. Leiden: E. J. Brill.
Oettinger, Anthony G. 1959. Automatic (transference, translation,
    remittance, shunting). On Translation, ed. by Reuben A.
    Brower, 240-67. Cambridge, Mass.: Harvard University
    Press.
    _____. 1961. A new theory of translation and its application.
    Proceedings of the National Symposium on Machine Transla-
    tion, ed. by H. P. Edmundson, 363-6. Englewood Cliffs,
    N.J.: Prentice-Hall.

Sanday, Peggy R. 1968. The 'psychological reality' of American-
    English kinship terms: an information-processing approach.
    American Anthropologist 70. 508-23.
Turbayne, Colin Murray. 1962. The myth of metaphor. New Haven:
    Yale University Press.
Vinay, J. P., and J. Darbelnet. 1958. Stylistique comparée
    du français et de l'anglais. Montreal: Beuchemin.
Weinreich, Uriel. 1963. On the semantic structure of language.
    Universals of language, ed. by Joseph H. Greenberg, 114-
    71. Cambridge, Mass.: MIT Press.
_____. 1966. Explorations in semantic theory. Current trends
    in linguistics, III, Theoretical foundations, ed. by T. A.
    Sebeok, 395-477. The Hague: Mouton.
Weisgerber, Leo. 1962. Die Sprachliche Gestaltung der Welt.
    Düsseldorf: Schwann.
Wonderly, William L. 1968. Bible translation for popular use.
    London: United Bible Societies.

6 | Semantic Structures

In Collaboration with Charles R. Taber

Most approaches to the problems of semantic structures may be classified as historical, territorial, componential, or generative. The historical approach[1] emphasizes the historical background of the meaning of a term or larger lexical unit, and usually attempts a logico-historical reconstruction or description. But though this may be useful in understanding what happened in the past, it is not very helpful in trying to analyze the synchronic functioning of such units on a semantic level.

The territorial approach[2] is one which describes the meanings of words in terms of domains, which are often described as contiguous, overlapping (e.g., varying degrees of synonymity), or included (i.e., hierarchically structured sets of related terms such as <u>animal</u>, <u>mammal</u>, <u>dog</u>, and <u>poodle</u>). This type of analysis is very helpful in understanding many semantic relationships, but it is not applicable to all types of lexical units. Moreover, in many instances the bases on which such domains are established and by means of which the territory covered by a term is described are both imprecise and impressionistic.

The componential approach[3] to semantic structure has provided some of the most useful leads and promises the greatest returns on investment in time and energy. But in most instances componential analysis has been restricted to very limited sets of terms, in fact principally to kinship terms, for which non-linguistic structures have provided an easily applicable set of corroborating relationships. Moreover, componential analysis has usually been applied only to the 'central' meanings of such terms and little or no attention has been paid to figurative or extended uses. For example, <u>father</u> in English has been treated as meaning only 'male, first prior generation, direct line of descent', and no consideration has been given to such expressions as Father God, Father Murphy, father of his country, or father of the idea.

The generative approach[4] has typically made use of sets of semantic markers to classify the terminal meanings of a term as the final elements in a generative 'tree'. But not only has this approach proved to be overly simplified, but the focus of attention has been too much the marginal problem of the resolution of ambiguity.[5] Though of course the resolution of ambiguities is an important factor, it is by no means central to semantics, and the marking of meanings in normal discourse is accomplished in far more subtle and extensive ways than any binary 'semantic tree' would suggest.[6]

1. Basic Considerations in Semantic Analysis

In contrast with these four approaches with their specific techniques and immediate concerns, and to supplement them, we have adopted as a point of departure two very important facts about semantic relationships.[7] In the first place, languages exhibit in use surprisingly little genuine ambiguity, despite the fact that they use somewhere between 25,000 and 50,000 lexical units to describe literally millions of different objects, experiences, and features of such objects and experiences. Though linguists can readily construct numerous ambiguous utterances, one finds relatively few such expressions in real discourse. Obviously languages have very efficient devices for sorting out the various meanings of terms. In the second place, the different meanings of single lexical units are far more separate in semantic space (i.e., they are far more different from each other) than the related meanings of different terms. For example, the meanings of run in such diverse expressions as a run on the bank, a run in her stocking, a shanty up the run, run the business, and run in the first race share far fewer components of meaning than the related meanings of run, walk, skip, hop, and crawl when they designate physical movements by a human being.

The fact that different meanings of the same word tend to be farther apart in semantic space than related meanings of different words, which may be said to compete for the same semantic domains, is of great importance, not only for the theory of semantics but also for the practical functioning of language. If this were not true, there would be serious difficulties in using the same word in different senses. However, when the different senses of a word are quite far apart in semantic space, one can readily mark these by a number of different techniques.[8]

In view of these practical and theoretical considerations, it has seemed best to concentrate attention upon those features of the semantic structure which are most evident in the normal functioning of language, i.e., in regular discourse. The questions which we must ask are therefore related to (1) how languages mark the meanings of words so as to avoid the frequent ambiguities which should theoretically occur, (2) what structures, in terms of classes and relationships, are revealed by these marking systems, (3) how componential analysis may be applied, both to related meanings of different terms and to different meanings of a single term, (4) what structural relationships exist between the components of such meanings, and (5) how these sets of meanings are structurally related to one another. Obviously, it is impossible within the limits of this paper to give fully adequate answers to these questions, but it is hoped that the following suggestions will be sufficiently programmatic to encourage further investigation and analysis, designed to confirm or to refute the observations herein presented.

2. The Marking of Meanings

In most discourse the intended meanings of terms are clearly marked by the context. The context, however, presents two quite distinct aspects: (1) the practical, i.e., non-linguistic, and (2) the linguistic. By practical context we mean those features of the circumstances and setting of the communication event which serve to signal the intended meaning. For example, the expression he has three degrees may have quite different meanings when uttered in a hospital ward and at an academic function. Similarly, when a woman shows her dislike of a particular man by saying What a rat!, the circumstances indicate quite clearly that she is not talking about a rodent. Again, when a preacher says from the pulpit our Father, he is most

likely to be talking about God, and not about a human male relative of
one prior generation in direct line of descent. Though linguists quite
naturally emphasize the linguistic contexts which mark meanings, in
reality the practical contexts of actual communication events are
probably much more relevant in giving the audience clues as to which
meanings are intended. Perhaps an undue preoccupation with written
discourse has tended to lessen our appreciation of the non-linguistic
factors which enter into the marking of semantic distinctions.

The linguistic context comprises two principal types of features, (1) syntactic and (2) semotactic features. Syntactic markers
of meaning are easily recognized and well documented. For example,
three meanings of stone are quite clearly distinguished by the syntactic use of the term in the contexts He picked up a stone, They will
stone him, and He is stone deaf. Pronominal reference provides
frequent clues; for example, in the contexts It is a fox and He is a
fox, it is the difference between it and he, anaphoric substitutes for
non-human and for human objects respectively, which marks the
literal meaning 'animal of a certain species' in the first sentence and
the figurative meaning 'crafty, deceptive person' in the second. Transitive and intransitive constructions may also identify differences in
meaning, e.g., in He ran fast vs. She ran him.

The semotactic features involve semantically defined classes
of terms. These semotactic classes are far more numerous than the
syntactic classes, and they are also far more arbitrary.[9] Nevertheless, they are the very essence of language, for they not only mark
the meanings of terms but to a great extent characterize the 'genius'
of each language. There are, for instance, four principal meanings
of run in English: (1) 'movement in space by an animate being' (e.g.,
The man runs, The horse runs); (2) 'movement of a mass' (e.g., The
water runs, The flour runs out of the bin, The faucet runs, and His
nose runs); (3) 'internal movement of a mechanism, organ, or organization' (e.g., The motor runs, His heart runs, The business runs);
and (4) 'linear extension' (e.g., The vine runs over the door, The
line runs off the page). These four meanings are clearly signaled by
the semotactic classes of the co-occurring terms. Unless otherwise
indicated, any object in the animate class which is capable of pedal
or analogous movement through space will mark the first meaning of
run (there is a fuzzy border between individuals as to what animals

can run; some find The snake ran across the road acceptable, some
do not). On the other hand, a term identifying a mass (e.g., sand,
flour, oil, salt, gasoline) or an object associated with the movement
of a mass (e.g., faucet, tap, spout, hose, nose) marks the meaning
of run as 'continuous movement of a portion of a mass'. Words which
designate a mechanism, an organ, or an organization (e.g., watch,
turbine, heart, corporation, club, church) which are capable of internal movement of related parts mark the third meaning of run. Finally,
things which are capable of linear extension (a rather limited class)
mark the fourth meaning of run.

Such patterns of co-occurring semotactic classes[10] seem so
utterly logical within a language that one scarcely realizes how arbitrary they often are. When, however, one compares the usage of
other languages, the arbitrariness becomes evident. In French, for
example, a motor does not run, it walks (French marcher). But the
differences between languages become even more evident when one
analyzes the semotactic usage of persons who have a limited knowledge
of a language. For example, a Korean friend wrote in English about
the difficulty he experienced in chairing a meeting of rival factions
by saying, I squeezed all the wisdom I had and began the meeting.
There are many objects one can squeeze in English, but wisdom is
not one of them.

The patterns of co-occurring semotactic classes represent
such an elaborate structure that a foreigner rarely masters them.
It is estimated that by diligent application in second-language learning
one can usually attain full mastery of the syntactic patterns in five
years or so; but to control fully the highly intricate structure of co-
occurring semotactic classes one must usually have some twenty years
of continuous active exposure to the language. Even then few people
acquire completely native ability in a second language.

3. Principal Syntactic and Semotactic Classes

The principal syntactic classes which are important for the
marking of meaning are the major word types. In English, these
are verbs, nouns and pronouns, adjectives, adverbs, conjunctions,
prepositions, etc. Within certain of these classes there are important

subclasses which are semantically significant. We have already mentioned the crucial distinction in nouns, marked by the appropriate
pronominal substitutes, between human and non-human objects, and
the distinction in verbs between transitive and intransitive uses. There
are also often important differences between event verbs and action
verbs. [11] Words such as rain, hail, snow (e.g., in It is raining)
specify events without agents, while most verbs require specific
agents, goals, and/ or instruments, as in John killed him, The poison
arrow killed him, and He died.

In addition to such syntactic classes, all languages also
exhibit certain major semotactic classes: objects, events, abstracts,
and relationals. Objects are semantic elements which designate
namable entities such as tree, house, river, man, dog, spirit. Events
are semantic elements which designate actions or processes (e.g.,
changes of state) such as run, think, eat, see, grow. Abstracts are
essentially features of objects, events, or other abstracts, which
have no independent existence but which can be conceptually abstracted
from the 'real' element in which they inhere, such as red, big, fast,
once, very. Finally, relationals are elements or features which mark
the meaningful relationships between the three major classes; typically, they include such items as word order, affixes, prepositions,
conjunctions, copulas, etc. The use of the term 'element' in defining
object and event reflects the very important fact that these kinds of
semantic items do not stand in any one-to-one relationship with words
as defined morphologically. [12]

It must be added that the functioning of a particular term
depends upon its actual use in a specific context. For example, stone
designates an object in He picked up a stone, an event in They will
stone him, and an abstract in He is stone deaf. But this applies only
when we are dealing with distinct senses at the same time. Membership of a term in a particular semotactic class, provided we are
dealing always with the same sense, does not shift with changing syntactic usage. For example, reign in George III reigned during a
crucial period in English history is an event; but it is equally an event
in the reign of George III, where it is a noun but retains the same
meaning. In both instances, George III is the agent of the event.

Furthermore, a single lexical item may express simultaneously more than one semotactic class. The term buyer in the buyer

of the property includes components of three classes: an object (the agent morphologically represented by -er), an event (buy) and the agent relational between them; the same components in the same relationship appear in the sentence He buys the property. It must not be thought, however, that semantic complexity of this sort is always reflected by morphological complexity. In heir of the property, heir contains precisely analogous semotactic elements even though it is morphologically simple. Apart from the specific components which distinguish buy from inherit, the semotactic patterns are identical.

These four basic semotactic classes show up most promi- nently in the kernel structures of languages, in which objects are normally represented by nouns, events by verbs, abstracts by adjec- tives and adverbs (or, as in some languages, by stative verbs), and relationals by particles, word order, affixes, etc. It is in the kernel structures that the syntactic and semotactic classes meet with the highest degree of correspondence. On the various levels of the sur- face structure there are numerous and radical types of non- correspondence, [13] since all languages have techniques whereby objects, events, and abstracts may be shifted from one syntactic class to another in order to change the focus. Compare, for instance, She sings beautifully, the beauty of her singing, her beautiful singing, and Her singing is beautiful, in which the three major components (she, sing, beautifully) are restructured in order to shift the focus. [14]

Within the major semotactic classes of object, event, ab- stract, and relational, there are a number of subclasses. At the highest level, objects are subdivided into countable and non-countable (or mass) objects; this division is made on the basis of the attributes and events which can be meaningfully related to the two kinds of ob- jects. Masses, for instance, can flow, drip, pour, etc. The appro- priate abstracts of quantity include much rather than many and some of rather than one of or several of. Countable objects are further subdivided on the basis of the various events with which they may co-occur. Animate objects can live, grow, die, etc., while inanimate objects cannot. Among animate objects we differentiate between per- sons (who alone can think, vote, gossip, speak, etc.), animals (which can do some things impossible for plants, such as run, swim, etc.), and plants (which can sprout, wither, and wilt). Animals can also do things impossible for persons, such as hibernate, estivate, and moult.

The basic distinction between animate and inanimate, and between persons, animals, and plants, has been found to be highly significant in scores of languages in which translators, for example, have tried to sort out the patterns of co-occurrence. In addition to these broad classes, there are also of course highly specific collocational sets, such as duck and quack, and dog and bark.

Inanimates reflect two types of cross-cutting factors in their classification: (1) manufactured vs. natural, e.g., axe vs. stone (teleological statements are normally made with respect to manufactured objects) and (2) degree of mobility. This last comprises a threefold distinction between (a) normally moving objects, e.g., waves, (b) readily movable objects, e.g., drum, axe, canoe, stone, and (c) not movable, e.g., house, garden, mountain. Obviously, movable objects are far more likely to be instruments than unmovable ones, while the latter are far more likely to be used to specify location.

Masses are often subdivided into three classes on the basis of patterns of co-occurrence with events and abstracts: (1) liquids, e.g., water, oil, sap, juice; (2) gases, e.g., steam, wind, vapor; and (3) dry substances, e.g., grain, sand, flour.

Events may also be classified on the basis of co-occurring participants and abstracts; commonly found classes include the following:

(1) Psychological, e.g., think, reason, compute, add.
(2) Sensory, e.g., feel, hear, see, smell, listen.
(3) Communicative, e.g., talk, scream, sing, signal, gesture.
(4) Physiological, e.g., eat, digest, sweat, defecate, reproduce.
(5) Physical movement, e.g., run, walk, swim, climb.
(6) Meteorological events, e.g., rain, snow, thunder, hail.
(7) Position, e.g., lie, stand, sit, lean against.
(8) Change of state, e.g., die, age, wither, sour, collapse, increase.
(9) Change of position, e.g., rise, fall, come, go, stand, sit[15].
(10) Making, e.g., make, fashion, carve, build, tie, cut.

These ten classes are by no means exhaustive, but they illustrate the kind of classification of events which can be made on the basis of co-occurring terms.

Though many semotactic classes have scores or even hundreds of members, some classes are very small. For example, baked and roast occur in very restricted, and basically arbitrary, situations. One says roast beef and baked ham, not *roast ham and *baked beef. On the other hand, we say roast pork, not *baked pork. Historically, there was a basis for the differences of usage, but at present there is no one-to-one correlation between the manner of cooking and the term used.

When confronted with such sets of co-occurring semotactic classes, some persons contend that they are merely the 'linguistic counterparts of the natural world', or that they are simply an expression of 'the logic of things'. However, an examination of the range of usage of terms in other languages soon indicates the fundamental arbitrariness of semantic domains and of limitations in patterns of co-occurrence. In English, for example, one can use the term kill with a number of goals, e.g.:

> He killed the man.
> He killed the dog.
> He killed the tree by spraying it too heavily.
> He kills time every day down at the park.
> He killed his chances of success.
> They killed the motion when it came from the committee.
> He killed himself by overwork.
> He killed the spirit of the group.

All of these uses seem to be a quite logical development of the central meaning of kill, but not all languages share the same logic. For example, in Kisonge (a language of central Congo), one may use the term for kill in relation to animals and persons, but not to plants. One may speak of killing oneself, but the expression means to hurt oneself, not to commit suicide.[16] But one cannot kill time, nor kill the chances of success, and certainly not kill a motion. On the other hand, one can kill almost all kinds of interpersonal relationships: one may kill a marriage, kill praise, kill friendship, kill peace, kill a promise, and kill a covenant.

4. Componential Analysis of Related Meanings of Different Terms

Though for the most part discussions of componential analysis have been restricted to the treatment of sets of terms which correspond to structured relationships in the external world, e.g., kinship terms, one need not be so restricted. One can equally well make componential analyses of other types of expressions, provided one makes certain distinctions as to the nature of components. For example, one can make use of componential features in the analysis of a series such as run, walk, skip, hop, and crawl; but in doing so one must observe certain important restrictions.

In the first place, it is impossible to compare in a single componential analysis all the meanings of a series of words such as run, walk, hop, skip, and crawl, for one would be dealing with too many completely incommensurate semantic dimensions. One must restrict the analysis to those particular meanings of the individual words which actually occur within the same general semantic domain. Run, for instance, has different meanings in run the business, time runs out, run the race, a run in her stocking, etc.; but one cannot compare all of these simultaneously with the meanings of walk (e.g., in He walked and He built a walk around the house) and crawl (e.g., in He crawled under the fence and They crawled through traffic) and skip (e.g., in He skipped class).

In other words, one cannot usefully compare all the meanings of a set of words, but only particular meanings of such words. Otherwise, the analysis becomes altogether too multidimensional and there is no relevant structure into which we can fit all the meanings. Eventually, of course, by systematic comparison of all the meanings of each term with the meanings of other terms which tend to occupy contiguous or related semantic space, one may hope to build up an elaborate structure which will provide an overall view of the multidimensional relationships, but this cannot be done in a single componential structure. Accordingly, we must restrict the meanings of run, walk, hop, skip, and crawl to 'activity of a person involved in physical movement through space'.

In so restricting our analysis, we are also by implication indicating what components are common to this set of meanings. The 'common components' are (1) physical movement through space (not internal movement of parts as in The watch runs well) and (2) by a human being. We could, of course, add any animal or insect, but this would entail a number of problems involving the order of the pedal movements and the relationship of the feet to the surface. It is, therefore, better to begin with a very restricted set of common components and to define essential differences on the basis of these, rather than to try to include too much and end up with a confusing picture of the diagnostic differences.

In applying componential analysis to a set of related meanings, it is essential to distinguish clearly between three types of components: (1) common components, i.e., those which are common to all of the meanings in the set and which therefore define the set, (2) diagnostic components, i.e., those which are essential (in the sense of being necessary and sufficient) to distinguish between the various meanings, and (3) supplementary components, i.e., additional features which may be very important for an extensive definition of a meaning but which are not diagnostic in specifying basic differences.[17] For example, one may feel that run is faster than walk and so wish to set up a component of < speed >[18] as a diagnostic feature of run. However, some people can walk faster than others can run; furthermore, one can even do stationary running. Speed is not therefore diagnostic, but it is undoubtedly an important supplementary component.

A componential analysis of the relevant meanings of run, walk, hop, skip, and crawl in terms of diagnostic component shows the structure given in Table 1.

Certain features of this analysis require comment:
(1) The matrix of components is not arranged in a strictly

TABLE 1

	run	walk	hop	skip	crawl
1. Limbs involved:	pedal	pedal	pedal	pedal	four limbs
2. Order of movement:	121212	121212	111 or 222	11221122	1-3, 2-4, 1-3, 2-4
3. Relationship to surface:	one foot not always on surface	one foot always on surface	one foot not always on surface	one foot not always on surface	two limbs always on surface

plus-minus structure. One could, of course, set up such components as (a) < pedal involvement >, (b) < four-limb involvement >, (c) < 12121 order >, (d) < 1111 or 2222 order >, etc. But there would be eight different components for such plus-minus marking and the results would reveal the structure far less satisfactorily than does this grouping of components in terms of the limbs involved, the order of movement, and the relationship of the action to the surface.

(2) It is also possible to walk on one's hands, but such a meaning is better treated as an extension of the more normal meaning, rather than by setting up variants of the components to cover such marginal cases. [19]

(3) It is also possible to be more specific in the description of certain components. For example, in skip there is not only the difference in the order of movement in the < 11221122 > component, there are also differences of spacing and timing. But it is the order of movement which seems to be primarily diagnostic. Note again that we are not including the meaning found in skip rope, which involves a number of different rhythms.

(4) Crawl may, of course, be done in more than one way, but in general one arm and one leg on opposite sides of the body move together.

(5) Not all persons may be aware that the distinction between run and walk is precisely the fact that in walking at least one foot must always be in contact with the surface, while in running there is an instant between each contact with the surface in which neither foot touches the ground.

(6) Strictly speaking, it is not necessary to introduce any more components than are absolutely necessary to establish the differences between the various meanings. On this basis, crawl would be distinguished from the other terms on the basis of any one of the three componential contrasts. It is only for run and walk that the full series is necessary. But in a componential structure it is important to carry through the series across all the components, so as to indicate clearly not only the nature of the contrasts, but also their extent. Furthermore, points at which such redundancy appears are points at

which different persons may establish the necessary distinctions on the basis of different components.[20]

Though these three sets of components are sufficient to distinguish the denotations of the relevant meanings of run, walk, hop, skip, and crawl, an analysis of the differences of meaning would certainly not be complete without some consideration of the supplementary components, which are especially important in the connotations of these terms. As we have seen, run in this sense carries the supplementary component < speed >; it also suggests < extra energy > and < necessity for greater coordination >. Walk carries such supplementary components as < the usual means of human locomotion >. Crawl, on the other hand, suggests < slowness >, < low position >, < associated with small child >, etc. Hop and skip carry the supplementary components of < play >, < activity of children >, and < necessity for greater coordination (than walking)>.

A comparison of certain meanings of chair, stool, bench, and hassock reveals other aspects of componential structures as found in series of terms with related meanings. Just as before, however, we must restrict our analysis to the particular meanings of these four words which share sufficient common components to place them in the same semantic domain. This means that we are concerned only with those meanings which share the components (1) < manufactured object > (2) < for sitting > and (3) < readily movable >.[21] We exclude the meanings of chair found in Address the chair, chair of philosophy, and condemned to the chair (which will be treated in a later section); also excluded are the meanings of stool as 'laboratory specimen', bench with reference to a position in the judiciary; and hassock as 'small stool for kneeling (as in Anglican churches)'. Hassock is taken in the sense of 'a seat, about 18 inches high, usually round, covered with leather, firmly stuffed'—an object quite common in North Africa.

The diagnostic components of the four related meanings arrange themselves into the structure shown in Table 2.

Certain aspects of this analysis require explanation.
(1) In this structure, it is possible to use a plus-minus notation, for the components are not particularly complex or diverse.

TABLE 2

	chair	stool	bench	hassock
1. A back:	+	−	±	−
2. Number of persons:	1	1	2 or more	1
3. Legs:	+	+	+	−

(2) The designation of an object as a chair or a stool may depend to a certain extent on its function. For example, an object which would normally be called a chair may be called a stool if it is near a bar. This is particularly true if it is somewhat higher than most chairs and has only a very low back. [22]

(3) Though stools tend to be either higher or lower than chairs, height is not a diagnostic component.

(4) One may be tempted to specify as diagnostic components the materials of which an object is made; but this is not satisfactory, for in this series the range of materials used in the manufacture of the objects is so varied: wood, plastic, steel, aluminum, etc.

(5) While chairs, stools, and hassocks are always movable, there is a tendency to label as benches certain built-in structures. In such instances they do not normally have legs. This type of exception, however, is best treated as a special case of the more usual meaning, rather than as a distinct meaning with its own diagnostic components.

The supplementary components associated with these meanings of chair, stool, bench, and hassock are quite numerous. Chair implies < ordinary piece of furniture for sitting >; it covers the widest variety of forms. Stool involves such supplementary components as < used in certain types of work > or < associated with bars >. Bench carries the supplementary components < often in a public place >, < less elaborate construction (than a chair)>, and < less comfort >. Hassock suggests < rare item >, < novelty >, and < casual setting >.

5. Componential Analysis of Different Meanings of a Single Term

Componential analysis has not usually been applied to the different meanings of a single term, even though the tree structures of Katz and Fodor[23] are based upon essentially this type of analysis. The reasons for the reluctance to use componential analysis in this area are, of course, readily understandable, for the meanings are often so diverse as to reveal few if any common components. There may in fact be no components which are shared by all the meanings of the term, i.e., there may be no common components at all. There are often instead 'chains' of related meanings linked by components common to a subset of meanings. The association of meanings within the same structure often depends upon purely supplementary components. When there are absolutely no componential links between various meanings, then of course one is no longer dealing with polysemy but with homonymy.

The fact that people differ from one another in their judgments as to the existence of componential connections between meanings does not invalidate the relevance of componential analyses. It only means that on the semantic level as at other levels of a language there are dialectal and idiolectal differences, and that structures may be in the process of change. Some people today may see a connection between arm ('upper limb of a person') and arms ('weapons'), even though historically these are unrelated; the same is true for corn ('grain') and corn ('horny growth on foot'). On the other hand, they may see no connection between the two meanings of ruler as 'one who rules over people' and as 'measuring stick', though historically these are related.

If we wish to analyze componentially the four meanings of run in (1) The man (boy, child) runs, (2) The water (faucet, flour) runs, (3) The motor (heart, business) runs, and (4) The vine runs over the door, we can postulate one common component, < movement >; this can be actual or implied, and in space or internal.

The diagnostic components of these four meanings of run constitute the structure shown in Table 3.

TABLE 3

	run_1	run_2	run_3	run_4
Analysis of movement:				
1. Actual:	+	+	+	−
2. Rhythmic:	+	−	+	−
3. In relation to object:	total	partial	parts	point

A number of features of this analysis require explanation.

(1) The basic analysis of these four meanings must depend upon the nature of the movement, not upon the types of objects involved in the movements. It would be easy enough to line up the componential structure in terms of the four semotactic classes of objects which mark these meanings, namely, animate beings, masses, mechanisms, and linear objects. But these are not components of the meanings of run, but contextual specifiers of the particular meanings.

(2) The component labeled < actual > indicates, when it is marked +, that the movement actually takes place in time and space. Note that meaning 4 does not imply any such actual movement; movement is only suggested.

(3) The component < rhythmic > indicates that there are repeating or alternating elements within the overall movement. This is applicable to the running of persons and to the movement of parts within a mechanism, but not to the flow of a mass or to the extension of a vine, a line, or time.

(4) The movement in the various meanings of run is, however, related to a certain extent to the objects involved, in that the movement may involve the entire object (meaning 1), a portion of the object (meaning 2), the parts of the object (meaning 3), or a point (meaning 4), in which the only movement which can be understood is essentially the extension of a point.

Several other types of problems may be noted in a componential analysis of various meanings of chair, as in (1) He bought a

chair at the furniture store, (2) He occupies the chair of philosophy
at the university, (3) Please address the chair, and (4) He was condemned to the chair, i.e., he was executed.

Some persons may see no connection whatsoever between
some of these meanings. There seems to be, however, a relationship
between meanings 1 and 4, since both of these objects are manufactured and both are used for sitting. The connection of 2 and 3 to 1 and
4, however, is more tenuous, and may be felt by some to be nonexistent; in that case, we would be dealing with homonyms. On the
other hand, persons aware of the historical development (i.e., full
professors occupied certain chairs in faculty assemblies, and persons
presiding at meetings occupied conspicuous chairs at the front of the
room) may well connect all of these meanings. If this is done, one
finds the componential structure given in Table 4.

TABLE 4

chair$_1$	chair$_2$	chair$_3$	chair$_4$
manufactured object	position	person	manufactured object
for sitting	academic	parliamentary	for sitting
for resting	prominent	prominent	for execution

While the componential structure of the meanings of run
exhibited a high degree of parallelism among the components, this is
much less true for the meanings of chair. Meanings 1 and 4 share
the first two components, but differ in the final one which specifies
purpose. Meanings 2 and 3 also share certain types of components,
but there is really very little connection between these two meanings.
This confirms, of course, our intuitive expectations, because we
sense that the semantic distance between the two meanings is very
great.

We could, of course, distinguish the first three meanings on
the basis of a single series of components. It is the recurrence of
the component < manufactured object > in sense 4 which forces us to
add other series of components so as to distinguish 1 and 4. If we

were concerned merely with finding minimal contrasts, it would not
be necessary to add <for sitting> to 1 and 4: we could indicate only
that one was <for resting> and the other <for execution>. However,
in order to show ultimately the connection of these meanings of chair
with the componential structures of other meanings of chair for manufactured objects (not analyzed here), we find it advisable to introduce
here this highly generic component.

For meanings 2 and 3, it is likewise not necessary to introduce any components other than <position> vs. <person>, since
these provide a diagnostic contrast. However, the other components
help to establish a tenuous link between them: they are also important
in order to spell out more clearly the restrictions upon the use of
chair in these kinds of contexts. Chair$_2$, for instance, is not used in
any kind of position, e.g., in a bank, on a ship, or in the army; therefore <academic> must be specified. Similarly, chair$_3$ is used only
in connection with <parliamentary> occasions.[24] Furthermore, it
is not enough for chair$_2$ to specify <academic>, for it is used only
of the particularly prominent position of a full professor. The component <prominent> is also shared by chair$_3$.

This type of componential analysis is not esthetically very
appealing because of the highly miscellaneous types of components
involved. What we have done is simply to set up the diagnostic components required for minimal differentiation of meanings. This type
of structure is precisely what we find in a high percentage of cases
of different meanings of a single term—a fact which clearly confirms
the statement made earlier, that the different meanings of a single
term are generally much farther apart in semantic space than the
related meanings of different terms.

6. The Relationship of Components to One Another

The components of meanings may stand in a variety of structural relationships to one another. They may, for example, be unordered, as in the case of kinship terminology. When we define father
in English as being (1) <immediately prior generation>, (2) <male>,
and (3) <direct line of descent>, there is no logical or temporal priority of any component over another. Similarly, in the componential
structure of chair ('piece of furniture for sitting') the components

<with back>, <for one person>, and <with legs> exhibit no built-in priorities of one over another.

For many sets of meanings, however, there are well-defined structural relationships between the components. The internal structures of these relationships may be ordered according to different principles; they may form chains, constellations, etc. If, for example, we analyze the relationship between the common and diagnostic components of run in The man runs, we find the following dependency relations:

1. movement
   2. through space
   3. by a human being
      4. using the lower limbs
         5. in 121212 order
         6. with recurring movements when neither foot touches the ground

Component 1 is primary, and components 2 and 3 are unordered restrictions on component 1. Component 4 is a restriction on component 3, while components 5 and 6 are unordered restrictions on component 4. When one takes the set of components of a meaning, both common and diagnostic, and arranges them in logical order of their dependency, the result is a definition of the meaning. One can, of course, do the reverse and turn a well-formulated definition into a componential structure.

It may therefore be asked just what componential analysis does which good definitions have not already done. In a sense, nothing; but there is an appalling lack of good definitions of meanings, that is, definitions which contain all the necessary and sufficient components to place the meaning in a domain and to distinguish it from all other meanings which compete for similar or related semantic space.

Ordered sets of components may, of course, follow a logical-temporal ordering. For example, an analysis of redeem, in the context redeem a slave, reveals three diagnostic components, arranged in chronological order: (1) <alien possession>, (2) <payment of a price>, and (3) <release>. Such linearly-ordered series may be called 'chains', in contrast with the sets of dependencies described above as 'constellations'.

7. Relationship of Related Meanings of Different Terms

Not only are components structurally related to one another, but related meanings of different words also exhibit significant, structured relationships to one another. These structural relationships are of four major types: (1) juxtaposed, (2) included, (3) overlapping, and (4) polar. These are diagrammed in Diagram 1.

The juxtaposed relationship may be illustrated by such terms as run, walk, hop, skip, and crawl, which share common components putting them into the same domain, but which contrast sharply on at least one diagnostic component. That is to say, in at least one diagnostic component there is a clear case of either plus-minus distinction or a difference which can be assimilated to a plus-minus opposition. Kinship terms also fall into this category of juxtaposed meanings.

Included meanings are illustrated by the related meanings of poodle, dog, mammal, and animal. All the components of animal are also found in mammal, but mammal has additional components to distinguish mammals from other kinds of animals. Similarly, dog has all the components of mammal (i.e., it is a kind of mammal), plus those components which distinguish dogs from horses, cats, and other kinds of mammals. Finally, poodle contains all the diagnostic components of dog, plus those components which distinguish poodle from terrier, boxer, etc. In just the same way, the meaning of march[26] in They marched him off to jail or He marched in the parade is included in the meaning of walk, with the addition of at least one component: <externally imposed rhythm>. One meaning of stroll is also included in this meaning of walk, with the added components <slow gait> and <indefinite goal>.

Juxtaposed   Included   Overlapping   Polar

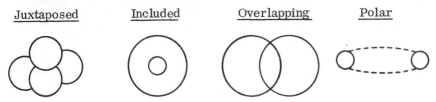

Diagram 1

Overlapping meanings present the most complex problems
for semantic analysis; for though there are common components which
bring such meanings together in the same semantic space (e.g., cer-
tain meanings of <u>peace</u> and <u>tranquility</u>, <u>joy</u> and <u>happiness</u>, <u>love</u> and
<u>affection</u>, <u>mercy</u> and <u>grace</u>), the differences between them cannot be
defined in terms of a plus-minus contrast, as in the case of juxtaposed
meanings. In many cases the differences are found only in supplementary components, while in other cases the differences are definable in terms of the degree to which the meanings overlap in having
in common a plus or a minus in relation to certain components.

Meanings which are polar opposites consist of such pairs as
<u>good:bad</u>, <u>tall:short</u>, <u>big:little</u>. Such terms possess the same types
of components, but completely opposite values for these components.
Because of this opposition or 'semantic tension', we have chosen to
diagram the relationship in terms of a magnetic field of polar opposition.

8. The Relationship of Different Meanings of a Single Term

Though the types of relationship existing between related
meanings of different terms can be stated with relative ease, since
the types are readily identifiable and classifiable, it is far more difficult to describe the relationship between the different meanings of
a single term. As has already been said, this is so fundamentally
because such meanings are so far apart in semantic space.

One can, of course, always employ traditional historical
methods to reconstruct just how certain meanings were derived from
other meanings, but in the ultimate analysis this is not very helpful
in determining how the language works on a synchronic level. Moreover, even in the case of languages with relatively well-documented
histories it is quite difficult to know precisely what the semantic
history of most terms has been. Obviously when we attempt to recon
struct semantic developments in languages for which there is no
documented history, we soon realize that what we are doing is pure
speculation—and not very profitable speculation at that.

What we need, then, is a relatively simple method of describing some of the more evident relationships without introducing the
complications which are almost inevitably involved if one tries to

define the relationships too closely. For example, in dealing with
the four meanings of chair, we sense a relationship, but we cannot
indicate precisely by means of a genetic tree just what happened. But
we do realize that the first meaning, namely 'piece of furniture' is
probably basic, for it is almost inevitably the meaning people give
when asked to define chair in a completely unmarked context. If we
do choose this meaning as central (we shall see below that some terms
do not have such a central meaning), then meaning 4 can be said to
be a 'satellite' of meaning 1. Meanings 2 and 3 are also satellites,
but in quite different 'orbits' from meaning 4. These orbits are,
however, somewhat related. That is, they are not very far apart in
semantic space. By indicating that meanings 2 and 3 have quite a
different type of orbit, i.e., elliptical rather than circular, we suggest that they may soon fly off into their own semantic space, no
longer attracted by the 'gravitational pull' of the central meaning;
they would then be homonyms, with no further connection with the
central meaning. We can diagram these relationships in a quite
impressionistic way, as shown in Diagram 2.

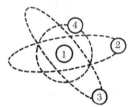

Diagram 2:   Meanings of chair

If we were to analyze the four meanings of coat in (1) He put
on his coat, (2) The house needs a coat of paint, (3) He will coat it
with grease, and (4) The dog has a heavy coat, and to diagram the
relationships of these meanings, we would draw the diagram given
in Diagram 3.

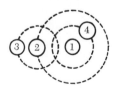

Diagram 3:   Four meanings of coat

In this diagram of the relationships of the meanings of <u>coat</u>, two features require explanation.

(1) It is difficult to decide which of the two meanings, 2 and 4, should be in orbit closer to the central meaning 1. In view of the fact that an animal's coat serves many of the same functions as a coat worn by a person, however, one may be justified in putting 4 closer to 1.

(2) Meaning 3 is obviously related to meaning 2 as its satellite. However, this type of diagram cannot do justice to the relative distances of peripheral meanings from a central meaning; no doubt the representation of the distance between 2 and 3 involves distortion.

A number of additional problems in determining the relationships between different meanings of a term are well illustrated by some of the meanings of <u>rule</u>: (1) <u>He ruled the people wisely</u>, (2) <u>The rules of this organization prohibit such an action</u>, (3) <u>As a rule, one would not make such an offer</u>, (4) <u>He ruled the page carefully</u>, and (5) <u>He has a rule on his desk to line up parallel columns</u>.

Some persons may not feel that these five meanings represent the same word, since they do not seem to share many components. Most dictionaries do, however, put all these meanings under the same entry, no doubt partly because of their derivation from Latin <u>regula</u> 'straight stick, often used for marking'. However, there is certainly no one meaning which is central, one from which, on a synchronic level, the others are derivable or to which they can be related. At the same time, one does sense that there are certain common components which may serve to link these meanings into a related set. These components, which may be stated as <a standard> and <conformance>, are not represented precisely by any single sense. Accordingly, it is advisable to use a 'dummy' meaning to serve as the core around which the actual meanings of <u>rule</u> can be said to orbit. This would mean that around the dummy (consisting of the two common components) there would be two quite distinct sets of meanings in two quite different types of orbits. The first group would comprise meanings 1, 2, and 3, each of which is structurally a satellite of the preceding meaning. The second group would consist of meanings 4 and 5, with 5 a satellite of 4. The following diagram, Diagram 4, represents these relationships.

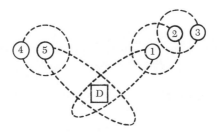

Diagram 4:   Meanings of <u>rule</u>

This description of the relationships between the various meanings of a single term is by no means fully satisfactory, for the relationships themselves are highly diverse and represent rather tenuous connections. However, this is as far as we can presently go in trying to describe the multidimensional relationships which underlie these highly disparate patterns. If, of course, we could ever reach the position of having described all the domains of related meanings of different words, we might then be in a position to state much more precisely the relationships between the different meanings of a single word. But until such a time—which is surely not in the foreseeable future—we shall have to be content with the insights which come from more limited analyses. Nevertheless, these insights and the techniques which have made them possible provide considerable promise for more effective exploration of semantic domains and structures than has been possible through the use of more traditional methods.

NOTES

[1] An early study along these lines was Michel Bréal's <u>Essai de sémantique</u> (Bréal 1897). More recently, Stephen Ullmann has done similar work: Ullman 1957 and 1963. The many semantic studies of Meillet and Benveniste are also basically historical.

[2] This approach is associated chiefly with the name of Jost Trier and his colleagues in Germany in the 1920's. A useful summary of their work is Ohman 1953.

[3] Most of the best work along these lines has been done by such anthropologists as F. G. Lounsbury (Lounsbury 1964a and 1964b) and W. H. Goodenough (Goodenough 1956).

[4] See Katz and Fodor 1963.

[5] For penetrating critiques of this misplaced emphasis, see Bolinger 1965 and Weinreich 1966.

[6] There is a sense in which this preoccupation with the peripheral phenomenon of ambiguity resolution parallels the tendency of a number of linguists to pay primary attention to the peripheral structures on the outer limits of grammaticality, i.e., the borderline between what is grammatical and what is not. As interesting as this approach may be, it will never reveal the structure of a language satisfactorily. The really relevant structures of a language are discovered by extensive analysis of the core or central features, rather than by concentrating on peripheral problems. Another parallel may be seen in the experience of phoneticians who attempt to work out sets of tonal contrasts merely by handling minimal pairs. As useful as these pairs may be to test the analysis, they rarely yield the really important insights into the structure. Only by careful and often tedious work on the principal, central features can one determine the structures into which such contrasts fit.

[7] This paper represents certain of the major lines of theory and application which are being further developed in the preparation of a volume to be entitled "An Introduction to Semantic Structures".

[8] Some may object to such a statement about the diversity of meanings of a single term by contending that this depends upon the grid used to determine whether the different meanings of a term should be separated or grouped. It is interesting to observe, however, that when students are asked to classify and group meanings, there is generally a high degree of agreement as to the resulting groupings. There is, of course, a reason for this: it is the semotactic classes (to be discussed below) which provide the structural basis for these groupings.

[9] It is in part a failure to distinguish these two kinds of classes, i.e., a conflation of syntactic and semantic features in a very traditional way, which makes Noam Chomsky's selectional and subcategorization rules (Chomsky 1965) so incredibly complex and ultimately quite unworkable. What he does is to make of what we call semotactic classes subtypes of the syntactic classes.

[10] Such British linguists as M.A.K. Halliday and R. H. Robins use the term COLLOCATION to refer to these patterns.

[11] Cf. Mathiot 1967 and 1968.

[12] This lack of correspondence between semantic elements and morphological units is what S. M. Lamb has called "discrepancy"; he describes seven types of discrepancy in language. See, for example, Lamb 1965: 41.

[13] These also fit into the category of Lamb's discrepancy; see footnote 12 of this article.

[14] One could say that the labels object, event, abstract, and relational are merely the syntactic-semantic designations of the major elements of kernels in all languages. Such a view would naturally result if one contends that all the semotactic structures are to be buried in the deep structure of the syntax. However, it seems far more relevant to make a clear separation between the syntactic structures and the semotactic structures and to note the precise degree of formal correspondence between them at the level of the kernal structures. As is evident, this approach represents a basically stratificational orientation.

[15] Note that in English stand, sit, and lie may refer either to a position or to a change of position. In other languages there may be quite distinct sets of terms.

[16] The use of kill in the sense of 'to hurt' is widespread in Africa, where life and death are not radically contrasting terms tied to one crucial moment of passage from life to death. To live actually means 'to increase in life force' and to die means 'to diminish in life force'. Therefore to injure oneself, or to grow old, is often spoken of as to die, since these involve a diminishing of the life force.

[17] Included here would be what Edward H. Bendix calls (confusingly) "connotation"; by this he means features of meaning which are in general implicit in the semantics of a term but which can be specifically excluded without destroying the sense under discussion (Bendix 1966: 23ff.) (Componential Analysis of General Vocabulary: The Semantic Structure of a Set of Verbs in English, Hindi, and Japanese (Bloomington, Indiana, 1966), pp. 23ff.

[18] We are adopting for clarity the convention of enclosing components in < > brackets. This does NOT imply the same thing as in the usage by Katz and Fodor (1963).

[19] Lounsbury has done essentially the same kind of thing in his "transformational rules" to extend the basic meanings of kinship terms; see Lounsbury 1964b.

[20] The non-uniqueness of the means by which speakers of a language actually establish crucial distinctions was one of the sources of Robbins Burling's skepticism in Burling 1964.

[21] The component <readily movable> is important to distinguish _chair_ from _seat_: one has a _seat_ at the theater, but a _chair_ at home. In a box at the theater, one may of course use either a _chair_ or a _seat_. _Seat_ is used to designate the position and the function, while _chair_ additionally indicates a movable object.

[22] At the December 1964 meeting of the Linguistic Society of America, William Labov presented a fascinating study of the effects of specified circumstantial details upon the labelling of objects as _cup_, _bowl_, and _vase_.

[23] See Katz and Fodor 1963.

[24] Katz and Fodor (1963) tried in their early work to distinguish between what they called markers (= rigorously diagnostic components) and what they called distinguishers (= components which are not rigorously diagnostic, but which impose co-occurrence restrictions on the use of a term); but as Bolinger has shown (see footnote 5 of this article) one can go on indefinitely "atomizing" the distinguishers and extracting from them markers required to disambiguate newly constructed contexts. In more recent work, Katz and Fodor no longer make this distinction.

[25] It is most important to repeat that we are not describing all the meanings of _march_, e.g., in _The band played a stirring march_. We do not say that a word is included in the meaning of another word, but that a specific meaning of a word is included in the domain of a specific meaning of some other word. Similarly, we do not speak of synonymous words, but of overlapping meanings.

REFERENCES

Bendix, Edward H.
    1966   Componential Analysis of General Vocabulary: The Seman-
                tic structure of a set of Verbs in English, Hindi, and Japa-
                nese (Bloomington, Indiana University Press).

Bolinger, Dwight
  1965   "The Atomization of Meaning", Language 41: 555-573.
Bréal, Michel
  1897   Essai de sémantique (Paris).
Burling, Robbins
  1964   "Cognition and Componential Analysis: God's Truth or
          Hocus-Pocus ? ", American Anthropologist 66: 20-28.
          (A discussion by Dell Hymes and Charles Frake in the
          same periodical, pp. 116-122).
Chomsky, Noam
  1965   Aspects of the Theory of Syntax (Cambridge, Massachu-
          setts Institute of Technology Press).
Goodenough, W. H.
  1956   "Componential Analysis and the Study of Meaning", Lan-
          guage 32: 195-216.
Katz, Jerrold J., and Jerry A. Fodor
  1963   "The Structure of a Semantic Theory", Language 39: 170-
          210.
Lamb, S. M.
  1965   "Kinship Terminology and Linguistic Structure" in Formal
          Semantic Analysis, E. A. Hammel, ed. (American An-
          thropologist 67: 5, Part 2), pp. 37-64.
Lounsbury, F. G.
  1964a   "A Formal Account of the Crow- and Omaha-Type Kinship
          Terminologies" in Explorations in Cultural Anthropology,
          W. H. Goodenough, ed. (New York, McGraw-Hill).
  1964b   "The Structural Analysis of Kinship Semantics" in Proceed-
          ings of the Ninth International Congress of Linguists, H. G.
          Lunt, ed. (The Hague, Mouton).
Mathiot, Madeleine
  1967   "The Place of the Dictionary in Linguistic Description",
          Language 43: 703-724.
  1968   An Approach to the Cognitive Study of Language (Blooming-
          ton, Indiana University Press).
Nida, Eugene A.
  In press Componential Analysis of Meaning; An Introduction to
          Semantic Structures (The Hague, Mouton).
Öhman, Susanne
  1953   "The Theories of the 'Linguistic Field'", Word 9: 123-134.

Ullman, Stephen
   1957   Principles of Semantics, 2nd ed. (Glasgow).
   1963   "Semantic Universals" in Universals of Language, J. H.
           Greenberg, ed. (Cambridge, Massachusetts, the M. I. T.).
Weinreich, Uriel
   1966   "Explorations in Semantic Theory" in Current Trends in
           Linguistics, Vol. III, Theoretical Foundations, Thomas A.
           Sebeok, ed. (The Hague, Mouton).

Part II. Language and Communication

7 | Indigenous Pidgins and Koinés

In Collaboration with Harold W. Fehderau

0. Misconceptions about pidgin vis-a-vis creole, trade language, lingua franca, koiné

There are a number of popular, but erroneous, ideas about pidgin languages. One particularly widespread view is that pidgins are only very much simplified forms of standard languages, with self-evident concessions to the ignorance or linguistic peculiarities of so-called 'natives'. Moreover, it is assumed that within a few minutes any speaker of the dominant language can adjust his speech so as to talk pidgin, or at least so as to understand it. In addition, it is assumed that pidgins really have little or no stable structure; that is to say, each speaker merely improvises as he goes along. Nothing could be further from the truth. Pidgin languages are not merely simplified world languages, and one simply cannot throw words together in any form or order and expect local people to understand. In fact, learning to speak a pidgin language well can be as difficult as mastering any foreign language, except for the fact that many of the lexical forms are at least familiar, but deceptively so, since the meanings assigned to them in the pidgin language are so often radically altered.

Some people regard any so-called hybrid language as being a pidgin, long after such a language has become the only language of a relatively large speech community. In early colonial days the form of French spoken in Haiti by the slave population from Africa and the European plantation managers was obviously only a pidgin, but rapidly this form of speech became the only language for the largely Negro population. In this process it evolved from a pidgin into a creole, with all the structural elaboration and vocabulary enrichment which is involved in any full-scale language.

Another misconception about pidgins is that they consist
merely of the vocabulary of one language and the grammar of another.
The dominant language, normally foreign to the area, is supposed to
provide the vocabulary, while the local language or languages provide
the grammar. Another view of pidgins is that they are merely a kind
of local mélange, in which the ingredients from various languages are
so mixed up that one cannot determine any genetic relationship. But
a careful study of pidgins has indicated that both these views about
pidgins are unjustified.[1] It is true that certain important structural
features of the dominant language are altered by the speakers of local
languages, but the essential structure of the dominant language remains.

Many people have thought that all pidgin languages were the
result of contact between (1) some great 'world language', such as
English, French, Portuguese, or Spanish, and (2) the local languages.
Most of the pidgins which have developed within the last few centuries
have involved such combinations, e.g. Taki-taki, Papiamento, Wes-
cos, Neomelanesian, and Chinese-English Pidgin, but this is certainly
not a universal feature of pidgins, even as we shall be pointing out
later in this paper, in referring to Kituba, spoken in the Congo, and
to Police Motu, spoken in Papua.

The assumption that any 'trade language' is a kind of pidgin,
is also quite incorrect, for a number of trade languages are simply
dialectal extensions of a regional language. In classical times the
Greek language spread throughout most of the countries bordering on
the eastern portion of the Mediterranean. Attic Greek became somewhat changed in this process of becoming a trade language, but at no
time was there a Greek pidgin, a form of language which was structurally distinct from and mutually unintelligible with Greek as spoken
by Greeks themselves. Koiné Greek did undergo typical modifications
in the direction of simplification of morphological and syntactic structures, but when any language extends over wide areas as a commer-
cially important tongue for bilinguals, such structural simplifications
are common. These types of linguistic modifications must, however,
be carefully distinguished from typical pidgin developments.

Though a number of important studies have been made of
pidgins and creoles,[2] there are two phases of such studies which have

not been adequately dealt with. First, insufficient attention has been
paid to the fact that pidgin languages do arise in so-called indigenous
situations, that is, in circumstances in which there is no world language present and therefore in which the pidginization is not the result
of contact between colonizers and 'natives'. Second, the distinction
between pidgins and Koiné languages has not been sufficiently recognized. Any trade language tends to be regarded as a lingua franca,
and lingua franca is equated with pidgin. Such an identification leads
to quite erroneous conclusions about the nature of the linguistic structures of such koiné forms of language. The present paper is an attempt
to correct these two gaps in the record.

1. Kituba, an indigenous pidgin language of Congo

Kituba[3] (also commonly known as Kikongo ya Leta) is spoken
by some 1,500,000 persons in the Lower Congo and in the Kwango-
Kwilu region of Congo-Kinshasa, and in southwestern Congo-
Brazzaville. It arose toward the early part of the 16th century in the
Lower Congo as a means of communication between various Bakongo
tribes engaged in slave and ivory trade. The dialect center of Kituba
was Manianga, a focal point in the trade routes which came from the
upper Congo basin and which separated at Manianga to various coastal
ports from Angola to Gabon. Kituba evidently flourished for more than
300 years with only minimal linguistic influence from the outside, for
white traders were strongly discouraged from penetrating inland.

It was only toward the end of the 19th century that there was
any significant linguistic influence from speakers of French, English,
or Portuguese, but by that time the Kituba pidgin was well established
among the various tribes in the Lower Congo and became a natural
means of communication with Whites from the outside. The white
traders and administrators, of course, appreciated Kituba, for it
permitted them to communicate with a minimum of effort, since Kituba
was so much simpler than the tribal tongues, and with a maximum
audience, for the Kituba was widely used. It is little wonder, therefore, that Kituba received considerable governmental sanction and
later became one of the four more or less official languages of the
Congo, alongside Lingala, Swahili, and Tshiluba.

A number of theories as to the origin of Kituba have been suggested. Some persons claimed that it had been introduced in the early days by the Portuguese. Others insisted that it was a Congolese response to the linguistic inadequacies of white administrators. Still others insisted that missionaries had invented the language, largely through the corruptions which they introduced into Kikongo, the local tribal language; and still other persons contended that Kituba was only the natural result of a linguistic 'melting pot' throughout the area wherever a number of different Kikongo dialects came into contact. As Fehderau has pointed out (1967), none of these theories as to the origin of Kituba can be justified. The only valid explanation is that Kituba is a typical pidgin language, arising as all pidgins do, namely, in the practical circumstances of people from different language backgrounds attempting to communicate with one another. Kituba is also typical in that it represents essentially one basic form of language, the dialect of Kikongo as spoken in the Manianga area. Moreover, it is fully understandable how such a trade center would provide the dominant linguistic form, since speakers of this dialect would be the continuing initiators of communication with the various traders who would come to and through Manianga.

Kituba reflects the modifications characteristic of all pidgins. It is not merely a simplified form of standard Kimanianga, but a form of speech which is mutually unintelligible with Kimanianga and the other Kikongo dialects of the area. The following features of this simplification process are significant: (1) The prefixal aspect-tense forms are drastically reduced. In Kimanianga there were about seventeen of these forms, but in standard Kituba today there are only nine aspect-tenses and these are formed by means of free particles, which form analytic verb phrases rather than tightly knit morphological units of a synthetic type. (2) The subject prefixes to the verbs are replaced by independent pronouns. (3) The noun classes, with six alliterative prefixes in the plural forms, are reduced to four non-alliterative prefixes. (4) The immediate past perfect, which in Kikongo has a complex morphophonemic structure, has been replaced by a simple verb phrase. (5) The tonal distinctions, which are quite important for the syntactic structure of Kikongo, are greatly simplified. There has been no special simplification in the phonological structure of segmental phonemes, for the phonological structure of Kimanianga was similar to the surrounding related dialects and actually simpler than other languages (adjacent to the Bakongo tribes) whose speakers learned Kituba.

Kituba is now in the process of becoming a creole, since there are now many speakers for whom Kituba is their only or principal language. Creolization, however, means very rapid reversal of some of the very structures which are characteristic of a pidgin. A new class of verbs has arisen in the western region, consisting of French borrowings; and the free forms of the verb phrases are rapidly being reduced to affixal structures. For example, the oldest generation will use munu imene kwenda I have gone, while the middle-aged generation says munu mekwenda, and the young people say mumekwenda. If this tendency continues (and there is every indication that it will), another generation will see a complete reversion to an affixal structure, similar to what occurs in Kikongo.

2. Police Motu, an indigenous pidgin of Papua

Speakers of standard Motu,[4] a Melanesian language, live in twelve villages near Port Moresby on the south coast of Papua. There is some speculation that these Motu speakers are relatively recent arrivals on the mainland of Papua, since the people do not possess much land behind their coastal villages. At any rate, the Motu people either preferred or were forced to engage extensively in commerce, and in the process they succeeded, in cooperation with their trading partners, in developing a pidgin form of the Motu language, which now extends for several hundred miles to the east and to the west of the Motu area proper.

This pidgin form of Motu spread in precolonial times, but it was seemingly very much aided by Sir Hubert Murray, the first governor of the region, who was so bitterly opposed to Neomelanesian pidgin English that he encouraged the use of pidgin Motu, apparently as the lesser of two evils. At any rate, pidgin Motu became known as Police Motu, for it was adopted as the language of local police and army units and was encouraged by some of the missions in the region. At present, however, only some 60,000 persons speak Police Motu, and then only as a second language. In fact, in the Motu villages usually only the men can speak Police Motu, for they are the only individuals having

any special need for it. Moreover, in view of the rapid inroads of
Neomelanesian (English pidgin), of which there are more than 800,000
speakers, Police Motu is definitely on the decline, and will probably
die out, even as many other pidgins have in the past.

    Police Motu, however, is definitely a pidgin language, and
not a koiné. Even though the vocabulary of Police Motu is at least
90 percent derived from Motu, the two languages are by no means
mutually intelligible. Of course, the Motu speaker will recognize
some of the words and he might 'get the drift' of a conversation, but
he would find it quite impossible to comprehend what was really being
said, for as in the case of all pidgins the structure of the dominant
language has undergone certain very severe modifications.

    In the first place, the relatively complex verb structure of
Motu is drastically simplified in Police Motu. This has meant that
only one form of the verb, the third person singular, is selected as
the base for all the analytic phrases. In the second place, instead of
complex person-aspect-tense complexes preposed to the verb, the
pronominal elements are represented by independent pronouns and
the aspect-tense elements become independent particles (often adverbs). These pre-verb structures in Motu are quite complex and
involve a number of morphophonemic alternations. It is not strange,
therefore, that they have been ready candidates for restructuring into
simpler combinations. For example, in Motu asina itamu I did not
see you (sg.) consists of a pre-verb asina, a fused pronominal element of the first person singular with the negative past-tense marker,
and itamu, the root ita- see with the object second person singular
suffix -mu. In Police Motu all of this has been restructured as oi lau
itaia lasi, literally you I see not.

    The interaction between the dominant language and the local
language in the process of formation of a pidgin may be readily seen
in the influence of Toaripi upon Police Motu. In standard Motu the
future is indicated by a preverb structure, marked by an initial b-.
In Toaripi, however, the future is characteristically indicated by a
particle aite, meaning later, and occurring between the pronominal
subject and the main verb. Speakers of Police Motu do not, however,
use aite, but employ the Motu word dohore, also meaning later, with
this same future significance and in the same position which it would

have in Toaripi. Similarly, in Toaripi completed action is indicated
by a post-verb expression roroka, meaning that's finished or that's
the end. Accordingly, in Police Motu speakers use the Motu word
vadaeni, which has the same meaning in isolation as Toaripi roroka
and place it at the same point in the verb phrase as the Toaripi counter-
part would be employed.

In addition to these important structural modifications Police
Motu also undergoes a complete loss of irregular verb forms and a
rather important series of phonological reductions. For example,
the Motu voiced velar stop and continuant fell together, and similarly
/ l/ and / r/ were reduced to a single phoneme. Complex patterns
of stress alternation, which in Motu signals differences between singular and plural in a number of words, was lost entirely.

3. Significance of pidginization in the light of information theory

To note the kinds of restructuring which occur in the processes of pidginization is all very interesting, but what is significant is
the nature of such changes, as they reflect certain basic factors in
communication. In the first place, a high percentage of changes
occurring in pidginization of languages are directed toward greater
redundancy. Free pronouns, rather than affixal forms, result in a
longer stretch of sound to signal the same amount of information.
Similarly, the use of independent adverbial particles, rather than
inflectional forms, to denote various tenses and aspects points in the
same direction of greater redundancy. In the second place, the simplification of structures, e.g. elimination of morphemic alternations,
reduction of grammatical classes, and preference given to single
unaltered forms of lexical units (i.e. with inflectional modifications
reduced to a minimum or eliminated entirely) suggests the attempt to
improve the efficiency of decoding for the person with strictly limited
experience in the dominant language. By always hearing only one form
of any lexical unit, the receptor can much more readily identify it,
since the 'search procedure' in his memory is so greatly simplified.

These two companion procedures of preference for longer
free forms and unitary symbolization of lexical units are constantly
at work in all languages, pidgin or standard. When procedures of

formal coalescence seem to have progressed too far, as, for example, in the verb inflection of Classical Latin, there is a tendency to substitute free forms in phrase structures, as in the case of Romance developments of the future and the perfective tenses. At present, the future of French and Spanish is undergoing a still further analytical development by the introduction of periphrastic forms with verbs meaning 'to go'. At the same time, analogical formations tend to level out some of the complex morphophonemic alternations which develop within linguistic units, so that from time to time such units are restructured in the direction of single rather than multiple forms.

4. Procedures in the development of pidgin languages

On the basis of what we know about the problems of intercommunication between persons attempting to overcome rather formidable linguistic barriers, we can readily reconstruct the major outlines of what actually occurs in the development of pidgin languages. In reality there is no special mystery about the ways in which pidgins arise—they are simply the normal and easily predicted reactions to special sets of circumstances. To understand what happens we need to look at this process first from the standpoint of the speaker of the dominant, or 'source', language and then from the standpoint of the speaker of the nondominant, or what may perhaps be better described as the 'feedback', language.

In describing the role of the dominant language, we might use the designation 'aggressor' language, for this is the language of the one who generally takes the initiative in establishing contact and who provides the basic linguistic material out of which the resulting pidgin is constructed. We could also speak of the nondominant language as the 'reactor' language, to emphasize the function of the receptors. However, the terms 'source language' and 'feedback language' are probably more satisfactory in view of the various types of contexts in which the names need to be used.

In a specific, concrete situation in which speakers of a source language wish to develop communication with persons who do not understand the source language or who have only a very limited knowledge of it, the following procedures will almost inevitably be followed:

(1) the source-language speaker will use the simplest and fullest possible free forms to identify (a) objects to which he can point, e.g.
fish, nets, shells, axes, pieces of money, ivory tusks, baskets of
betel nuts, (b) events which he can demonstrate or mimic, e.g. buy,
sell, carry off, eat, and drink, and (c) quantities which he can show,
e.g. one, two, three, much, and little; and (2) the source-language
speaker will then attempt to put these three classes of terms into the
simplest possible syntactic constructions, normally following the
structure of his own language.

At this point, however, there is almost immediate influence
from the feedback language, for the speakers of the feedback language
inevitably exhibit two important tendencies. First, they tend to reproduce the words with certain phonological changes, depending on the
structure of their own language. If the source-language speaker really
wants to do business, he will usually adjust his pronunciation of words
in order to accommodate the sounds to the phonological structure of
the feedback language. Furthermore, even in the incipient bargaining
that takes place in initial contact, the speakers of a feedback language
are likely to reorder the words on the basis of the syntax of their own
language. Again, the source-language speaker is very likely to shift
to this order, for he wants to make his point as effective as possible.

As communicative contacts continue between speakers of the
source language and the feedback language, speakers of the latter will
acquire more and more of the vocabulary of the source language, but
without the elaborate grammatical structure into which it fits. They
will almost inevitably, therefore, fit this vocabulary into their own
syntactic structures, but as isolated free forms, not as bound forms.
What occurs is 'translation borrowing', i.e. borrowing of lexical
items from the source language but with meanings and usage distinctive of the feedback language. The speakers of the source language
normally do not object to such modifications of their own language,
for the motivation of commercial advantage prompts them to forego
any strong emotional feelings based on puristic ideas they might have
about their mother tongue. Moreover, being the aggressive parties
in the transactions and having in general a sense of security about the
superiority of their own culture, they do not hesitate to speak this
'debased form' of their own language, for they attribute all of this to
the cultural 'inferiority' of those who speak the feedback language.

For those who speak the feedback language there is usually an important prestige value in being able to do business in the pidgin. The first men to learn the pidgin are usually the more progressive members of the community and they become the pacesetters. In view of the fact that speakers of the feedback language normally do not go to live with speakers of the source language, there is no pressure to learn the standard forms of the source language. Moreover, members of the source-language community usually are not too anxious for other people to learn their language in its correct form. This means that pidgin serves an additional function of making people available, when their presence or help is required, but also of keeping them at a distance when one does not wish to be bothered. In other words, speakers of a feedback language who have acquired the use of a pidgin are economically useful while not being socially threatening.

The ambivalent role of a pidgin is well illustrated in the traditional value of Chinese-English pidgin. As Hall has pointed out (1966, p. 8) the early English merchants in points such as Canton regarded learning 'heathen Chinese' as quite impossible and hence were only too happy to simplify their own language for the benefit of the Chinese. At the same time, the Chinese did not wish to stoop to learn the real language of the 'foreign devils,' but thought this pidgin form of language much less debasing to themselves. Hence, this form of pidgin served the interests of both parties in keeping one another at arm's length. All this, however, was changed with the introduction of western forms of education into China. Persons aspiring to learn about the outside world wanted the standard forms of English and persons who really wanted to do business in China found that pidgin was simply not enough. As a result pidgin rapidly became merely a symbol of the domestic servant and the poor factory worker, and soon largely ceased to exist, though at one time it was perhaps more widely used than any other pidgin of which we have record.

Because of the special nature of pidgin languages they may arise very quickly—they can be the creation of only a few days or months—when the communication factors are just right. At the same time, however, they can disappear almost as quickly, whenever the circumstances which gave rise to them have radically changed.

5. Koiné forms of language

The koiné form of a language presents no such structural break as is clearly present in the case of pidgins. Koinés are always mutually intelligible with at least some forms of the standard language. Of course, one who knows only a koiné form of a language would find it difficult to understand the high-flown language of traditional literature, but an uneducated speaker of the standard form of the language would likely have a similar degree of difficulty.

Perhaps one of the most interesting koiné developments in language at the preset time occurs in Swahili, which spread from the East Coast of Africa inland through major parts of Kenya, Uganda, Tanzania, and Eastern Congo. One may actually distinguish two principal levels of koiné development. First, there is the simpler language used in interior Tanzania, Kenya, and slightly more of a tendency to koiné structures as one moves from Tanzania, to Kenya, and then on to Uganda. Nevertheless, all these forms of Swahili can be roughly classified as East African Swahili, but of a simpler variety than one encounters among educated persons in Dar es Salaam and Zanzibar.

The second koiné area includes the central and southern parts of eastern Congo and Bukavu. The inhabitants of Albertville (now Kalemie) speak a form of Swahili which most closely approximates the form of language used in East Africa, but from Albertville south the Swahili takes on a distinctive koiné structure, in which verb forms are analogically regularized, noun classes are simplified, and syntactic structures become progressively less complex. A further development of Swahili involves a pidginization, Kingwana, which is much despised by some educational authorities and often strongly denounced by mission leaders, but which still persists, especially in the rural areas considerably to the north of Albertville. In Kingwana the verb structures are radically simplified, the noun classes have almost disappeared, and the sentence structures are very limited.

Congo Swahili as spoken in the area of Lubumbashi has been regarded by some persons as a pidgin and therefore as something to be condemned. There are, however, two very important differences which mark the status of Congo Swahili as a koiné, and not as a pidgin. First, Congo Swahili is mutually intelligible with the form of Swahili as spoken and understood in rural Tanzania; and second, speakers of standard Swahili do not shift their language completely when they attempt to communicate with Congo Swahili speakers. They may choose to employ less complex grammatical structures, but they do not radically modify their speech. They may recognize certain dialect differences, such as may occur, for example, in different dialects of French, but they certainly do not regard Congo Swahili as a foreign language.

In the case of a pidgin language this total shift in manner of speaking is almost always clearly evident. On a recent occasion in Mount Hagen, New Guinea, Nida noticed how an Australian government official was attempting to communicate with one of the servants at the hotel. He first addressed the servant in standard English, on the assumption that he might be a school graduate and should be given the opportunity to respond in proper English. When the servant obviously did not understand, the official rephrased his communication in simple English to which the servant again gave no response. At that point, the official adopted an entirely different attitude, complete with distinctive intonation, and facial and hand gestures, and began to speak Neomelanesian. A shift from English to French would not have brought out any more striking differences. At last the servant reacted, as though only then had he really been addressed in meaningful forms.

The two levels of koiné development in standard Swahili represent really two different dialects of the same language. Only Kingwana is a pidgin development. The different koiné forms of Swahili reflect the same types of modifications which occurred in Ancient Greek as it spread through the Eastern Mediterranean regions, in English as it has developed distinctive forms in the Philippines, and in Portuguese as it has evolved in Brazil.

The Lingala language of Congo should also be classified as a koiné. As it spread from its up-river origin, it underwent a series of analogical simplifications and regularizations. But speakers of Lingala could always understand one another, even though they could detect certain regionalisms. The furthest extension of Lingala has been to Kinshasa, where it has largely taken over as the trade language of the capital city. At present, probably half of the speakers

of Lingala live in Kinshasa or nearby, and due to the importance of
Kinshasa in the life of Congo this distinctive Kinshasa form of Lingala
is beginning to play a dominant role in influencing the up-river form
of the language.

In reality koiné forms of language are much more common
than pidgins. In Africa, for example, there are a number of languages
which are undergoing modifications as the result of their being used
as trade languages by persons of nearby tribal groups. Languages
such as Bambara and Hausa in West Africa are particularly important
as trade languages, but there are many less conspicuous languages
which exhibit koiné tendencies as the result of their extensive use in
bilingual contexts, e.g. Tshiluba and Yaounde.

Though traditional colonialism, which spawned a number of
pidgin forms of language, is largely an institution of the past, it would
be quite presumptuous to think that future circumstances would not
provide settings for the development of new pidgins. Of one thing we
may be sure, however, the pressures of multilingualism throughout
the world will most certainly give rise to many more developments
in the direction of koiné forms of languages, especially in a continent
such as Africa.

6. Summary of degrees of response to situations of language contact

In most situations there is one of three different types of
languages in use: (1) international (so-called world) languages, e.g.
English, French, and Spanish, which are used in countries of various
nationalities and accepted as vehicles of communication in international
affairs; (2) national languages, e.g. Polish, Dutch, and Greek, which
are used as vehicles of communication within a given country; and
(3) ethnic or regional languages (or dialects), e.g. Welsh, Kikongo,
Zulu, and Cree, which serve as vehicles of communication for more
restricted groups within a given country.

When people speaking mutually unintelligible languages come
into social contact with each other, one of four main responses can
take place: (1) each group rejects the language of the other group as
a means of verbal communication; (2) a third language acceptable to

both is chosen to be the means of communication; (3) one group accepts the language of the other group; or (4) a 'compromise' is reached by drastically restructuring the language of one of the groups to create a new vehicle of communication acceptable to both.

The languages involved in (2) and (3) (by mutual acceptance) and in (4) (through restructuring) constitute what are called 'trade languages'. The differences between these responses to a contact situation are not so much a matter of kind as of degree. In (4) there is a great deal of linguistic change involved, but even the outright acceptance of a major world language, for example, as a vehicle of communication by people of another country (such as the use of French in government, education, and business in the Congo) does not preclude linguistic change, a certain amount of restructuring, and the development of regional dialects of the world language. In fact, such changes are bound to take place.

It seems helpful to recognize four degrees of response to language contact. In the past, a great deal has been said about C (below). Nothing more need be said about A, but we feel that it is useful to distinguish and isolate B and D.

A. The aggressor language is accepted with very little or no linguistic change.
B. The aggressor language is accepted with some accompanying widespread modifications but without loss of mutual intelligibility. The resulting language can be called a koiné.
C. An international aggressor language undergoes drastic linguistic change in contact with a local reactor language. The resulting language can be called, for lack of a better name, a 'hybrid pidgin'.
D. A regional or ethnic aggressor language undergoes drastic linguistic change in contact with other regional or ethnic reactor languages. The resulting language can be called an 'indigenous pidgin'.

Koinés are distinguished from pidgins in that pidgins are mutually unintelligible with the originating aggressor and reactor languages while koinés remain largely mutually intelligible with the originating form.

World languages, national languages, ethnic languages, and koinés can be the primary, secondary, or tertiary language of certain groups of speakers. Pidgins, by definition, are never primary languages, i. e. no one calls a pidgin his 'mother tongue'. If a pidgin develops into a primary language for a segment of the population it is called a creole, and creolization means fairly rapid linguistic change, as the vocabulary and grammar of the language are elaborated.

Following the above framework, one can see how the same language can undergo different developments in different areas: Swahili spreads as a koiné (with slight linguistic modifications and continued mutual intelligibility) in Kenya, Tanzania, and most of Eastern Congo. But it develops as a pidgin (Kingwana) in the northern areas as it undergoes drastic changes.

Kikongo is drastically reduced in the Lower Congo to a pidgin Kikongo (Kituba) by native traders and is used as such for decades. Then it spreads (koiné-like) to other areas to the east (actually far into the Kasai in the early days of this century). This same Kikongo base (the Kimanianga dialect) is taken by the Protestant missions of the area and used for teaching, preaching, Bible translation, and vernacular literature, thus creating what is today a church koiné Kikongo, which has spread throughout the Bakongo area. The Roman Catholic church has done the same with the Kintandu dialect of Kikongo.

NOTES

[1] See Hall (1966).
[2] Some of the more important treatments of pidgins and creoles include the following: Broomfield (1930), Jacobs (1932), Hall (1944, 1948, 1952, 1961, 1966), Cole (1953), French (1953), Nida (1955), Samarin (1955), Taylor (1956), Voorhoeve (1957), Berry (1959).
[3] For data on Kituba see Fehderau (1967).
[4] Most of the data of this section is derived from Wurm (1964). Supplementary information was furnished by Mr. H. Brown, for many years a missionary among the Toaripi of Papua.

BIBLIOGRAPHY

Berry, Jack. 1959. The origins of Krio vocabulary, Sierra Leone Studies 3: 12.

Broomfield, G. W. 1930. The development of the Swahili language,
    Africa 3.516-22.
Cole, Desmond T. 1953. Fanagalo and the Bantu languages in South
    Africa, African Studies 12.1-9.
De Camp, David. 1961. Social and geographical factors in Jamaican
    dialects, Creole Language Studies 2.61-84.
Fehderau, Harold W. 1967. The Origin and Development of Kituba.
    Kisangani: Université Libre du Congo.
French, A. 1953. Pidgin English in New Guinea, Australian Quar-
    terly 23:4.57-60.
Hall, Robert A. , Jr. 1944. Chinese Pidgin English: Grammar and
    Texts, Journal of the American Oriental Society 64.95-113.
_____ 1948. The linguistic structure of Taki-Taki, Language 24.
    92-116.
_____ 1952. Pidgin English and linguistic change, Lingua 3.138-
    146.
_____ 1961. Pidgin, Encyclopaedia Britannica 17.905-907.
_____ 1966. Pidgin and Creole Languages. Ithaca (New York):
    Cornell University Press.
Jacobs, Melville. 1932. Notes on the structure of Chinook Jargon,
    Language 8.27-50.
Nida, Eugene A. 1955. Tribal and trade languages, African Studies
    14.155-8.
Samarin, William J. 1955. Sango, an African lingua franca, Word
    11.254-67.
Taber, Charles. 1964. French loan-words in Sango: a statistical
    study of incidence. M. A. thesis, Hartford Seminary Foun-
    dation.
Taylor, Douglas McR. 1956. Language contacts in the West Indies,
    Word 12.399-414.
Voorhoeve, Jan. 1957. Missionary linguistics in Surinam, The Bible
    Translator 8.179-90.
_____ 1961. Linguistic experiments in syntactic analysis, Creole
    Language Studies 2.37-60.
Wurm, S. A. 1964. Motu and Police Motu, a study in typological
    contrasts, Papers in New Guinea Linguistics, No. 2, 4.19-
    41.

8 | Communication Roles of Languages in Multilingual Societies

In Collaboration with William L. Wonderly

1. Introduction

The purpose of this paper is to provide a model for studying languages in reference to their communicative functions, especially in multilingual societies; and to point out some of the factors that should be taken into consideration by educators and policy-making bodies who are concerned with the development of national languages and with making optimal use of other languages in their areas.

The role of language in society has often been studied and described. As a result, there are a number of classifications of language usage, but these are based primarily (1) on the function of language within different contexts, e.g. education, legal proceedings, governmental decrees, trade, religion, etc.; or (2) on different levels of status, e.g. official, national, tribal; or (3) levels of usage, e.g. colloquial, literary, vulgar, slang; or (4) on differences of historical setting, e.g. ancient, traditional, archaic, obsolescent, and modern.[1] These classifications have never been fully satisfactory, since one and the same language may function in so many different ways and diverse groups within the society may make use of languages for quite different purposes. Though such classifications are obviously helpful, they generally fail to highlight the dynamics of language usage and as a result they prevent us from seing similarities of function on a broad cross-cultural base.

In contrast with these valuable but somewhat limited classifications of language use, this article shifts the perspective from the particular language itself to the communication needs of the society, with primary emphasis on the typical multilingual or multidialectal society. Our purpose is thus to study the relationships between language (or languages) and the communication needs of a particular group of interacting persons.

2. Major Communication Functions of Language

A study of language in terms of the needs for adequate communication within a particular society has led to the recognition of three major communication roles: (1) communication with people of the in-group, (2) communication with people of the out-group, and (3) communication involving specialized information. Quite naturally, within multilingual societies there is a tendency for certain languages to be primarily "in-group languages" while others function as "out-group languages"; and finally, certain languages may have the function of "languages of specialized information".

3. The In-group Language

The in-group language is the one used in any society for the basic face-to-face relationships with other speakers with whom the individual in question fully identifies. In so-called primitive societies this would quite naturally be the indigenous or tribal language. In certain large language communities such a face-to-face language might be the regional dialect as, for example, in the case of Swiss-German.

In a large linguistic community which is relatively heterogeneous, in the sense that it has many so-called "vertical dialects" (socio-economic distinctions in speech), the in-group form of language may be one of these levels, or it may be characterized by the use of colloquial levels involving special slang expressions, or it may even be a highly specialized jargon which is particularly important for in-group identification. Such forms of speech have been important for groups such as beatniks, and the in-group speech of English-speaking teen-agers reveals certain of these characteristics. Relatively elaborate underworld jargons have been known and studied by various language specialists. [2]

4. The Out-group Language

Almost all people living in a face-to-face speech community have some need for contacting people of groups outside their own community. The only exception to this situation might be some of the isolated tribes in Amazonia, but even among groups such as the Guaica (or Shiriana) Indians in northern Brazil and southern Venezuela (where some of the dialects are mutually unintelligible), there is a highly developed form of language used on all occasions when different tribal groups meet together. Even under these so-called "primitive" circumstances an out-group form of language has developed.

In many parts of the world a trade language serves the purpose of out-group communication. In the lower Congo and the Kwilu valley a trade language called Kituba serves for most intertribal contacts. The Kituba language is actually a koiné form of Kikongo, which has spread throughout the area as a medium of out-group communication. In the process of spreading, it has become greatly simplified in its linguistic structures. In eastern New Guinea the language of out-group communication is a local pidgin language called Neomelanesian, a name designed to give the language some status. [3]

It is important to recognize, however, that there are certain very essential differences between a pidgin language and a koiné language. The former tends to have its vocabulary and grammar derived from a foreign source, but to be very heavily influenced by the structures of the local languages. This is true, for example, of Weskos pidgin of West Africa, of Neomelanesian in New Guinea, and of Taki-taki in the northern part of South America. As long as such a form of language is only a second language for people and used under relatively restricted circumstances, it may continue to have a rather restricted vocabulary and limited grammatical structures; as, for example, in the case of Chinook, used as a type of pidgin in the north-western part of the United States. However, just as soon as such a pidgin becomes the only language of a sizeable constituency of interacting persons, for example, a hundred thousand or more, it develops very rapidly and becomes known as a creole language.

A koiné language, on the other hand, is a form of language which preserves in very large measure the basic vocabulary and structure of its source, but is considerably simplified as it spreads over "foreign" territory. It quite naturally tends to pick up vocabulary from local languages in the area, and it may also acquire certain of their grammatical devices. The general simplification of classical Greek as it spread throughout the eastern Mediterranean in post-classical times is the typical example of a koiné. Similarly, the spread of Swahili from Zanzibar and the contiguous coast of East Africa through a number of areas of East Africa represents the same kind of simplification process. Likewise, the manner in which Tagalog is now being promoted in the Philippines as a national language under the name of Pilipino is a similar example of this tendency toward simplification, with the retention of the basic vocabulary and structure of a single language.

5. The Language of Specialized Information

In many areas where there are both in-group and out-group languages, there is also the need for a language of specialized information. This is often the language of higher education or of specialized formal training. For example, in the Camerouns many of the speakers of local languages, e.g. Bafia, Bassa, Meka, and Kaka, also know the trade language Yaoundé (closely related to Bulu which was promoted as a trade language by Protestant missionaries). Yaoundé serves as an important out-group language, but any person wanting to acquire specialized information, that is, information which comes from the world culture and not from the culture of the immediate out-groups, must learn French. Similarly, in the Philippines speakers of such languages as Cebuano, Hiligaynon, Pampango, and Samareño must learn Pilipino if they are to enjoy movies, watch television, read certain newspapers, and carry on trade in areas outside of their immediate tribal areas. But these persons must also learn English if they want to go on to secondary school or the university and if they wish to take positions of leadership in politics, business, or social life.

6. Multilingual and Monolingual Linguistic Structures

Though in the preceding description of in-group languages, out-group languages, and languages of specialized information we may have given the impression that such uses of language occur only in strictly multilingual situations, it must be clearly recognized that these three basic functions of language exist in a number of different linguistic settings. The setting in which these functions are most obvious is no doubt the "three-language structure"; but it would be misleading if we were not to recognize also certain essential features of a two-language structure as well as those of a one-language structure. What we are dealing with here is not primarily multilingual patterns but the essential functions of language. Hence, even to appreciate such functioning in a multilingual structure, it is important that certain essential comparisons be made with other structures.

7. The Three-Language Structure

A typical three-language structure may be found in Kenya where people who speak various in-group languages, e.g. Lugaroli, Kipsigis, Lango, Acholi, Kikamba, and Kikuyu, find it highly desirable to learn Swahili if they wish to have much outside contact. At the same time, if such persons want to obtain a higher education or to participate as leaders in national life, English is indispensable.

In a typical three-language structure a so-called "world language", e.g. English, French, Spanish, or Portuguese, tends to be the language of specialized information. This is due to the fact that technical information from the world culture comes to people primarily by means of such a language. However, a three-language structure does not always involve a so-called world language as the language of specialized information, for the linguistic world of a particular speech community may be highly restricted. For example, in the Kwilu area of Congo a Kihungana speaker certainly must learn Kituba if he is to have contacts with other tribal groups. Kituba thus becomes his out-group language. However, the language of the army and of many local Congolese government administrators is Lingala. Within his restricted context, therefore, Lingala may be said to constitute the language of specialized information for him.

A similar situation exists in the northern part of the Philippines. Some of the small tribal groups learn Ilocano as the out-group language, but if they are to have much contact with the national life, then it is essential for them also to learn Pilipino, which thus becomes for them the language of specialized information.

There are, of course, some speakers who might be said to have a "four-language structure". Their own tribal language constitutes the in-group language, and there may be two different out-group languages, representing different "grades" of usefulness and serving to communicate with different out-groups. Finally, they may have a fourth language for specialized information. However, this kind of four-language structure is relatively rare and does not usually involve any large number of individuals. Furthermore, the possession of more than one out-group language usually represents not so much a different functional level as the presence of diverse out-groups with whom the person has occasion to interact. It is thus only the exceptional situation in which a person is so placed as to find it important to know four languages representing four distinct levels of communication. Therefore, we have not set up a four-language structure as being one of the basic structures for communication.

Focusing upon a three-language structure for different levels of linguistic usage does not mean, of course, that people necessarily restrict themselves to learning three languages. Quite the contrary, in Africa where there is a greater percentage of multilingualism than in any other large speech area of the world, many persons know four, five, or six languages. However, these do not represent distinct grades in out-group language contacts, but rather the learning of specific neighboring languages under circumstances where their acquisition has proven obligatory, inevitable, or highly useful. It is therefore necessary to distinguish between the learning of a specific out-group language which serves as a basis of contact with one particular group, and the learning of an out-group language which may serve as a means of communication with a number of different groups. It is within the context of this type of distinction that the recognition of a three-language structure seems to be fully justified.

8. The Two-Language Structure

In many places in the world, speakers participate in a two-language structure rather than in a three-language structure. The

second language serves both as the language of out-group contacts
and also as the source of specialized information. For the indigenous ,
groups of Latin America, for example, the various Indian languages
constitute the in-group forms of speech. The out-group languages,
both for communication between Indian groups and with the leadership
in the national life, are primarily Spanish and Portuguese. These
languages at the same time serve as the languages of specialized
information, including all levels of higher education.

   In Haiti there is a special form of two-language structure.
Practically all persons speak Haitian Creole, but only about 10 percent
speak what would be called standard French; though quite naturally a
much higher percentage understand at least the simpler forms of such
standard French. Haitian Creole, which is essentially a form of
French with a number of rather radical structural changes, serves
as the in-group language; but if one is to identify with the cultural
heritage of Haiti (which is proudly French) and with higher echelons
in the government, or is to have the advantages of higher education,
then standard French is indispensable.

   In some "two-language systems" the out-group language and
the language of specialized information may actually be multiple. In
Holland, for example, there are three languages which serve simultaneously as languages of the out-groups and of specialized information. These are German, French, and English. A good secretary
must be able to take dictation and to transcribe in all three languages.
At the same time, however, Dutch, which is the in-group language,
serves as the language of university education and hence must also
be regarded as a vehicle for specialized information. Nevertheless,
it cannot possibly serve all of the requirements of a highly technological society which must depend upon the world's most recent resources
of technical information. Moreover, the economic condition of Holland requires constant contacts beyond those which can be maintained
through Dutch, in terms both of out-group contacts and of specialized
information.

   The Dutch language may thus be regarded as a kind of anoma-
lous development. On the one hand, it approximates a "one-language
structure" since at least in certain regards the same language serves
for all three basic purposes. It is, for example, the in-group language

of Dutch people generally; it becomes the out-group language for the linguistically proud Frisians, and for many Dutch people it also serves as the language of specialized information, since it can be used throughout a university course. Nevertheless, the size of the Dutch-speaking community, the necessity for commercial contacts, and the requirements of technological information superimpose upon this one-language system a two-language structure in which the upper levels may actually be served by several different languages, primarily, English, German, and French.

Switzerland might be cited by some persons as an exception to the rule of having only a single language as the in-group language, for this country has been traditionally regarded as basically multilingual. This is not quite the case, however, for each person identifies strongly with his own linguistic group, whether French, German, Italian, Romansch, or Ladin. Nevertheless, there is also the need for an outside language, usually French or German. In the German-speaking portion of Switzerland, local Swiss dialects serve as the in-group language while standard High German serves as the language for out-group contacts and as the language of specialized information.

9.   The One-Language Structure

Native speakers of major languages, e.g. English, French, German, Spanish, Russian, or Chinese, have typically a one-language structure. They may actually speak a local regional dialect, for example, southern U.S. or Liverpool English, as the language of in-group identification; but the standard form of the language is used for most out-group contacts and for specialized information. Since there are so many millions of speakers of these individual languages and since there is such a wealth of information contained in books in such languages, most people feel little or no compulsion to learn a foreign language.

Within such one-language structures there are always those who specialize in out-group contacts. The persons dealing with tourists and foreign representatives are language specialists, but this does not have any great effect upon the broad segment of the population.

Of course there are, within many of the larger one-language societies, minority ethnic groups that have originated through immigration and maintain a two-language structure, in which the language of their country of origin constitutes the in-group language. Examples are Spanish, German, Polish, etc., in the U.S.A., and Italian, Japanese, German, etc., in Brazil. These languages tend to disappear within a few generations, but the rate of disappearance depends upon many factors. If the ethnic group has social prestige in the country and speaks a language which also enjoys prestige (as in the case of English or German-speaking immigrants in Latin America), their language may be maintained almost indefinitely; but if the prestige factor is lacking due to poor social and economic conditions of the ethnic group (as in the case of Spanish or Polish-speaking groups in the U.S.A.), the language suffers a "social handicap" and is apt to be rejected by the newer generations in their desire to extend their in-group beyond the borders of their own ethnic group.

In one-language structures, the theoretical need for additional languages of specialized information has been recognized, but in many instances the recognition is far more theoretical than practical. For example, German and French have traditionally been regarded as essential for a candidate for the Ph.D. degree, but there is an increasing tendency to make requirements in these two languages only nominal and not to insist upon a level of competence which would actually be required if one is to do any research in the languages in question. Nevertheless, the very fact that such requirements do remain in most universities is at least a "nod" in the direction of languages of specialized information.

In those languages in which there are less adequate resources of specialized information, there is almost always a greater tendency for persons to acquire a more adequate grasp of some foreign language. For example, university students in Latin America find it almost necessary to learn a language such as English, especially if they are specializing in sciences.

Japan is a country in which an amazing effort has been made to provide a one-language structure. Japanese publishing houses undertake an almost incredible amount of translating. This means that Japanese is probably the only language outside of Europe where

a national language has succeeded in becoming an adequate vehicle
for specialized information. This, of course, has been possible only
because of a sound economic base, a high degree of literacy, and large
numbers of avid readers interested in specialized information. There
are very few other countries in the world with resources such as to
make possible the duplication of this effort.

10. Languages and Political Action

        The above description of three-language and two-language
structures has not indicated anything of the tensions or problems
involved in such multilevel systems; but obviously the importance of
language for interpersonal relationships and its symbolic value as a
means of group identification (it is the most important because for
one thing it is the hardest to change or falsify) make languages politically and socially very strategic. Hence, languages naturally become
a prime element in the struggle for national unity. From the very
beginning of the independence movement in Indonesia the trade language Bahasa Indonesia was proclaimed as the language of national
unity. This was a fortunate choice, for though at the time that it was
adopted as a language of national unity it probably did not have more
than ten million speakers, it nevertheless was a very effective instrument for rallying the total constituency of Indonesia. Even today there
are only about thirty million speakers of Bahasa Indonesia, of whom
perhaps not more than three to four million speak it as their mother
tongue. In view of the presence of Javanese, which is spoken by some
sixty million people, it is in a sense surprising that Bahasa Indonesia
was chosen as the language of unity. But if Javanese had been chosen,
the attainment of national unity would have been highly questionable.

        Bahasa Indonesia did have certain very distinct advantages
as a national language. In the first place, its speakers were widely
scattered throughout the whole region of Indonesia. In the second
place, its structure is relatively simple and is closely related to all
of the languages within the Indonesian area except those very few
which are spoken in the highlands of West Irian. The very fact that
Bahasa Indonesia was politically neutral did a great deal to make it
acceptable to various groups who would have been unwilling to accept
any other language as a dominant form of speech.

Bahasa Indonesia itself is derived from the Malay language as spoken in the northern part of Sumatra and the Malay peninsula. As it has spread throughout Indonesia, it has adopted certain typically simplified structures which mean that it may be classified as a type of koiné.

In the Philippines the linguistic situation was somewhat different. The obvious choice for a language of national unity, in terms of the number of speakers, would have been Cebuano since it is spoken by more persons than any other. However, Tagalog, as the language of the region of Manila, had much greater prestige and had been acquired by a number of speakers of other languages as their "second language". The influence of Tagalog as the language of Manila was, however, increasingly decisive, for the population of Manila is somewhat over three million persons out of a total population on the islands of thirty million. In other words, at least one-tenth of the total population of the country lives in Manila, and a very high percentage of persons go to Manila from time to time.

If, however, Tagalog was to be accepted by people generally throughout the Philippines, certain concessions were regarded as essential. As one concession the national language has been called Pilipino, not Tagalog. This means that promoters of the use of Pilipino have rejected the pressures which have come from the strict Tagalog purists, who wanted to establish Tagalog in its classical form as being the norm of the national language. Some persons, of course, promoted the use of English as a national language since it was spoken at least in some measure by as many persons as any other one language of the Philippines. Nevertheless, English had a very decided disadvantage as an out-group language and as the language of national unity, since its structure is so completely different from that of the Malayo-Polynesian languages of the Philippines. Actually, a person who speaks any one of the Philippine languages can usually learn Pilipino within three to four months of residence in a Tagalog-speaking area. Moreover, the learning of Pilipino in school is much greater than would ever be the case with English. Even though English has been retained as the language of advanced primary and secondary education and of university instruction, there is mounting pressure for the use of Pilipino as the medium of instruction throughout the secondary schools, except for courses in science, where it is

recognized that students obviously need to be prepared to receive
specialized information in a language in which a greater abundance
of such information is available.

In contrast with the situations in Indonesia and the Philippines, India has presented quite a different perspective as to language
usage. English has become a kind of de facto national language by
virtue of the extensive British school system during colonial times.
English was particularly acceptable to Dravidian-speaking groups in
the south who seemed to feel that in language matters they fared somewhat better under British rule since the interests of language groups
such as the Tamils, Telugus, and Malayalams were "protected" from
domination by persons speaking the Sanskritic-based languages of the
north. On the other hand, making English an actual national language
would be an enormous economic task for India, and hence political
leaders inevitably turned to Hindi, a kind of linguistically neutral
amalgam, and essentially a trade language of central India. However,
enforcing Hindi as a national language has been an entirely too explo-
sive issue. For one thing, it meant that northerners would tend to
have distinct advantages in examinations for government positions,
and the whole movement would thus prove prejudicial to the interests
of the Dravidian-speaking groups of the southern part of India. The
reaction of people to the language issue became so violent that bloody
riots resulted. Under such circumstances it has been impossible for
India to develop a unified language policy, particularly in the face of
an increasing tendency toward regionalism, not only in government
but also in educational policy. For example, in a number of states
the language of university education is shifting from English to such
regional languages as Tamil, Telugu, and Malayalam. [4]

11. Nationalism and Regionalism

The very pressures that create the needs for some national
language as a unifying force almost inevitably also create a contrary
reaction in favor of regional languages. Whether people actually feel
threatened by the emphasis upon national unity in language is hard to
say, but certainly the emphasis upon a single language very frequently
makes them more and more aware of their own regional language.
As already noted in the case of India, regional languages have been

winning out in certain situations. Also, more and more languages of
Sanskritic stock have been recognized as official and therefore author-
ized for education. The political realities of such a situation almost
force politicians to accept regional languages as vehicles of education
and even as potential instruments for specialized information. However, here is where the real problem arises, since the regional language communities rarely have the economic resources sufficient to
publish current specialized information in such languages. Almost
by the time a book is translated and published it is out of date if it
deals with some of the rapidly developing technological phases of
modern society. In a world in which the information explosion is
even more significant than the population explosion, emphasis upon
regional languages produces serious economic and social hindrances.

This local emphasis on regional languages depends partly
upon the degree of cultural vitality of the particular regional group,
and upon the group's sense of identification or non-identification with
the national society. In Latin America most of the indigenous groups
have, through more than three centuries of uninterrupted Spanish and
Portuguese-speaking colonization and government, developed a feeling
of inferiority with respect to their own Indian languages; while main-
taining the Indian languages for purposes of in-group communication
and identification, they have shown little interest in extending their
use to that of out-group communication or the communication of
specialized information. And as these groups progressively identify
with the national society, they show increasing interest in the use of
the national language, Spanish or Portuguese. The resurgence of
Guarani in Paraguay is only an apparent exception, as this language
has now taken on national status alongside Spanish, and has become
a symbol of national, not just regional, identity.

In the Camerouns the emphasis in education has certainly
been on French, and though there is no tendency to repudiate French
as the national language nor as the language of specialized information, there has certainly been an emphasis upon regional language,
particularly within the Christian community. Here there has been a
rapidly increased interest in the translation of the Scriptures into
various languages. On the whole, however, this emphasis is not at
the expense of the national language, but at the expense of some
former out-group languages. For example, Protestants in the
Camerouns are no longer content to have their Scriptures in Bulu,

which had become a kind of "Protestant Latin" to many of the people.
They insist that they want the Scriptures in French and their own local
language, but not in a kind of "half-way language" such as Bulu has
seemed to be.

12. A National Language

For a language to become a national language certain very
important features are needed. In the first place, it should be politically neutral. If it is not characterized by political neutrality, it
is too often regarded merely as a tool by which a particular language
group seeks to extend its domination. Quite naturally, this is a cause
for alarm among other language communities. In this respect, the
development of Bahasa Indonesia has been very instructive, for under
the circumstances there has been very little opposition to Bahasa
Indonesia and almost no reaction in favor of regional languages. In
the Philippines, making Tagalog appear politically neutral has been
exceptionally wise; and in East Africa Swahili has at least seemed to
afford a neutral linguistic medium, especially in a nation such as
Kenya where the political center of the country is not associated with
traditional Swahili dominance.

In Nigeria there is simply no politically neutral language.
In fact, the division into three major regions reflects the three language poles: Hausa, Yoruba, and Ibo. The political survival of
Nigeria as a country would be even more seriously threatened than
it is if any one of these languages were promoted by the government
as being the one national language.

If a language is to be a national language, it should also be
linguistically related to the various local languages of the area. One
feature which makes Tagalog and Bahasa Indonesia so acceptable in
their respective areas is that they are so closely related to all of the
other languages. For example, a generative grammar of Tagalog,
Ilocano, and Cebuano can be almost completely identical up to the
point where morphemes have to be identified. In other words, the
grammatical structure is essentially the same. It is only that individual lexical items tend to be different. With languages so very
closely related, people can learn the national language in a very short

time. It is so much easier than having to master an entirely foreign
structure. In contrast, the fact that Spanish and Portuguese, as
Indo-European languages, are so radically different from the Indian
languages of Latin America, is no doubt one of the important factors
which has hindered the indigenous groups from learning the national
language in these countries. Moreover, when persons are required
to learn a completely foreign grammatical structure they often tend
to develop a relatively distorted form of that structure as, for example, in the rather widespread modifications of French structure as
now spoken in Congo.

For a national language to succeed it should also be spoken
as a mother tongue by a substantial community of speakers who can
serve as fully satisfactory models. In Indonesia an average of one
person in ten could speak the language Bahasa Indonesia—with, of
course, certain minor local variations, but always with complete
mutual comprehension. The persons who serve as models for such
a language should also be well distributed geographically and not concentrated in one place. The problem of French in the Congo is that
after independence the number of people who spoke French as their
mother tongue became increasingly more restricted (even a high
percentage of the Roman Catholic missionaries in the Congo were
Flemish-speaking). The increasing absence of valid models creates
a serious problem, for with rapid expansion of the school system and
fewer and fewer native speakers as models for the language, students
often become separated by a four-to-five "generational gap" between
the native speaker of French and the local teacher of French. As a
result, a native French speaker often has real difficulty in recognizing
his own language as spoken by such people. Almost the same thing is
true of English as it is often taught in local schools in the Philippines.
Accordingly, many persons speak of this form of English as "bamboo
English".

13. The National Language and the Language of Specialized Information

Almost inevitably, leaders of any nation attempt to make the
national language also the language of specialized information. This
is precisely what has happened in the case of Indonesia. At an earlier
stage Dutch was the language of the university system in the area, but

shortly after independence all instruction was carried out in Bahasa Indonesia. The rejection of Dutch is understandable, not only because of its association with colonialism and the fact that its structure differs from that of Malayo-Polynesian, but also because it has certain limitations as far as being a "world language" is concerned. Dutch thus seemed to be an inadequate instrument for keeping abreast of technological developments throughout the world. English was considered as a language of specialized information, but only for certain restricted types of material. As a result, Bahasa Indonesia was not only established as a national language, but every effort has been made to raise it to the status of a language of specialized information. For the most part, however, language planners in Indonesia have had no adequate appreciation of the technical and economic problems involved. No provision, for example, has been made for the translating and publishing of necessary textbooks. There has even been drastic restriction on the importation of books, and as a result the level of training in the universities has suffered.

In making the national language a language of specialized information, Japan has often been regarded as the model of what an Asian nation could do on its own. However, most Asians do not realize that when Japan finally did become open to Western technology, it already had a 38 percent literacy rate, a highly disciplined society, an intense emphasis upon education, and a viable economy which was able to support a broad program of translation and publication of foreign titles—something which has not been true of any other country outside the Western world.

The very problem of specialized information is becoming more and more acute, for nothing in the history of the world has quite equalled the information explosion during the last thirty years. It is estimated, for example, that of all the scientists who have ever engaged in research and publication, at least 90 percent are now alive and producing. Moreover, progress in the present-day world depends far more upon technological information than upon any other one factor. Therefore, if so-called developing nations do not wish to condemn themselves to perpetual dependency and to an ever-increasing lag, they must make provision for either (1) a sufficient number of persons fully educated in a language of specialized information and continually provided with books in such languages, or (2) adequate

programs of translation and publication of such materials in the
national language, or (3) even better, a combination of these two
approaches. Perhaps the basic difficulty is that governmental bureaus
move with tragic slowness in such matters, and by the time books are
approved, translated, and published they are very likely out of date.
So rapid is the advance of knowledge in our day.

14. Means for Promoting a National Language

        The most obvious means for the promotion of a national
language would certainly appear to be the school system, and this is
no doubt largely true. However, it is absolutely essential that in any
such school program a sufficient number of years of instruction be
included so that a person actually develops adequate control of the
language. Furthermore, he needs to have continued contacts with a
national language or he soon loses facility. Where there are only
three or four years of primary education in a national language, the
tendency is to lapse into illiteracy or semi-literacy, and the continued
influence of instruction in the national language becomes minimal.
Such persons may know the alphabet and be able to write their name
and read signs, but they are not really participants in the national
language community. The failure of continued contacts through papers,
magazines, and inexpensive books also means that much of the value
of primary education may be lost, for there is no continuing reading
habit. In this respect, goals defined or carried out by government
bureaus are often entirely too shortsighted.

        Without at least certain supplementary means of promoting
the national language, even a school system is likely to be largely
ineffective. In reality, the informal means by which people learn
languages are often far more satisfactory than the formal ones. In
the Philippines and Indonesia, for example, movies constitute one of
the very important techniques by which the national language is promoted in the provinces. In the Philippines, comic books are particularly important. There are at least one hundred and twenty different
publications put out every two weeks, ranging in size of edition from
four thousand to thirty-four thousand each. The contents include
everything from Donald Duck stories to horror comics, but the important factor is that all of these are in Pilipino and they reach a very

wide audience. In fact, these books are no doubt more important in spreading the use of Pilipino than any and all of the textbooks printed by the government.

An important means of promoting the national language, but one which has not yet been sufficiently exploited, is that of serious literature on a level of language within reach of the poorly educated reader. Most serious reading matter tends to be on a level suitable only for the person who is well-educated in the national language, leaving a gap between the primer stage and the stage of the experienced reader. Many persons who learn to read, therefore, lapse into semi-literacy or, at best, continue to nourish their intellect on comics and similar publications. However, techniques are available by which writers can be taught to prepare serious materials on a "common" level which will be accessible to the poorly educated reader while still acceptable to the better educated—i. e. in a form of the language common to both groups. [5] Bible translations in such common or popular language are being made available in Spanish, French, English, and a number of other languages, and the same techniques used in preparing these could also be used for preparing all kinds of material of cultural and educational value.

Increasingly in the Philippines television is an important instrument for the spread of Pilipino. Local radio is often in regional languages, but it is economically impossible to provide television in the various local languages and therefore the use of Pilipino serves an important function with an ever-increasing audience. The situation is no doubt similar in the case of other national languages; however, the persons who do not speak the national language frequently tend to be economically underprivileged and thus their limited access to television places certain limitations upon the use of this medium for spreading the language.

15. Gaps in Vocabulary of Out-group Languages and of Languages of Specialized Information

It is a common assumption that a person educated in an out-group language or in a language of specialized information will have a vocabulary fully sufficient to cover the totality of his experience, for example, greetings, business, politics, family life, religion, and technology. This, however, is by no means always the case. A person may have received a relatively adequate technological education in such a language but still have little or no experience with that language in certain areas of his life, such as interpersonal relations and religion. It is, of course, possible for such individuals to have a "consumer vocabulary" in such areas but to be pitifully inadequate as far as their "producer vocabulary" is concerned. [6]

In the Philippines the national language Pilipino serves quite well as an out-group language for speakers of many other languages except in the areas of family and religion, where almost inevitably people revert to the local language if this is at all possible. One must recognize, however, that with the emphasis upon the national language rather rapid progress in vocabulary acquisition is being made by many individuals. This is especially true in the case of families in which the father speaks one local language and the mother another, for in such cases the tendency is to change either to the national language Pilipino or, depending on the level of education, to English, since both Pilipino and English are regarded as being distinctly advantageous to the children.

There are some situations, however, in which religion seems to be primarily a subject for discussion in an out-group language, or in a language of specialized information. This type of behavior may reflect some degree of insecurity as far as the local language is concerned. People may feel that a language other than the in-group language is necessary as a symbol of prestige due to the deity, and not infrequently the use of such a language expresses a people's desire to identify with a group of which they are not an immediate part. In Roman Catholicism the traditional tendency to use Latin reflects something of this same type of prestige status for a language of specialized information.

In circumstances where people do discuss religion (at least on certain levels) in a language other than that of the in-group, there are usually two quite distinct levels of religion. The religion of the home is actually discussed primarily in the local in-group language. This is essentially the "lower storey" of religion—what might be called the lower stratum of religious expression which lies beneath the veneer of a theologized form of expression. In contrast with this, the religion of the temple or the church may be expressed primarily in the out-group language or in a language of specialized information. Where there are two quite distinct languages involved in religious expression one will usually find quite distinct forms of religion, and in many instances people do not bring these two "levels of religion" together. Examples of this may be seen among Latin-American Indians in the existence of folk-Catholicism or Christo-Paganism alongside of more orthodox forms of Catholicism, and of African religious elements in the Voodoo and similar religions of the Caribbean; [7] in the preservation of pagan elements of belief and practice by Christians in many parts of Africa; and in the practice of folk-Buddhism alongside of more orthodox Buddhist practices in different parts of Asia. In fact, even seminary graduates many times find it quite impossible to discuss their religious beliefs in the in-group language if their education has been carried on entirely in an out-group language or in a language of specialized information. The use of two different languages certainly accentuates the tendency toward departmentalization or compartmentalization of religious belief. At the same time this compartmentalization reinforces the seeming need for different languages in which to discuss the diverse though related systems of belief.

16.   The Multiple Roles of Language

        For the sake of simplicity of presentation the previous discussion has focused primarily upon the diverse roles of different languages in the distinct patterns of communication. Actually, however, the situation is far more complex than what might appear on the surface, for one and the same language may occur at different levels, even within a so-called three-language structure. For example, in Congo (Kinshasa) French may serve as an out-group language for certain types of general business contacts while at the same time serving as a language of specialized information. A language such as Lingala, which is an in-group language for many people, also serves as an out-group language for many others, especially on the lower levels of out-group contact in a capital such as Kinshasa.

        Similarly, in the Philippines Pilipino serves as the medium of interpersonal communication on the lower level of the out-group

contacts, while English functions on the upper level of the same type
of interpersonal communication. Though at the present time English
is distinctly the language of specialized information, there is considerable pressure, particularly from school teachers, to make Pilipino
a language of specialized information, reaching at least through the
secondary school system.

It is interesting to note that in the Philippines pressures for
extending Pilipino to secondary education are coming primarily from
the teachers themselves. One could expect such pressures to arise
with nationalistic politicians or from such groups as might feel themselves handicapped because of inadequate preparation in the English
language. However, the pressures actually have arisen from teachers,
all of whom are theoretically competent to teach in English.

It is true, of course, that some teachers find it difficult to
teach in English because their own preparation in the language is not
especially good; but no doubt their real motivations (whether consciously so or not) stem from the fact that they have found it to be
much easier to communicate in Pilipino than in English. In other
words, the real problem does not lie with the inadequacy of the teachers so much as with the inadequacy of students in the processes of
decoding or comprehension. It is instructive, threfore, to see that
"ease of communication" is gradually taking precedence over the
strategic value of a language for purposes of communicating specialized information. Such an attitude becomes justified on the basis that
the number of individuals actually engaged in assimilating, using, and
passing on technological information is likely to be relatively small.
Therefore, the immediate gain in communicating information to a
broad segment of the population outweighs any concern for promoting
the use of what is essentially a "foreign" language.

Though the basic distinction between in-group languages,
out-group languages, and languages of specialized information is
fundamental, one must, of course, recognize that particularly in two-
language and one-language structures different levels exist. The
situation in Holland is particularly instructive in this regard. On the
in-group level, for example, Dutch (in several of its minor dialectal
forms) and Frisian serve as in-group languages. For most contacts,
Dutch is also an out-group language in that it serves for a high

percentage of those contacts which are beyond the face-to-face constituency. Dutch also functions as the out-group language for most Frisians, since Frisians all learn Dutch while only a few persons learn Frisian.

If, however, a person in Holland knows only Dutch, then the out-group contacts are relatively restricted, and this means that Dutch persons increasingly learn English, German, and/or French. Otherwise, the out-group range is too restricted for a technological and internationally oriented society.

Dutch, however, also serves the people of Holland as a language of specialized information since it is used on all levels of university training. Nevertheless, it does not serve as the exclusive language of specialized information, and any individual who wishes to go very far in his academic pursuits must master one or more foreign languages.

17.   Language and Levels of Style

The distinction between in-group language, out-group language, and language of specialized information is closely parallel to certain distinctions in the level of style within an individual language. For example, an English-speaking person in the United States will generally use an informal or casual level of style in in-group contacts. For out-group contacts his level of style will probably be formal, sometimes called "regular", while as a language of specialized information the level of style is rather largely technical.[8] A native speaker of English can regularly shift between these levels, and in fact is hardly aware of the existence of such differences. Nevertheless, a person who does not speak English as his own mother tongue and has learned only one of the levels becomes immediately conspicuous when he tries to communicate in an area for which his linguistic experience has not prepared him. For example, many students from India studying in the United States have mastered a form of English which is distinctly "bookish". Though such students are quite competent in the area of technical or formal speech, their attempts at casual or informal use of English quickly betray their background.

As suggested in the previous paragraph, the same language often serves on radically different stylistic levels. Perhaps this is nowhere more vividly illustrated than in the different forms of English used in Liberia. The differences in vocabulary, pronunciation, and grammar of a Bassa-speaking person using English on the Firestone Plantation and of a high-level politician in Monrovia using English at a formal reception represent such a wide diversity of linguistic forms as to be scarcely identifiable as representing the same language.

In some multilingual situations, the functions of informal or casual style as over against a more formal or technical style are distributed among two or more languages. For example, bilingual speakers of Haitian Creole use the Creole in social situations that call for informal or casual speech, but standard French for more formal speech; so that standard French in Haiti tends to lack, for want of occasion for their use, the informal and casual expressions that are available in Parisian French, and the Creole of the same speakers tends to lack the potential for more formal use.[9]

18. Limitations of the In-group Language for Use in other Functions

Linguists have generally assumed that any language is adequate for communicating any and all ideas that the members of its speech community have occasion to deal with—granting, of course, that new terms may need to be borrowed or new expressions coined with the intrusion of new ideas. However, where the different communication functions are distributed among two or more languages, each of the languages is thereby, in actual practice, subject to certain limitations. The vocabulary gaps in out-group languages and languages of specialized information, as mentioned in a preceding section, are an example of this; as are also the limitations in style level in a case like that of Haitian bilingualism.

This is not a case of inherent inadequacy in either of the languages involved, but rather of a "social handicap"—that is, of limitations placed on one or both of the languages by the society itself. An in-group language therefore tends to be limited in its function to the communication of the kinds of information normally transmitted

in interpersonal relationships within the local society, largely on an
informal or casual level. In many two-language or three-language
situations, the in-group language is unwritten, and is usually not
standardized. "Outside" information, whether communicated in
spoken or written form, tends to be limited to the out-group language
or the language of specialized information, at least until such a time
as it has been taken into the society and assimilated as "inside"
information. Stewart mentions the possibilities of habilitating an in-
group language such as Haitian Creole through standardization, to
make it acceptable for other functions; but warns that a premature
attempt to use it for other functions can lead to difficulties, "since
the use of a language outside of its prescribed function without an
accompanying change in its status is likely to be considered locally
as inappropriate or even ludicrous."[10]

19. Language as a Class Privilege

        In view of the increased importance of communication as a
means of control of human beings, it is not at all strange that language should figure more and more prominently as a politically
important instrument. The acquisition of a prestige language is thus
regarded by many persons as one of the essential keys to success and
social advancement. It is for this reason that many Indians in Latin
America place such a high premium upon gaining a command of Spanish. Similarly, many Africans are keenly concerned about mastering
English, French, or Portuguese, for such a language means not only
acceptance by a ruling class but the possibilities of participation in
the national life of the society.

        If, however, language acquisition can thus be viewed as an
instrument of upward mobility, the converse is also true. That is,
the exclusive possession of certain language abilities can be regarded
as a technique for perpetuating an oligarchic control. If a particular
language is the exclusive language of education and if it is the essential medium for controlling technical information, it may for this very
reason serve also to "keep people in their places" and thus guarantee
a larger share of control for a privileged few. It is no wonder, therefore, that language policies are regarded by so many people as being
the touchstone of class mobility and the guarantee of personal rights.

20. The Inevitability of Multilingualism in Many Parts of the World

Though the ideal of one nation and one language is a worthy goal, it is quite impossible for many present-day nations to think realistically in such terms. The close relationship between local languages and indigenous cultures means that people are not going to give up readily what seems to them to be their most distinctive heritage. Moreover, the diverse ethnic groups within any multilingual society have certain distinctive contributions to make; and making such a contribution almost inevitably requires a multilingual context if these different groups are to function in a way which is significant for the nation as a whole.

A very small language community may, of course, lack the necessary features of linguistic viability, and therefore over a period of a generation or two will lose its language. However, the number of languages which actually die out is far less than most people imagine. Therefore, new nations are obliged, if they are to be realistic at all, to face the necessity of a multilingual society for at least seventy-five to a hundred years.

Multilingualism need not, however, mean linguistic or political anarchy. Unity is, of course, more difficult in a multilingual society; but it certainly is not impossible. Moreover, monolingualism in a society by no means guarantees political uniformity or social agreement.

What is required in many new nations is not the elimination of linguistic minorities but sound principles of "linguistic engineering" by which the legitimate functions of various groups and the communication roles of their languages can be recognized and encouraged, so that within a two-language or three-language structure the highest degree of "mobility in ideas" may be guaranteed. The optimal utilization of existing languages is far more important than any enforced suppression of any of these means of communication.

NOTES

A shorter version of this article was first published in <u>Language Use</u> <u>and Social Change</u>: problems of multilingualism with special reference

to Eastern Africa: studies presented and discussed at the ninth
International African Seminar at University College, Dar es Salaam,
1968, edited, with an Introduction by W. H. Whiteley.   London: Oxford University Press for International African Institute, 1971.

[1] See especially William A. Stewart, "An Outline of Linguistic
Typology for Describing Multilingualism", in Frank A. Rice (ed.),
Study of the Role of Second Languages in Asia, Africa, and Latin
America, pp. 15-25 (Washington, D.C., Center for Applied Linguis-
tics, 1962). (This volume contains several important articles and
bibliographies related to the subject of the present paper.) Another
volume of importance, both for the articles it contains and for its
bibliographies, is John J. Gumperz and Dell Hymes (eds.), The
Ethnography of Communication (Part 2 of American Anthropologist,
Vol. 66, No. 6, 1964).

[2] For a discussion of some of the varieties which can be found
within a large linguistic community, see William L. Wonderly, Bible
Translations for Popular Use, chapters 2 and 3 (London, United Bible
Societies, 1968).

[3] For a study of the characteristics of pidgin and creole languages, see Robert A. Hall, Jr., Pidgin and Creole Languages (Ithaca,
N.Y., Cornell University Press, 1966). For a listing and discussion
of African pidgins and trade languages, see William J. Samarin,
"Lingua Francas, with Special Reference to Africa", in Rice, op. cit.,
pp. 54-64.

[4] For various other aspects of the linguistic situation in India,
see Charles A. Ferguson and John J. Gumperz (eds.), Linguistic
Diversity in South Asia, Indiana University Research Center in Anthropology, Folklore, and Linguistics, Pub. 13 (1960).

[5] Some of the techniques for preparing this type of literature,
and of the problems relating to its preparation, are discussed in
Wonderly, op. cit.

[6] Ibid., pp. 35 ff., for concepts of "producer" and "consumer"
language.

[7] Cp. E. A. Nida, "Christo-Paganism", Practical Anthropology 8.1-14 (1961); A. Metraux, Voodoo in Haiti (London, 1959).
See L. J. Luzbetak, The Church and Cultures (Techny, Illinois, 1963),
pp. 239-64, for discussion and bibliography.

[8] Martin Joos, The Five Clocks. Indiana University Research
Center in Anthropology, Folklore, and Linguistics, Pub. 22 (1962);
see also Wonderly, op. cit., pp. 13-17.

[9]William A. Stewart, "The Functional Distribution of Creole and French in Haiti", in Georgetown University Monograph Series on Languages and Linguistics, No. 15.

[10]William A. Stewart, "Creole Languages in the Caribbean", in Rice, op. cit., pp. 34-53; quoted from p. 49.

9 | Varieties of Language

Most people know that there are a great many different languages in the world, but no one knows exactly how many. Various estimates have been made, but figures based on exact data are simply not available. To some extent, this uncertainty is due to the fact that in some parts of the world no detailed linguistic surveys have been carried out. New Guinea, for example, is reputed to have more than 700 different languages, but there are some sizable areas of this large island where no linguistic surveys have as yet been made. Moreover, determining whether two different forms of speech should be regarded as related dialects or as separate languages depends largely upon the criteria of mutual intelligibility. In some classifications of languages, for example, all the so-called dialects of Chinese are lumped together as being one language, when in reality several of them (for example, Amoyese, Hakka, and Cantonese) are mutually unintelligible. On the other hand, Spanish and Portuguese, although to a large extent mutually intelligible, are normally regarded as two distinct languages because they have two distinct national "standards". If we speak of mutually unintelligible forms of speech, we can probably arrive at a figure of approximately 2,500 languages in the world. Yet if we were to add up the total number of speakers of only the first hundred of these languages (those with the largest numbers of speakers), we would have a figure exceeding the total population of the earth. The reason for this is that so many people speak two or more of these major languages.

At the end of 1971, at least some portion of the Holy Scriptures had been produced in 1,457 languages, with 253 languages having the entire Bible and 330 more having the New Testament. These languages represent the mother tongues of fully 98 per cent of the world's population. This means, however, that there are approximately 1,000

additional languages (whose speakers comprise less than 2 per cent
of the world's population) which do not have any part of the Bible.
Certainly, even these languages should have at least some part of
God's word, and at present there are Bible translators who are working in fully half of them.

In addition to the multiplicity of languages, there is also the
existence of many different dialects within languages. In Norway
there are two competing literary dialects, one on a more traditional
literary level, the other a more colloquial form of speech. English
speakers are increasingly aware of some of the differences between
British and American usage. For example, there is the hood versus
the bonnet and the trunk versus the boot (parts of a car) and the drug
store versus the chemist's shop. In Spanish there is the frequently
mentioned distinction between the dialects which pronounce the letter
z the same as s and those which give it a th-like (theta) sound. In
Arabic there is the age-old conflict between the classical form of the
language, as standardized by the Quran and followed in literary pro-
ductions to the present time, and the distinctive colloquial forms
which are almost universally employed by speakers of Arabic. In
fact, in almost all languages speakers are aware of certain differences,
some of which carry very important information about the status of
the speakers and the relevance of the information involved. These
are the subtle varieties of language of which the translator must be
constantly aware if he is to do justice to the text which he must
reproduce.

Levels of Language

Any language spoken by a large structured society—this
applies to all national and world languages—has several distinct levels
of usage. In general, it is probably best to think in terms of five
distinguishable levels or styles: formal, consultative, casual, intimate, and frozen. [1]

The consultative level of language usage occurs between
people who do not know each other and who are talking about something
which is neutral in emotive value. This style is the most neutral of
all the levels, and in fact it is most easily defined by the absence of

features which are typical of the other levels. When people are using this level of language, the focus is normally on the message, and hence there is no need for rhetorical elaboration. There are, however, frequent occurrences of so-called "contact language" in which the respondent employs such expressions as <u>yes</u>, <u>I know</u>, <u>well</u>, and <u>that's interesting</u>, as a means of showing that he is participating in the conversation. The setting for this type of language is not formal, and therefore the source is not expected to employ formal language. What is distinctive about the consultative style, in contrast with formal style, is that some measure of feedback is expected.

The <u>formal</u> level of language is likewise used between persons who are unknown to each other, but in this case the setting is formal— for example, a university lecture hall, parliamentary chambers, or a public auditorium. One person does the speaking, and there is little or no feedback from the audience. Accordingly, an English speaker is likely to employ <u>may</u> rather than <u>might</u> or <u>can</u>; to use a clause such as <u>for whom did you get it</u>? rather than <u>who did you get it for</u>?; and an adverb outside rather than inside of the infinitive phrase—for example, <u>purposely to show</u> rather than <u>to purposely show</u>. There is also a tendency to use phrasal prepositions—for example, <u>on behalf of</u> in place of <u>for</u>, and <u>with reference to</u> in place of <u>about</u>. Many speakers using a formal level of language avoid the contractions of ordinary spoken English; they say <u>cannot</u> rather than <u>can't</u>, <u>will not</u> rather than <u>won't</u>, and <u>I shall see</u> rather than <u>I'll see</u>. Not all languages, of course, have the same types of differences between consultative and formal styles, but there are certain contrasts which are similar. The formal style employs (1) fuller and more precise forms, (2) closer conformity to written style, (3) avoidance of clipped phrases, and (4) reduction of colloquial expressions (or apologies for using such expressions).

The <u>casual</u> level of language normally occurs between people who know each other and in settings where the participants are relaxed. Furthermore, the topic of the communication is normally not too urgent, and therefore one can employ a degree of verbal play. The two prinicipal characteristics of this level are ellipsis and slang, often including some taboo terminology. This casual level of language may also occur between persons who do not know each other, but who are operating in a very familiar setting—bargaining in a market or store, in which case the conversation may include such clipped expressions

as <u>How much</u>? <u>One dollar each</u>. <u>Too much</u>! <u>How about these</u>? <u>Only</u>
<u>two bits each</u>. <u>Okay, gimme four</u>.

The <u>intimate</u> level of language occurs only between people
who are well acquainted and who have shared many linguistic and non-
linguistic experiences. As a result they may employ extreme ellipses
which would not be intelligible to outsiders. Persons employing intimate level of language often use highly specialized names, not only for
one another but also for common objects, especially body parts. In
intimate language much is communicated by supplementary codes of
proximity (such as facial gestures, smell, and touch), so that language
becomes quite secondary for conveying messages.

The fifth level of language style is aptly called <u>frozen</u> because
its form and content are largely predictable. Eulogies are one of the
most typical forms of frozen style, and in some churches sermons are
also largely frozen. Since the content of sermons is largely predictable, there is a tendency for elaborate rhetorical devices, somewhat
artificial pronunciation (to fit the ritual mood), and a fixed intonation
(often a compromise between formal style and a chant form). A fixed
liturgy is the most extreme example of the frozen style.

Though everyone will admit that these five levels or styles
(with certain minor subdivisions and modifications) are typical of all
large languages spoken by an urbanized society in which there are
several definable socio-economic classes, some people would hestitate
to think that some so-called primitive languages also have such levels
of style, but this is almost always the case. For example, in a number
of languages of Africa there is a very distinct form of language used
by a chief when he is making a formal proclamation. In fact, his
statement may be in such a "high" form that it must be explained to
the people by an official spokesman. In some tribes there is an official "praiser" of the chief who must employ a frozen form of language
in talking to and about the chief. In such societies the level of language
used by the elders when they are discussing some important event or
issue often takes on the characteristics of formal style.

The various levels of language often remain unnoticed until
one fails to employ the appropriate forms. For example, we quickly
react to the person who attempts to be "too friendly" by employing

casual or even intimate language before an appropriate period of
acquaintance. Spanish speakers are especially sensitive to those who
want to employ too soon the familiar second person pronoun tú and the
corresponding verbal endings. The use of slang in the wrong setting
is especially annoying and may even be shocking. The inclusion of
witticisms in a sermon may likewise have quite different effects in
different settings. In America, jokes from the pulpit are usually
acceptable—in fact, some of the best preachers regularly elicit laughs
from their congregations—but in Europe similar language in the pulpit
would generally be regarded as at least inappropriate, if not decidedly
uncouth.

Socioeconomic Dialects

        In a number of societies different socioeconomic dialects play
a much larger role than most people suspect. Traditionally, British
people have placed great emphasis upon the linguistic acceptability
of certain dialects such as "public school English" and "the speech of
Oxford and Cambridge". With the current social revolution in England,
much of this dialectal snobbery is disappearing. Even the BBC is
admitting to the air some persons whose pronunciation would have been
considered quite unacceptable for its programs not long ago.

        In the United States there has been a tendency to deny the
importance of dialectal differences, though some prejudice has long
existed against certain forms of language. For example, the pronunciation of bird to rhyme with toyed (as in he toyed with the idea) has
been frowned on. Recently William Labov made a detailed analysis of
certain features of the dialects of New York and found some rather
amazing situations.[2] He studied the occurrence of the r sound (or the
lack of it) in such words as bared, guard, dark, car, beer, beard,
and board, and found that some speakers pronounce bared like bad,
guard like God, etc. When he compared the r and r-less pronunciation of such words with the socioeconomic class and age of the speakers
and the contexts in which the words were uttered, he discovered that
the occurrence or non-occurrence of r was not simply a matter of
free variation but that it correlated very well with class membership
and context of use. In casual speech, the upper-class speakers were
found to use r forms only 18 per cent of the time, but in reading paired

words they used the r forms 60 per cent of the time. Among the lowest
socioeconomic class, the r forms did not occur at all in casual speech;
but in reading paired words, speakers from this class employed the r
pronunciation 38 per cent of the time. Middle-class speakers shifted
from 5 per cent used in casual speech to 78 per cent in reading paired
words—considerably higher than even the upper class. The middle-
class speakers were obviously more linguistically insecure and hence
tended to overdo the correction, so as to imitate what they regarded
as the proper forms of language.

Many people judge the value of dialects merely in terms of
their correlation with socioeconomic classes. They conclude that
the speech of the upper class is intrinsically superior, since it carries greater prestige and rewards its speakers with greater material
benefits. Generally upper-class persons conclude that the failure of
lower-class persons to use the "proper form" of language is due
either to laziness or to linguistic incompetence. Such judgments,
however, are entirely superficial. Any form of language which is
maintained in a society must have certain positive values or it soon
disappears. In New York City, for example, the use of upper-class
forms does improve one's chances of getting a better-paying job, but
at the same time the lower-class usage is a much better indicator that
the speaker of such a dialect will come out on top in a local fight.
Though lower-class speakers may admit the prestige value of upper-
class usage, they often adhere to their own language forms with surprising tenacity. This is not primarily because it is too hard to learn
the upper-class usage, but rather because they find their own form of
language an important mark of social identification, a symbol of the
constituency with which they feel at home. Furthermore, there is a
marked tendency for lower-class persons to feel that though the upper
classes may have certain economic advantages, the people of these
classes are less trustworthy, more inclined to exploit others, and
less valuable to cultivate as friends.

Attitudes of Speakers Toward Other Dialects

The attitude of many people toward a dialect which is not their
own is largely conditioned by their evaluation of the speakers of that
dialect. They may regard them as being "lazy", "snobbish", "uncouth",

"high hat", "low down", "country bumpkins", or "city folks", and their
attitude toward the speakers will be projected to the dialect which they
speak. In general, however, judgments are often projected onto the
various forms of language so that dialects themselves are frequently
characterized as being "soft", "musical", "guttural", "harsh",
"sweet", "barbarous", "refined", etc. In most instances, people
have positive evaluations of their own dialect and negative evaluations
of the dialects of others, but that is not always the case. New Yorkers,
for example, tend to depreciate their own forms of language, while
Bostonians and Philadelphians tend to regard their forms of language
as being superior. There is a tendency for the speakers of Arabic
each to regard his own national dialect (whether of Beirut, of Damascus,
of Amman, or of Bagdad) as superior to other national forms of the
language, but the Bedouin dialects are almost universally thought to
be superior to any metropolitan forms, since the relatively conserva-
tive Bedouin dialects retain so many features of Quranic usage.

Alternative Use of Dialects

        Many persons imagine that most speakers use only one form
of speech, namely, their own "mother dialect", but this is far from
being the case. Just as there are bilingual or multilingual persons,
there are also bidialectal or multidialectal persons. In the Philippines
many children switch easily back and forth between Philippine English
(often called "bamboo English") and standard American English—but
one must be very certain of the setting in which such shifts can take
place. A wrong choice can be very offensive. American children
growing up in England often employ two quite different forms of
English. One teenage girl made it a practice to use American English
in speaking to her boy friends, but British English in speaking with
her girl friends. American English had a prestige value (even something of the exotic!) with the boy friends, but for identificational purposes British English was much more acceptable to the girl friends.

        Language switching is especially conspicuous in Haiti where
practically everyone speaks Haitian Creole (a creolized form of
French) and some 15 per cent of the population speaks normal French.
All formal schooling is, of course, in French. When boys and girls
are in school together they usually speak Haitian Creole, at least

outside the classroom, but the moment courtship begins they use French exclusively and this continues right through the marriage ceremony. But as the couple leave the church, Haitian Creole begins again!

The questions is often asked as to why alternative forms of language are preserved. Would not the principle of economy of effort soon eliminate one form of language in favor of another? The fact is that human behavior does not respond directly to the degree of energy expenditure. Tradition (itself a form of inertia) has a good deal of influence, but quite apart from tradition there are a number of values which keep alternative usages alive. The more specific of these are group identification, secret communication (ability to communicate without everyone else knowing what is being said), pleasure in variety, the association of language with particular topics and contexts (e.g. Latin for the Roman Catholic mass), and sense of increased verbal competence in being able to manipulate more than one linguistic code.

Attitudes toward Speakers of Other Dialects

When there are alternative forms of speech within a single society, certain attitudes toward the speakers of other dialects or languages almost inevitably develop. In Latin America Spanish speakers usually have a very superior attitude toward the speakers of Indian languages and regard the Spanish language as being inherently and innately superior to any of the Indian tongues. Almost the same kind of attitude exists in Tanzania by speakers of Swahili toward those whose mother tongue is one of the minor languages of the hinterland. What is interesting about such situations is that the persons who belong to a lower socio-economic class often share these disparaging views concerning their own languages or dialects. Many Indians in Spanish-speaking America, for example, will agree, at least overtly, with the judgment that their language is somehow inferior. Covertly, of course, many Indians hold a number of adverse judgments against the Spanish-speaking constituency and their use of language.

Some very interesting research was carried out by W. E. Lambert and others in French-speaking Canada to determine what attitudes were held by the people toward English-speaking and

French-speaking persons.[3] For this experiment they recorded the
speech of persons who were equally fluent in both French and English.
Persons who knew both French and English were then asked to characterize the personalities of the speakers on the basis of their speech,
without, of course, being told that the same persons had recorded both
an English and a French portion of the test. Quite to the astonishment
of most persons, not only did the English persons who spoke English
as a mother tongue rate the speakers of the French passages as being
smaller, darker, less honest, and more deceptive, but even those who
spoke French as a mother tongue had relatively similar judgments of
the speakers of the French passages. No doubt French speakers have
certain compensating positive values associated with their own language, but it is important to recognize that a set of cultural values
held by a dominant section of society can be shared by those in a less
favorable socioeconomic class.

Varieties of Language and the Translator

        One of the most complete and subtle problems which faces a
translator is the proper matching of stylistic levels of language. The
Bible translator cannot afford to select a level of language which is so
high as to make the message inaccessible to the people to whom it is
directed. At the same time the language of Scripture cannot be such
as to debase the contents. For example, in some parts of the Arabic-
speaking world completely colloquial forms of language are employed
only for comic strips and pornographic literature. A strictly colloquial form of language is therefore quite unacceptable for the New
Testament, despite the fact that it would no doubt be more widely
understood.

        But even after one has chosen a level of language which is
presumably adequate for the Bible, one must still make a number of
further choices, since the Scriptures reflect more than one type of
style. What may be appropriate for the Epistle to the Hebrews is
certainly much too elegant for the simple, straightforward style of
the Gospel of Mark. Likewise, the language of the Psalms should be
quite different from the narratives of Joshua and Judges.

        In some languages the levels or styles which must be used
between exposition and reported conversation differ appreciably. That

means that when conversations are quoted (for example, the conversation between Jesus and the woman of Samaria), one must use quite a different form of language from what is employed when a discourse is reported (for example, the upper room discourse of John 14-16).

Translating involves much more than finding corresponding words between two languages. In fact, the words are only minor elements in the total discourse. In many respects the tone of a passage (that is, the style of the language) carries far more impact, and often even much more meaning, than the words themselves.

NOTES

This article is based on a lecture given at a Translators' Seminar in Halle, DDR. 1971.
[1] See Martin Joos. 1959. The isolation of styles. Monograph Series on Language and Linguistics (Georgetown University) 12.107-113; and 1960. The Five Clocks. International Journal of American Linguistics 28, No. 2, Part V. Note also the contribution of Szabo Zoltán. 1970. The types of stylistic studies and the characterization of individual style: an outline of problems. Linguistics 62.96-104.
[2] William Labov. 1970. The reflection of social processes in linguistic structures, in Joshua A. Fishman, ed., Readings in the Sociology of Language (The Hague: Mouton), pp. 240-275.
[3] W. E. Lambert, R. C. Gardner, R. Olton, and K. Tunstall. 1970. A study of the roles of attitudes and motivation in second-language learning, in Joshua A. Fishman, ed., Readings in the Sociology of Language (The Hague: Mouton), pp. 473-491.

10 | Words and Thoughts

Since so many thoughts can be associated with particular words, it is little wonder that most people assume that in some way or other words are directly tied to thoughts and that for every culturally significant thought there must be a word. Furthermore, people reason that if words exist, they must represent relevant thoughts, and the thought must stand for some kind of reality. Therefore, if there is a Hebrew word translated leviathan, many persons assume that leviathans (whatever they were) must have existed in ancient times. Likewise, the Greek word for dragon must also signify that at some time or other—whether in the past or future—there have been or there will be dragons. Since most people assume that words and concepts are learned together, the two are often regarded as merely the two sides of the same coin. Moreover, since each language has its own set of words, just as each nation has its own kind of money, and no two sets of words in different languages match exactly, many persons argue that the speakers of any two languages must in some way or other have quite different sets of thoughts. In fact, some have even concluded that people think the way they do precisely because of the language which they speak.

The idea that language determines thought is as old as the ancient Greeks, and such a theory about languages was first formulated in a detailed manner in modern times by von Humboldt.[1] Whorf[2] elaborated von Humboldt's thesis and insisted that grammatical categories serve as important determiners of thought. Weisgerber has been particularly insistent upon the influence of language structure upon world views and ethnic characteristics, and he has claimed an overwhelming influence of the German language upon the German character.[3] In spite of the attractiveness of such theories, however,

they simply do not stand up to careful scientific investigation. In the
first place, they are usually based on a comparison of only two languages and related cultures, with the result that many coincidental
features appear to be far more significant than they really are. It is
not enough to compare the Ancient Greek and Hebrew languages and
to relate them to what is known about the world views and cultural
features of the respective societies, as many Christian theologians
have done. Modern Hebrew is essentially the same language as ancient
Hebrew, but Hebrew speakers in present-day Israel do not have the
same world view or psychological outlook as Hebrew speakers of
Biblical times. Nor do present-day Greeks continue to have the same
ethnic characteristics as ancient Greeks. Furthermore, the changes
which have taken place in the Hebrew and Greek peoples cannot be
correlated with changes in their languages. If one were to make a
thorough analysis of related languages and cultures, it would be necessary to analyze all languages which have certain structural features
and to find corresponding traits in the speakers of all these languages.
Linguists have explored these possibilities extensively and have found
no basis for concluding that language determines thought.[4]

Nonconformities between Words and Thoughts

Though the lack of evidence for a one-to-one relation between
grammatical structure and thought has been conclusively substantiated,
most people still feel that in some way or other words and thoughts
must be intimately connected. In a sense this is true, for there are
many distinct words for many distinct thoughts. But there are even
more thoughts which are not expressed by single words, and there are
many single words which symbolize whole series or bundles of thoughts,
e.g. Reformation, Renaissance, democracy, existentialism, and relativity. Only by carefully examining some of the many nonconformities
between words and thoughts can a translator fully appreciate certain
of the essential problems encountered in finding satisfactory equivalents.

One of the nonconformities between words and thoughts is
that there are often no words for certain quite specific concepts. For
example, English does not have separate terms for three kinds of
aunts: (1) mother's sister, (2) father's sister, and (3) the wife of an

uncle (i. e. an aunt by marriage). Many languages do have quite different terms for these three kinds of aunts, but this does not mean that the speakers of these languages have such concepts while we as English speakers are not able to think such thoughts. In the Kaka language of the Cameroun there is no word for incest, but the people are quite aware of what incest is and frequently speak of it. To do so, they employ a descriptive phrase, rather than a single word. The fact that incest is not identified by a single lexical unit does not mean that the concept is nonexistent for Kaka speakers.

Very frequently one can identify the same concept by more than one verbal device. One may, for example, speak of a triangle or of a three-sided geometric figure. The lexical units are different but the concept is essentially the same. Languages abound in different ways of symbolizing the same concepts. The phrases in-group identification, sense of belonging, and social acceptance may be used in a single paragraph to refer to the same concept. Similarly, in the Bible there is no real referential distinction between demons, evil spirits, and unclean spirits.

The fact that in some instances the meanings of words may be transferred without any essential alteration in the related concepts is clear evidence that meanings are not inherently tied to certain forms. Since the publication of the King James Version in 1611 the meanings of ghost and spirit have completely shifted. In Elizabethan times ghost meant essentially what spirit means today (hence, the appropriateness of the rendering Holy Ghost), while spirit at that time meant an apparition. The two concepts have not changed in any appreciable way, but there has been a complete interchange of the words which are used to symbolize these concepts.

Quite frequently a word will be retained in a language even though it has changed its meaning in a very radical manner. For example, atomic was first employed to mean the smallest possible particle of matter—literally the term atomic means "uncuttable". Later scientific investigation has demonstrated that atoms are made up of many different parts. The word atomic remains, but the concepts associated with the term have been altered in profound ways. In theology, very similar changes have taken place in the conceptual content of terms such as redemption, atonement, revelation, and loving-kindness חֶסֶד· . Similarly, many people continue to use the term God, but mean by it some impersonal power or primal reality. Even the statement man is an animal must be quite differently interpreted, depending upon whether the speaker is an existentialist philosopher or a behaviorist psychologist.

The fact that different languages can be used to speak about essentially the same thoughts is an important factor in understanding the relations between words and thoughts. Most people in Paraguay speak Guarani, an Indian language, but the ancestors of many of these people were not Indians. They immigrated from Europe, largely from the Iberian peninsula, but they gradually gave up the Spanish language and shifted to Guarani. This shift, however, did not change their culture or the conceptual framework of their thoughts; they simply employed a different language to express them. Furthermore, the thousands of bilingual Guarani-Spanish speakers of Paraguay today show no sign of having two different conceptual structures because they speak two languages. In Mexico a number of Indian communities have given up their own native tongues and have adopted Spanish, but there is no evidence of any significant change in the concepts which they have. They simply use a different set of terms to talk about essentially the same old concepts.

It is also possible for persons speaking the same language to have quite different cultural viewpoints. A number of scholars have spoken of the distinctive orientations of upper-class and lower-class English speakers in England. Furthermore, a West African who employs excellent Parisian French is not really in heart and mind a Frenchman.

The fact that in historical developments concepts precede words or lexical units, e.g. neutrons, quasars, relativity theory, and binary units, should clearly warn anyone about mistakenly assuming that language determines thought. The reason why we tend to think that words precede concepts is that there is a basic difference between personal and cultural learning. As individuals we have often become acquainted with words before we have learned their meanings; but in the experience of the culture, the concepts come first and then words are selected or formed to symbolize the chunks of experience or thought.

The limitations in the specific vocabulary of a language is certainly no indication that its speakers cannot make detailed distinctions. All people are able to distinguish between an amazing number of variations in color hues and tones, but most languages have specific terms for only a few color variations. Some languages of Africa have only three so-called color terms, corresponding to black, white, and red. But that does not mean that the speakers of those languages are blind to numerous variations in hues and tones. While they have specific terms for only a few colors, they use descriptive terms to identify many others. Lack of vocabulary does not indicate conceptual or cognitive inferiority; it only indicates that the speakers of such languages have not found it necessary to make distinctions by means of specific color terms.

It is particularly significant that all languages contain terms which have multiple meanings. The English word board, for example, has a distinct meaning in each of the phrases board of managers, board and room, cut the board, and board the train. There is no doubt that, historically, the various meanings of board are related, but for most speakers of English there are simply no shared components in these distinctive uses. Etymology can be a very interesting study, but it may be quite irrelevant in determining how people actually use their own language and what concepts they may relate to one another. Some words indicate by their forms something of their meaning. One may, for example, say that breakfast is evidently derived from break and fast, but few English speakers are ever conscious of such a derivation. A hot dog is hot and poison oak is poisonous, but a hot dog has nothing to do with a dog and poison oak is not an oak, but a sumac. And pineapple is not related either to pine or to an apple.

Symbolization for New Concepts

As has already been suggested, new concepts are almost always symbolized by phrases before they are symbolized by words. In fact, at the very first instance a new concept may require a whole paragraph or even an entire article in a scientific journal for a satisfactory identification. In the development of information theory the smallest units of contrast were first described as binary units of information. Later, these were designated as binits, and at present they are usually spoken of as <u>bits.</u> Very similar developments take place in almost all areas of human inquiry. For example, though the term <u>trinity</u> does not exist in the Bible, theologians have consistently used it as a shorthand way of talking about relations which are variously spoken of in the Scriptures.

For one who is endeavoring to translate the Bible into a so-called "new language", that is, one which has not as yet had anything of the Scriptures, it is quite unnecessary to think that every concept symbolized in the Greek and Hebrew texts by a single word can or must be expressed by a single term in the receptor language. There is usually no existing term for <u>sanctification</u>, but one can certainly employ some phrasal equivalent, e.g. "the washing of the heart" or "making one's innermost clean". Too often Bible translators have been unduly concerned because they could not find particular words in a receptor language or could not discover similar expressions in the indigenous oral literature. One translator even insisted that he could not employ the figures of speech in Mark 1:3 (<u>Prepare the way of the Lord; make his paths straight</u>) since these did not already occur in the receptor language in which he was working. Accordingly, he rendered these two clauses as "Do good; stop doing bad; the Son of God is coming". This is a very worthy admonition, but it is not what Isaiah said and is certainly not a translation of what Mark wrote in his Gospel. The genius of language is precisely its capacity to express thoughts which the people have not heard before. Failure to appreciate the significance of this in the translation of the Bible may be an exaggerated form of paternalism.

Words and Conceptual Domains

Instead of relating words to thoughts as one does the two sides of a single coin, it is better to conceive of words as constituting a set of maps of conceptual domains.[5] First of all, a map is not the domain. It belongs to an entirely different dimension. Furthermore, it does not include all the details nor does it specify the content of each identified area or place. But most important of all, a map only marks off the boundaries and as such merely shows the limits of certain territories in relation to others. In addition, maps always lag behind actual developments. In the same way, the development of words and lexical units lags behind the cognitive progress of a culture.

Another way of looking at words and their relations to concepts is to conceive of the words in a sentence as being like a string of freight cars. Many cars have a number of different loads, but some cars are linked together to carry single long loads. Similarly, some words contain a series of concepts and others link together in phrases to specify closely integrated concepts. What is important in the hauling of freight is not what goods are loaded onto what wagons nor the particular order in which the wagons are connected to one another, but that all the contents get to their destination. The same is true in translation. It is quite unnecessary that what is one word in the source language be translated by a single word in the receptor language. The semantic load of such a word can readily be distributed over a phrase. Similarly, what may be a phrase in the source language can often be communicated in the receptor language by a single word. What is relevant about this procedure is that all the significant components of meaning arrive at their destination in such a form that they can be used by the receptors.

The task of the translator may therefore be defined in terms of reproducing in the receptor language the closest natural equivalent of the content of the source-language message. To do this, the translator will obviously want to preserve as much of the formal correspondences as are equivalent in meaning, but he must not be chained to any false ideas about inseparability between words and thoughts. The relevant unit of meaning for the translator is not the word, but the message.

NOTES

This article is based on a lecture given at a Translators' Seminar in Halle, DDR.

[1] Karl Wilhelm von Humboldt, 1836. <u>Über die Verschiedenheit des menschlichen Sprachbaues und ihren Einfluss auf die geistige Entwickenlung des Menschengeschlechts</u>. Berlin: Dummer.

[2] Benjamin Lee Whorf, 1956. <u>Language, Thought and Reality; Selected Writings</u>. John B. Carroll, ed. Cambridge (Mass.): M. I. T. Press.

[3] Leo Weisgerber, 1953-1954. Vol. 1, <u>Grundzüge der inhaltbezogenen Grammatik.</u> Vol. 2, <u>Die sprachliche Gestaltung der Welt</u>. Düsseldorf: Schwann.

[4] In this connection, the following two articles are of special importance: (1) Jane O. Bright and William Bright. 1967. "Semantic structures in northwestern California and the Sapir-Whorf hypothesis". American Anthropologist 67.249-258. (2) Lars Brink. 1970. "Semantic boundary lines in languages and their influence on cognition of the surrounding world". Acta Linguistica Hafniensia 13.45-74.

[5] One of the first persons to point out this relation between words and thoughts was Alfred Korzybski. 1948. Science and Sanity: an Introduction to Non-Aristotelian Systems and General Semantics. Lakeville, Conn.: International Non-Aristotelian Library Publishing Co.

Part III. Linguistics, Christian Missions, and Biblical Scholarship

11 | Linguistics and Christian Missions

In Collaboration with William L. Wonderly

0. Introduction and Scope

The extensive involvement of Christian missions in linguistics may be suggested at the outset by the fact that at least some substantial part of the Bible has, as of 1962, been translated into 1181 languages, whose speakers constitute at least 97% of the world's population. Of these languages, the entire Bible has been translated into 226 (over 90% of the world's population), the New Testament into an additional 281, and at least one book of the Bible into another 674.

Almost a century ago Max Müller wrote: "It was Christianity which first broke down the barriers between Jew and Gentile, between Greek and barbarian, between the white and the black .... When people had been taught to look upon all men as brethren, then, and then only, did the variety of human speech present itself as a problem that called for a solution in the eyes of thoughtful observers: and I, therefore, date the real beginning of the science of language from the first day of Pentecost .... The pioneers of our science were those very apostles who were commanded 'to go into all the world, and preach the Gospel to every creature,' and their true successors, the missionaries of the whole Christian Church." (Müller, pp. 128-30.)[1]

This missionary character of the Christian religion is one of the leading factors which has led to a two-way relationship between Christianity and linguistics, with contributions in different directions at different periods. During the pre-scientific period, such contributions were largely from Christian missions to linguistics in one form or another; with the development of linguistics as a science, there also developed a mutual relationship in which each field has contributed to the other, with linguistics now in our time reciprocating, so to speak, by providing basic concepts and tools that are significantly affecting the work of missions.

In contrast with Judaism and Hinduism, which were not primarily interested in extension by missionary effort, and with Islam, which was to conquer and impose upon its followers its language as the exclusive instrument of religious instruction and worship, Christianity was from the beginning concerned with an effective communication of its message to all men everywhere, such as could be accomplished only through the native idioms of the people. This concern early led to an interest in translation and to the production in many languages of documents that are important today as source materials. As early as the fourth century A.D., Jerome wrote on the problems of translating, in relation to his translation of the Bible into Latin.

At a later date, when the medieval church was being threatened politically from without, there came to be a greater concern for self-preservation, with an emphasis upon the use of Latin as part of an effort to maintain purity of tradition and unity of control. This trend, from which Protestant Christianity broke at the time of the Reformation, has been largely continued in the Roman Catholic Church. However, now threatened ideologically from within by secularization and by the diffusion of communist and other doctrines, Roman Catholics have within our own times begun to manifest a new concern for communication in the language of the people, as may be seen for example in the appearance of numerous Catholic translations of the Bible and the current interest in the use of the vernacular languages in its liturgy.

A missionary emphasis was similarly present in the Buddhist religion, which led to the early use of the Prākrit or vernacular dialects in preference to the classical Sanskrit for the promulgation of its teachings. Much of the Prākrit literature is Buddhist in origin, and Buddhist works were early translated into Tibetan, Chinese and Tokharian, the latter of course being of special interest to Indo-Europeanists as source material for historical linguistic studies.

Other religions, apart from missionary motives, have in many cases been concerned with language because of their interest in the study and accurate preservation of their sacred writings. The outstanding example is the Hindu study of the language of the Vedic writings, culminating in the grammar of Sanskrit by Pānini sometime about the end of the fourth century B.C. Moslem scholars of the seventh century A.D. developed a grammar of Arabic, stimulated by their desire to preserve and exegete the text of the Koran. In Judaism the Masoretes, beginning in pre-Maccabean times, built up a body of material concerned with the form of the text of the Hebrew Bible, and later developed the system of vowel points that came to be used in Hebrew. Similar interest in the sacred text has led Christian scholars in more recent times to develop important studies related to biblical languages, as will be noted in a later section of this paper.

The present paper is concerned primarily with the influences of Christian missions upon the history of linguistics, together with the contributions made in turn by linguistics to Christian missions; hence any elaboration of the relationships between linguistics and non-Christian religions lies properly outside the scope of our treatment, as does also any extended treatment of factors in the pre-Christian period.[2]

The present paper presents first a historical sketch, in which for each period prior to the 20th century we discuss first the language materials resulting from Christian missionary activity and then such theoretical work and discussions from that period as appear relevant to our subject. For the 20th century the historical presentation is modified to allow for emphasis on specific fields and on the contributions being made by linguistics to Christian scholarship and missions. The second section presents the major areas of interchange between linguistics and missions, with emphasis upon contemporary developments and implications.

1. Historical Sketch

1.1. <u>Early period</u>. During the Christian period prior to the Middle Ages, the missionary work of the church was accompanied by a new awareness of languages other than those of the Hebrew and

the Greco-Roman civilizations. This led to the production of religious
texts which now provide important source material on languages and
dialects of the period. The chief theoretical discussions of language
problems were by Jerome and Augustine.

1.1.1. Language materials. The Greek NT[3] itself, dating
from the first century A.D. and whose extant copies date from the
fourth century onward (with fragments from as early as the second
century), is in the Koine or non-literary Hellenistic dialect of Greek.
The Greek version of the OT known as the Septuagint, prepared after
the middle of the third century B.C. and constituting the earliest
known Bible translation in the ordinary sense of the term, is in a
similar type of Greek. Until the discovery of the Greek inscriptions
and papyri, which were not seriously studied until late in the 19th
century, the Greek NT and the Septuagint were practically the only
sources for this dialect. The Septuagint, being a translation, is
heavily influenced by the Hebrew of its original (though not as slavish
a translation as that of Aquila which was made in the second century
A.D.). The NT is a series of original documents written in Greek,
although many influences from Hebrew and from the Aramaic of
Palestine are present and provide on the one hand difficulties in the
study of Greek structure and on the other hand valuable sources for
studying the characteristics of Palestinian Aramaic.

Aramaic existed in several dialects. Besides the data from
the Greek NT, which has been studied from the standpoint of loan
translations and other Aramaic features, Aramaic dialects appear in
certain portions of the OT, in Egyptian papyri, and in Jewish sources
which include Targums and translations of parts of the OT, the most
important of which is a translation of the Samaritan Pentateuch
dating from the third and fourth centuries A.D.

Syriac, a Semitic dialect similar to but different from the
Palestinian Aramaic of the first century, has as its most important
source materials the translations of the NT, the earliest of which
were done in the second century and which were later followed by the
OT and by other Christian literature. A Syriac grammar was compiled by Jacob of Edessa (650-700 A. D.), a result of the study of
Greek by Syrian Christians for ecclesiastical purposes. It was based
on Greek grammar, with terminology similar to that used by the

Greeks. It succeeded, however, in systematizing the Syriac system of vowel points. This grammar became the basis for the later Syriac grammars of the 11th and 13th centuries.

In Latin, various versions were made of the Scriptures, the first being prepared near the end of the second century A. D. These early translations, known as the Old Latin versions, were made from the Greek (including the OT). In the fourth century Jerome prepared his monumental version known as the Vulgate, which was based upon the Hebrew OT and the Greek NT. We shall comment below on Jerome's approach to language and translation.

Coptic is the name given to Egyptian from the third century onward, written in an alphabet based chiefly on Greek. Its literature is exclusively of Christian origin, and began with the establishment of Christianity in Upper Egypt during the third century, Biblical translations exist in six Coptic dialects, the most important being in the Sahidic dialect, done in the third and early fourth centuries, and in the Bohairic dialect, dating from the seventh century onward. The latter came to be the literary and liturgical language of the Coptic Church after the 11th century.

Gothic, of special importance in Indo-European comparative linguistics, has come down to us almost exclusively in the Bible translation made by Ulfilas in the fourth century, using an alphabet devised by him (2.1.1., below). This translation was a direct result of missionary work of the Arian sect among the Goths of the Danubïan provinces. Most of the NT is extant in Gothic, besides a few fragments of the OT.

For Armenian the earliest documents, except for a few lines of poetry, are translations of the Bible made in the fifth century. The alphabet used was devised by Mesrop about 400 A.D. (2.1.1., below). Georgian has as its earliest materials a translation of the Bible which was begun in the fifth century. Two different alphabets were used, both said to have been introduced by the Christian church and one of which tradition attributes to Mesrop. Through the eleventh century the literature was entirely religious, produced by Christian clergy and monks.

Ethiopic is first known in inscriptions from the fourth century A.D. at Aksum, said to be due chiefly to King Aeyzanas, who introduced Christianity to the country. Although the oldest dated biblical manuscript is from the 13th century, it is generally agreed that this was transmitted from translations of the Bible first made in the fifth century. Arabic versions of the scriptures date from about the ninth century, but probably reflect earlier translations that are no longer extant.

Sources for Old Church Slavic, the earliest of the Slavic languages to be preserved, are also due to Christian missions. The brothers Cyril and Methodius, of Thessalonica, were missionaries in the Balkan Peninsula in the second half of the ninth century: using an alphabet developed by Cyril (2.1.1., below), they translated the Gospels and liturgy for use in the church which they had organized.

Although most of our materials for the Indo-Iranian languages are from non-Christian sources, the Middle Iranian dialects (Middle Parthian, Middle Sogdian, and Middle Sakian) are preserved chiefly in translations of Christian documents from Syriac and of Buddhist writings from Sanskrit. These date from around the eighth and ninth centuries.

1.1.2. Theoretical work. The early interest in the church in matters of language was related in part to the preparation of literature in the languages of the newly evangelized peoples, and this led, as has been mentioned above, to the development of alphabets for certain of the languages, especially Gothic, Coptic, Armenian, Georgian, and Old Church Slavic.

Differences between the Hebrew OT and the existing translations in Greek led early Christian scholars to concern themselves with matters of text and translation. In the third century Origen of Alexandria made a special examination of these relationships in his Hexapla, which consisted of the OT in six columns, with the Hebrew text, its transliteration in Greek characters, and four Greek versions including the Septuagint, marking in the Greek versions the points at which they differed from the Hebrew original. The Hexapla is of especial interest to Hebrew scholars today because in the transliteration

the Hebrew vowels are indicated according to their current pronunciation. (Roberts, 1951, pp. 128-38.)

   Jerome, who translated the OT from the Hebrew rather than
from the Septuagint which underlay the Old Latin versions, was
brought face to face with these differences and was criticized by
those who insisted upon the inspiration of the Septuagint and also by
those who objected to his degree of freedom in translating. In the
preface to his work and in replies to his critics, he expressed in
considerable detail his views on the principles of translating, stating
quite frankly that he had rendered 'sense for sense and not word for
word',[4] and emphasizing a philological approach to Bible translating
which brought him into conflict with the views of other churchmen,
including Augustine, who insisted upon what has been termed the
'inspirational' approach.[5] In one of his letters he wrote that the task
of a good translator consists in rendering idiomatic expressions of
one language into the modes of expression peculiar to the other.
(Schwarz, p. 34). On other occasions Jerome wrote that the order
of words should be preserved in translation; however, since his
practice was otherwise it would seem that such statements were made
in the heat of controversy and as part of the confusing theological
climate of the day rather than as reflecting his real convictions.

   Augustine (354-430 A.D.) knew the Phoenecian language and
something of its affinity with Hebrew, and insisted on the appointment
of bishops who could speak it. He included in his writings a treatise
on Latin grammar and discussions of obscurities, ambiguities, etc.
(1841 in bibliography). In his work De Magistro (1947 in bibliography)
he discussed different types of signs, the relationships of words to
reality and to other signs, and the difference between signs and the
things signified. His correspondence (1951 in bibliography) with
Jerome includes discussions of the authority of the Septuagint, which
Augustine considered as inspired as against the Hebrew OT, but these
letters do not otherwise appear of linguistic interest. (Compare
Schwarz, pp. 41-43.)

   Gray asserts that the writers of the early Christian period,
including Basil, Jerome, Augustine, and Chrysostom, adhered to
Plato and the Stoics in their philosophy of language and that they were
"practically obliged to maintain that language had its origin phusei

since God had given it directly to man. . ." (Gray, pp. 427-28.)
That this is not, however, entirely true had already been shown by
Müller, who writes, "St. Basil was accused by Eunomius of denying
Divine Providence, because he would not admit that God had created
the names of all things, but ascribed the invention of language to the
faculties which God had implanted in man." (Müller, p. 40, note.)
He then cites Gregory of Nyssa as having defended Basil's position. [6]

One of the factors which retarded linguistic progress was
the belief among early Christian writers and persisting well into the
Renaissance era, that all languages were derived from Hebrew.
Hebrew was supposed, without evidence from the Bible or elsewhere,
to have been the language of Adam; and much intellectual effort was
spent in attempting to relate other languages to it.

1.2. The Middle Ages. After the establishment of Christianity throughout the greater part of the known world during the early
period, there came a period of comparative inactivity as regards
missions. Written literatures already begun were of course continued in many languages, but expansion into new languages largely
ceased for a time to occupy the attention of the Church.

On the other hand, medieval philosophers, many of them
churchmen, began to give some attention to the problems of language,
with the result that the intellectual world began to be prepared for
the advances in linguistic knowledge which were to be made by their
successors and more fully realized still later, in the 19th century.
However, these medieval scholars did not for the most part grapple
with linguistic problems as realistically as Jerome had done.

1.2.1. Language materials. Old English, whose records
begin in the earlier period, is treated here since its materials extend
to an important degree into the Middle Ages and beyond. Christianity
was introduced into the British Isles near the close of the sixth century; written records begin in the eighth century and owe their preservation in large measure to Christianity. Over half of the old
English poetry deals with Christian motifs. Among the earliest of
such materials are Caedmon's poem (seventh century) and the poems
on Genesis and other parts of the Bible. These were followed by
Cynewulf's poems of about 800 A. D., also dealing with Christian

subjects, besides other Christian poems. Old English prose literature was developed by and under the inspiration of King Alfred (871-
901 A. D.). Among the works for which he was responsible are
translations of Pope Gregory's Cura Pastoralis and of Bede's His-
toria Ecclesiastica Gentis Anglorum. Early biblical translations
include ninth century interlinear glosses on the Latin Psalter, followed by the so-called Paris Psalter from the late ninth or early
tenth century, the Lindisfarne Gospels in the northern Northumbrian
dialect of the tenth century and the later Rushworth Gospels in the
southern Northumbrian dialect. There are also the West Saxon Gospels and Aelfric's version of several OT books, dating from about
1000 A. D. The first translations of the whole Bible were the Wycliffite versions of 1302 and 1388.

In German, the earliest biblical materials are a Frankish
version of Matthew from the year 738,. followed by a harmony of the
Gospels from the ninth century in an East Frankish dialect. More
than 200 biblical manuscripts exist from prior to the time of printing,
most of them from the 15th century. Records of Old Saxon, the early
form of what is now Low German, begin shortly before the Middle
Ages. The chief monument is the Hēliand, a Christian poem of some
6000 lines composed about 830 A. D.

Sources of Old Irish are some brief inscriptions from the
fifth and sixth centuries, followed by a large number of glosses
dating from the eighth to the eleventh centuries on the Bible and on
Latin authors, and the Cambrai Homily, an Old Irish religious com-
position. Other languages of the Celtic family become available during the Middle Ages, in a number of cases through Christian literature.
The oldest records of Breton and Cornish are dramas on biblical and
religious themes dating from the 15th century.

In Albanian, the oldest documents are a short baptismal
ritual of 1462 and a Bible translation of 1555, now preserved at the
Uniate Seminary in Palermo. The better known Albanian material
dates from the 17th century, consisting of folk songs and other literature.

The earliest documents of the Finno-Ugric family are in
Hungarian, beginning with a short funeral oration from the 13th

century and followed in the 15th and 16th centuries by other religious
manuscripts.

Among the important early documents of the Turkic group of
languages is the Codex Cumanicus (1303), which contains three
glossaries (Latin-Persian-Coman, Coman-Latin, and Coman-German),
riddles, penances, hymns, and other texts of Christian nature.

1.2.2. Theoretical work. Saint Isidoro of Seville (c. 570-
636) was a precursor of the Medieval period, and his Etymologies
(see reference to Spanish edition in bibliography) had a wide circula-
tion and influence during the Middle Ages. His approach was similar
to that of Plato's Cratylus of a millennium earlier; he used etymologies (some of which were far-fetched indeed)[7] to discover and teach
the real meanings of words, and wrote lengthy treatises on grammar,
geography, mathematics, medicine, agriculture, etc. in which the
nature of the real world was explained partly in terms of his etymologies for the names of phenomena.

With the development of medieval philosophy, some attention
was turned to the study of languages and their relationships. The
most important figure in this period, from the linguistic standpoint,
seems to have been Roger Bacon. We shall discuss briefly his views,
together with those of a few others whose interests included matters
of language studies.

St. Anselm (c. 1033-1109) wrote a treatise entitled Dialogus
de Grammatico. He divides meaning into two kinds: what a word
means per se or directly, and what a word may mean indirectly. He
argues that if a white horse is out of sight, the word 'white' is insufficient to tell one what it is; but that if one sees a white horse and a
black ox and is told to 'hit the white one', then the word 'white' indirectly identifies the horse as well as its color. Some words, such
as 'man' or 'horse', have a substance as their direct meaning; while
others, such as 'grammarian' or 'white' have a quality as their direct
meaning and may have also a substance as their indirect meaning
(e.g. 'grammarian' means 'man' indirectly, 'white' may mean 'horse'
indirectly). He notes also that words are classifiable one way as to
grammatical form but another way as to the nature of things (e.g.

lapis is masculine in form but not male, petra is feminine in form but not female).

Aelfric, 11th century author of the Old English homilies, prepared a descriptive Grammatica Latino-Saxonica and a Latin-Old English glossary. Aelfric was known as 'The Grammarian' in allusion to his linguistic interests and attainments.

Alexander de Villa Dei, a churchman in Normandy early in the 13th century, wrote the Doctrinale Puerorum, a Latin grammar in verse, modeled somewhat after that of Priscian of the sixth century. This came to be universally studied in the schools during the Middle Ages, being revised by other authors in the 15th and 16th centuries.

Robert Grosseteste (c. 1175-1253) was reader in theology at Oxford and later Bishop of Lincoln. He was a Greek scholar and translated Greek works into Latin. Grosseteste showed an enthusiasm for the study of languages, holding theories similar to those of Bacon, who however advanced beyond him in this respect. His endeavours to promote the study of ancient languages induced him to invite Greek scholars to England for this purpose. A work entitled Grammatica, unpublished, is attributed to Grosseteste; it was unfavorably criticized by Bacon, who was apparently unaware of its authorship. This work is cited by Thomson, who says, "It is rather [than a Greek grammar] an introductory treatise on language: the relation of language to knowledge, comparative phonetics, the eight parts of speech and the relations between them all with apt illustrations from Latin or Greek." (Thomson, pp. 101-102.)

Roger Bacon (c. 1214-1292), philosopher, theologian, and man of science, was a Franciscan and a devout follower of Christianity. His interest in the study of languages sprang largely from the fact that the entire European knowledge of theology and philosophy was derived from sources other than Latin. Languages were not to be studied for their own sake, as a scientia principalis like mathematics, but rather like logic as a necessary gateway to the acquisition of wisdom. His method, however, demanded none the less that language be made the object of independent and scientific research.

One of Bacon's strongest motives for promoting the study of other languages, especially Greek and Hebrew, was for purifying the current Paris Text of the Latin Vulgate Bible, which had become badly corrupted. He considered that not only the Bible, but Aristotle and the other Greek writers were unsatisfactory in their Latin translations, and insisted that scholars go back to the original languages in order to adequately understand them. In addition, Bacon also spoke of the value of knowing foreign languages for the purposes of commerce, international relations, and Christian missions. He wrote: ". . . the knowledge of language is necessary to the Latins for the conversion of unbelievers. For in the hands of the Latins rests the power to convert. . . Oh how we should consider this matter and fear lest God may hold the Latins responsible because they are neglecting the languages so that in this way they neglect the preaching of the faith." (Bacon, pp. 110-112.)

Bacon himself wrote a Greek grammar and began a Hebrew one; it was his desire to produce one in Arabic also, which he considered a third language indispensable to learning. His Greek grammar, written for pedagogical purposes, treats Greek in comparison to the more familiar Latin. He believed that, with a well prepared manual, a pupil could get a useful beginning in any of these languages in a matter of days; but also that their study required years for complete mastery.

Bacon's linguistic interests covered many aspects of what we today call philology; all this he included under 'grammar'. Even the problems of the origin of speech, whose study he considered essential to a proper understanding of theology and philosophy, he placed under this term. Although responsible for nothing new in basic linguistic theory, Bacon was in advance of his time in his emphasis on language study and his restatement of a number of the problems which were then considered a part of 'grammar'.

Bacon desired a systematic investigation of the theory of 'signs' in connection with linguistic studies, holding that words are arbitrary signs imposed by the mind. He further distinguished form from meaning in calling a word 'articulate' when it can be written down, regardless of meaning. A 'letter' is then the smallest part of such a written word, but is distinguished from its corresponding sound, which he called an 'element'. In this distinction between sounds and their graphic representation Bacon seems to have been considerably in advance of his time.

As to meaning, Roger Bacon held, with the allegorists of his time and earlier, that each word had in addition to its literal meaning three others: an allegorical, a tropological or figurative, and an anagogical or more hidden meaning. It was especially because of these non-literal meanings that he insisted the Bible could be adequately understood only in the original languages.

The Franciscan philosopher Duns Scotus (c. 1265-1308) was influenced by Grosseteste and Bacon in his interest in the study of languages. The treatise De Modis Significandi, sive Grammatica Speculativa is generally attributed to him. It incorporates much of Bacon's doctrine, and is 'one of the earliest attempts to give a scientific account of the meaning of linguistic forms'.[8] It contains some interesting conclusions concerning gender which were more recently reached on strictly scientific evidence. (Gray, p. 187.)

Archbishop Rodrigo Jimenez de Rada drew up in 1243 a list of languages of Europe which, according to Borst,[9] was the first attempt at classification on an empirical rather than a traditional basis. He seems to have been the first to note the existence of a West Germanic as opposed to a Scandinavian branch within the Germanic language family, and appears to have recognized the close relationship within the Romance family.

Much of the scholarship of both the Middle Ages and the Renaissance was due to the efforts of the church, and the European universities of that day were founded with a view to the promotion of Christianity. An impulse to linguistic study was given in 1311 at the Council of Vienna when Pope Clement V asked the four great universities to establish chairs in Hebrew, Arabic, and Chaldee, the motive being to enable students to dispute successfully with Jews and Mohammedans.

The work of the Jewish Masoretic scholars, beginning in the earlier period and reaching its climax in the Middle Ages, is of interest both linguistically and for the effect which their linguistic approach had upon the Christian attitudes toward the Scriptures.

For several centuries the Hebrew text of the OT, originally devoid of vowel letters, had been supplied sporadically with matres lectionis or the consonants aleph, he, waw, and yodh, used with vocalic values at places of potential ambiguity. From the fifth century A. D. onward there began the indication of vowels by auxiliary signs or points above and below the consonants. This was further developed by different schools of the Masoretic scholars, culminating in the work of the western Masoretes from the ninth century onward. Their purpose was to establish definitively the vowel pronunciation of the Hebrew biblical text as it had been handed down orally and by the use of the matres lectionis.

There were many differences in the work done by the various Masoretes, and their work as finally accepted for use in the Hebrew OT could not of course fully represent the pronunciation of an earlier millennium. The system developed a number of artificial forms and was also characterized by some archaizing tendencies in the elimination of certain of the genuine consonants in the belief that they were matres lectionis and the substitution of vowel points for them. Nevertheless, their work was a very meticulous study and led to a very accurate phonetic representation of the vowel sounds as they believed them to have been pronounced. [10]

The purpose of the Masoretic studies was to preserve the form of the biblical text which they considered inspired and authoritative. Although their work was demonstrably recent in date and therefore could not have the same textual authority as the consonantal Hebrew text, opinions were later voiced, especially in the 16th and 17th centuries, that divine inspiration and authority were actually extended to the vocalization of the text as written by the Masoretic points. Although this view was opposed by the better scholars, both Protestant and Roman Catholic, it was even officially approved by Protestantism in the Helvetian Council in 1675. (Roberts, 1951, pp. 68-69.) The weight of scholarship finally won the day, but the attitudes toward the inviolability of the sacred text which were developed in this connection continued to exert their influence among Christians and to contribute toward their attitudes regarding the text of the NT as well as of the OT.

1.3. Renaissance and post-Renaissance.

1.3.1. <u>Language materials</u>. After the discovery of the New
World and the invention of printing, linguistic activity increased and
new languages became known. Missionaries as well as other travel-
ers came into contact with other languages and added them, in at
least a superficial way, to the total of linguistic knowledge. Hence
by the end of the 18th century it was possible for Pallas to include
over 200 languages of Europe and Asia in his survey which appeared
in 1786, and eighty more in 1791. (Bloomfield, p. 7.) Hervás y
Panduro (1800) lists some 300, including American languages.

This period was also characterized by Bible translations
into a larger number of languages than even before. North (pp. 23-
27) lists 33 languages into which biblical translations had been made
prior to the invention of printing in Western Europe. Between that
time and the founding of the British and Foreign Bible Society (1806),
his lists show 47 additional languages in which biblical materials
were published. These include translations of the Bible, largely
Protestant, into all the major languages of Europe. During the same
period, Roman Catholic missionaries prepared translations of catechisms, liturgies, etc., in numerous new languages, including languages of the Western Hemisphere.

Among the previously unrecorded Indo-European languages
whose records begin with religious literature of this period are
Modern Greek, Manx, and Old Prussian. One of the earliest literary
records of Modern Greek is a polyglot version of the Pentateuch with
the Greek in Hebrew characters, published by Jews at Constantinople
in 1547. Manx is first recorded in a translation of the Book of Common Prayer made between 1625 and 1630 (printed in 1895). Old Prussian is represented by two versions of Luther's Catechism (both in
1545), the Enchiridion or Short Catechism of Luther (1561), besides
802 words in the Elbing Glossary of the early 14th century and some
material of lesser value from the early 16th century.

Mention has been made, in connection with the preceding
period, of the early materials in English and German. A most valuable source of materials for tracing the structural development of

Middle English and Early Modern English is in the various Bible
translations that were begun in the Middle Ages and made at almost
regular intervals during this later period. After the 14th century
Wycliffite versions, there appeared Tyndale's NT of 1525, followed
by a series of versions, chief of which are the Coverdale Bible (1535),
Matthew's Bible (1537), the Great Bible (1539), the Geneva Bible
(1560), the Bishop's Bible (1568), the Rheims-Douai Bible (1582-
1610), and the King James Bible (1611). During the same periods a
considerable part of the original literature in English is that pertain-
ing to religious and ecclesiastical matters. Important among these
writers may be mentioned Wyclif (c. 1320-1384), Chaucer (d. 1400),
the author of Peres the Ploughmans Crede (c. 1394), Tyndale (1477-
1536), Thomas More (1480-1535), Hugh Latimer (1491-1555). These
materials, together with other literature of the period, enable us to
trace the development of English from generation to generation during
the period of transition from Old to Modern English.

Of the other Germanic languages, the first to receive a
printed Bible was German; this appeared in 1466, the first Bible
printed in any modern language. The translation by Luther, of which
the NT appeared in 1522 and the entire Bible in 1534, was the first
complete Bible translated from the original languages into a modern
European language, and is considered a landmark in the history of
Bible translating. A Dutch translation made about 1300 became the
basis for the first printed edition of the OT in Dutch in 1477. In Ice-
landic a translation and paraphrase of parts of the Bible had been
made near the end of the 13th century, and the NT was published in
1540. Of the Scandinavian languages, the first Scripture in Danish
appeared in 1524, in Swedish in 1526.

All of the important Romance languages, including several
minor dialects, had Scripture translations by the 16th century; some
of these are among the important historical materials of these languages. The earliest biblical translations in Old French date from
the 12th century; the first published translation in French was the
NT in 1474. Earlier material than this appears for Provencal; the
Gospel of John was translated by Peter Waldo in the 12th century,
and a 14th century manuscript believed to be from this was published
in 1848. The NT was published in Provençal in 1887 from a 13th century manuscript. (Since 1800 there have appeared Scripture

translations in at least 14 modern French and Provencal dialects.)
For Romansch, there is a translation of the Psalms in meter form
published in the Lower Engadine dialect in 1562, the first book printed
in this dialect. The NT was published in two other Romansch dialects
in 1560 and 1648. For Vaudois, in northern Italy, a manuscript of
John's Gospel which probably dates from the 14th century was published in 1848, and the NT was published in 1890 from a 16th century
manuscript. In Catalan, translations of parts of the Bible were made
as early as the 13th century. Some 14th century manuscripts are
extant, and a fragment of the first Bible printed in Catalan, which
appeared in 1478. This Bible, translated by the brothers Bonifacio
and Vicente Ferrer earlier in the century, was the fourth whole
Bible printed in a European language. In Italian, manuscripts of
parts of the Bible are extant from the 13th and 14th centuries; the
first Italian Bible was printed in 1471.

Spanish, Portugese, and Rumanian were the last of the
Romance languages to possess published Bible translations. The
Liturgical Epistles appeared in Spanish in 1490, and the NT in 1543.
A harmony of the Gospels was published in Portuguese in 1495, but
the NT did not appear until 1681. The Rumanian translation of the
Gospels, published in 1561, was the second book printed in Rumanian.
This was followed by other biblical materials, and finally by the Bible
in 1688.

Six editions of the Bible or parts of it were printed in Czech
before 1500, under the influence of Jan Hus.

Among the Finno-Ugric languages, literary Finnish begins
with a translation of the NT in 1548. Esthonian literature begins with
a translation of the Liturgical Epistles and Gospels, dated 1632. The
first book printed in Hungarian was a translation of the Epistles of
Paul in 1533. A few 15th century manuscripts containing the Gospels
and some OT portions are also preserved. (North, pp. 37, 169.)

The earliest record of Basque, except for some place-names
dating from the eighth century, is a 16th century collection of poems
entitled Linguae Vasconam Primitiae by the priest Dechepare. Most
of the subsequent literature until about 1880 consists of translations
of religious works. The NT appeared in Basque in 1571.

Sanskrit, which was to play such an important part in the development of comparative linguistics in the 19th century, was first discovered by missionaries during the 17th century. Roberto de Nobili, who went to India in 1606 as a Jesuit missionary, was perhaps the first European to acquire a knowledge of Sanskrit. European scholars, however, remained for the most part quite unaware of its existence until the middle of the 18th century, when Father Pons and other French Jesuit missionaries succeeded in arousing their interest in it. The first European grammar of Sanskrit was published by the German Carmelite missionary Paolino de San Bartolomeo at Rome in 1790, after having lived in India from 1776 to 1789. It provided material to demonstrate some of the similarity between Sanskrit and the classical languages of Europe, and was an early attempt at a grammatical description of the language.

The greatest single field of language materials opened up during this period was that of the languages of the New World. By far the greater part of the early linguistic materials there, especially in Middle and South America, was produced by Roman Catholic missionaries. At the same time, Roman Catholic missionaries were also responsible for the destruction of most of the pre-colonial documents on the American continent, which if preserved would have been invaluable to linguists today in the study of American languages. But in their evangelistic efforts these missionaries soon realized the importance of using the native languages, and set about studying them. In Mexico, for example, "one of the first acts of these twelve [Franciscan] friars—called the 'Twelve Apostles'—was to found a language school in Texcoco for the study of Indian dialects and for teaching Spanish to the Indians. ... One friar, Bernardino de Sahagún, arriving in Mexico in 1529, spent his first few years mastering Náhuatl and other Indian dialects at the language school in Texcoco. ... (McHenry, pp. 51-52, 57.)

These New World languages were recorded in traditional Roman characters, in a very few cases with the use of diacritical marks where the Latin alphabet appeared to the missionaries to be insufficient. Grammars and dictionaries were written, incident to the learning of the languages and for the use of the clergy. These grammars were mostly in a Latin mold, generally that used by Nebrija for Spanish (1.3.2. below).

Some idea of the extent of this work may be gained from the fact that there are listed[11] for the 16th century alone a total of 212 works dealing with languages of the New World. Of these, thirty are languages of South America. The first grammar of Quechua was the Gramática o Arte de la lengua General de los Indios de los Reynos del Perú, by the Dominican Domingo de Santo Tomás (Valladolid, 1560). Josef de Ancheta (d. 1597) wrote a grammar and vocabulary of Tupí, with a catechism in the language. Antonio Ruíz de Montoya formed a grammar and vocabulary of Guaraní, published in 1639-40; he was among the first to use Roman letters with diacritics.

There are 27 works named for Central America during the 16th century on six or more languages. For Mexico 155 works are listed, on twelve languages. The language best represented is Náhuatl, with 92 works listed. Eleven of these were grammars, the first of which was a Grammatica et Lexicon Linguae Mexicanae, Totonacae, et Huaxtecae, by Fr. Andrés de Olmos (México, 1555-60, 2 vols.). Eight lexical works are noted, and twelve translations, including the Gospels, Proverbs, and other materials. Others include 48 original works in Náhuatl consisting of sermons, catechisms, commentaries, dialogues, etc.

For the seventeenth century over 250 works are listed which treat of Indian languages of Latin America. There was less activity of a literary nature in the already known languages, but new work was done in many languages of Mexico and especially of South America.

The most productive period was that of the Franciscans and the Dominicans; these were largely superseded in the 17th and 18th centuries by the Jesuits, who also worked among the Indians but with less accomplishment in the actual use of the languages. Still, 210 works are listed for the 18th century; and some of these represent perhaps a greater degree of systematization of materials, the culmination of which we find in the work of the Jesuit Hervás y Panduro, to be discussed below:

Protestant missionary work among the Indians of the New World was not begun until the 18th century. It is to their work that we owe most of the Bible translations which appeared in printed form both before the close of the 18th century, and to a greater extent,

since that date. Of the 18th century work, the first was that of the
Moravians in British Dutch Guiana; a harmony of the Gospels was
translated by them into Arawak and published in 1799.

In North America the first important Protestant missionary
work was that of John Eliot among the Massachusetts Indians. Eliot
reduced the Massachusetts language to writing about 1643 and translated the NT, which was published in 1661. The Bible appeared in
1663, said to be 'the earliest example of the translating and printing
of the entire Bible in a new language as a means of evangelization. '
(North, p. 39.) Massachusetts is a language of the Algonkian family
which is no longer spoken and is available to linguists only in such
records as these. Similar records in other Algonkian languages
appeared during the 19th century. Mohawk, an Iroquoian language,
was reduced to writing by missionaries and a translation of the
Prayer Book with selections from the Bible was published in 1715;
the Gospel of Mark was printed in 1787, and other portions later.

Greenlandic Eskimo was reduced to writing about 1730 by
Hans Egede, a Norwegian pastor. Poul Egede prepared a grammar
(1750; see Rosing, p. 64) and translated the Gospels (1744); the NT
appeared in 1766. Otho Fabricius prepared a version of the NT (1794)
and a grammar (1801). This was followed by Kleinschmidt's important work in the 19th century; see below, 1.4.1. and 2.2.

Missionary work in the Pacific area was begun as early as
the 17th century and carried on to some extent along with 18th century
explorations, but little linguistic progress was made until the 19th
century. In the early period, however, should be noted the work in
Malay and Formosan. Malay had been written as early as the 14th
century, but old inscriptions are rare. The oldest surviving manuscripts in Malay date from about 1600; the Gospel of Matthew was
printed in 1629. The NT, which was the first published in a language
of Oceania, appeared in 1662, and the entire Bible in 1733. In Formosan, a translation of Matthew and John was published in 1661.

1.3.2. Theoretical work. Of special significance during
this period is the developing interest in the relationships of languages
and the increasing awareness of Hebrew and Greek on the part of
churchmen. With a new concern for going back to the original

textual sources, 16th century scholars became interested in the study of the languages and turned their attention away from the purely traditional and authoritative interpretation of the texts toward a philological approach to them. The leading figure in this was Erasmus.

Greek studies were at a near standstill at the end of the 15th century, and were given an important impetus by Erasmus. His edition of the Greek NT was one of the most important events in the history of biblical studies. Erasmus insisted on a philological approach in preference to the traditional authoritative view, and this led to serious language study. He preferred the writings of Jerome to those of Augustine, expressing appreciation for Jerome's philological work and following him in his emphasis upon understanding the text of the original instead of considering the translations authoritative. He also emphasized the need for knowing not only the language of the original but the literature and usage of other authors in the language. Erasmus advocated translation of the Scriptures into the vernacular languages, and insisted upon a translation being meaningful: "Language consists of two parts, namely words and meaning which are like body and soul. If both of them can be rendered I do not object to word-for-word translation. If they cannot, it would be preposterous for a translator to keep the words and to deviate from the meaning."[12]

Erasmus' Greek NT, first published in 1516, became to all intents and purposes the Textus Receptus upon which most missionary translations were based until the work of 19th century textual criticism provided better texts.

Hebrew studies had been neglected and in the 15th century were actually opposed by such men as the Dominican Peter Schwarz on the theory that the discrepancies between the Latin Bible and its Hebrew sources were due to falsifications perpetrated in the Hebrew Bible by the Jews. Materials available for the study of Hebrew were few and inadequate. Johann Reuchlin, who has been called 'the father of the study of Hebrew among Christians', published a Hebrew grammar and dictionary in 1506 entitled De Rudimentis Hebraicis, which marked the beginning of serious Hebrew studies in Europe. In his work Reuchlin, like Erasmus, broke from the use of theological criteria in the interpretation of Scripture and insisted upon a philological method.

The publication in 1520 of the famous Biblia Poliglota Complutense, a version of the Bible in Latin, Greek, Hebrew and Chaldee, was the result of the combined labors of a number of scholars under the direction of Cardinal Jiménez de Cisneros at the University of Alcalá in Spain, and demonstrated the growing interest in languages and their relationships. It included a 75-page Greek-Latin glossary which was one of the first attempts at lexicography of the biblical literature.

One of the important philologists of the beginning of this period, and one who influenced the linguistic approach of missionaries of the period, was the Spanish scholar Elio Antonio Nebrija (1444-1532), of the University of Salamanca. Besides his work as a grammarian, he helped interest Cisneros in reviving the study of the ancient languages, and later helped in the preparation of the Biblia Poliglota. He insisted upon appealing to the Hebrew and Greek manuscripts for the authentic Bible text, and demonstrated the absurdity of the current belief that the Jews had corrupted the Hebrew text in order to confuse the Christians. (Bataillon, vol. 1, pp. 35-38.) Nebrija's most direct linguistic contribution was his Gramática de la Lengua Castellana, which was the first grammar published of the vernacular Spanish. This appeared in 1492, and during the century following was looked upon as an authority in grammar. As such it exerted a powerful influence on the work of the Spanish missionaries in America, many of whom modeled their grammatical descriptions of American languages expressly after the work of Nebrija, resulting of course in descriptions which reflected more the Spanish or Latin model than the real structure of the languages.

The work of the Jesuit Lorenzo Hervás y Panduro (1735-1809) entitled Catálogo de las Lenguas de las Naciones Conocidas was published in six volumes from 1800 to 1805 and is a fitting climax to the linguistic contribution of missionaries, especially in America, during the period which it closes. Hervás was a Spanish missionary in America. Upon his return to Europe he assembled materials of his own and of other Jesuit missionaries from various parts of the world, producing a survey which includes some 300 languages of Asia, Europe, and America. He is said to have himself formed grammars of some forty languages. (Müller, p. 140.) His Catálogo, while sharing many of the misconceptions of its day, is of considerable

linguistic interest, and in closing our discussion of this period we
shall treat the theories of its author in some detail.

Hervás y Panduro, like Bacon in an earlier day, emphasized
the need for the study of languages both for the administration of
government and the propagation of Christianity. (Hervás y Panduro,
vol. 1, p. 20.) He pointed out that a knowledge of affinities between
different languages is of value to the missionary who desires to learn
other languages related to the one in which he has worked. In another
connection, however (vol. 1, pp. 52 ff.), he implies that studies
relating to linguistic affinities and diversities are of little use as an
end in themselves; and one of his chief tenets is that the purpose of
scientific language study should be to illuminate history. He cites
(vol. 1, pp. 37 ff.) the work of various predecessors who had col-
lected specimens of the Lord's Prayer in different languages (Bibli-
andro in 1548, 14 languages; Rocca in 1591, 26 languages; Megisero
in 1592, 40 languages and later in 50 languages; Mullero in 1680,
nearly 100 languages; Schultz in 1748, 200 languages), but considers
this type of collector's approach as ultimately of little scientific
value. He says that it "sirve más para satisfacer a la vana curiosi-
dad, que para adelantar en las ciencias."

Hervás insisted (vol. 1, pp. 62 ff.) on the need for descriptive grammars and for vocabularies as a prerequisite for comparative studies. He suggested the need for phonetic alphabets by recom-
mending the use of diacritics such as his fellow-Jesuit Ruíz had used
for Guaraní in 1639 (1.3.1. above). He noted the importance of
grammar over vocabulary in determining linguistic relationships,
saying: ". . .el carácter de algunas lenguas no se llega a conocer
perfectamente por medio de sus vocabularios solos; mas se deben
consultar sus grámaticas para conocer su carácter propio por medio
de su artificio gramatical."

Rejecting the still prevalent notion that all languages were
traceable to Hebrew, Hervás (vol. 1, pp. 35 ff.) deprecated the
various attempts that had been made to derive all languages from one,
ridiculing, for example, Goropius Becanus and his theory of Dutch as
the original language. He pointed out that the discovery of new languages had already made Becanus' work out of date to say the least—
since other languages might equally well qualify as original tongues.

He showed equal impatience with Scaliger's hypothesis of 'recipro-
cally unrelated' languages in Europe. However, Hervás had not con-
ceived the idea of attributing linguistic relationships to descent from
a common prehistoric language. His idea was rather that of a number of lenguas matrices or existing languages from which others had
been derived. For example, he lists the various Mayan languages of
Central America, and suggests Maya as the lengua matriz (vol. 1,
p. 304). Coupled with this conception of linguistic relationships was
a belief suggestive of what has more recently been called the 'sub-
stratum theory,' which led him to the conclusion that each language
retains the pronunciation of an earlier period. He writes: "Cada
lengua matriz en su origen tuvo su propia y particular pronunciación
de sílabas, la qual dura y se conserva substancialmente invariable
en sus dialectos, como demostrativa y prácticamente nos lo hacen
conocer todas las lenguas matrices, y los dialectos que de ellos se
hablan." (vol. 1, p. 19.)

The first two volumes of Hervás' work, dealing with American and Malayo-Polynesian languages, appear to be of greater linguistic interest than the other volumes, which treat of the already known
European languages. His survey of the American languages was
probably better than any made previously. It is quite detailed, and
shows a good knowledge of the character as well as the diversity of
the languages of the New World. His treatment of the languages of
Mexico, for example, shows a fair conception of the major language
families. His classifications are largely on a geographical basis
except where he had data for linguistic classification.

The section by Hervás y Panduro on Malayo-Polynesian languages is less extensive than that for the Americas. In it, he was
the first to point out the relationship between Malay and the Polyne-
sian languages, an observation which Max Müller called 'one of the
most brilliant discoveries in the history of the science of language'.
(Müller, p. 141.) Hervás makes this observation in the following
words: "Verá que la lengua llamada malaya, la qual se habla en la
península de Malaca, es matriz de inumerables dialectos de naciones
isleñas, que desde dicha península se extienden por más de doscien-
tos grados de longitud en los mares oriental y pacíficos. . . La
lengua malaya se habla en dicha península, continente del Asia, en
las islas Maldivas, en la de Madagascar (perteneciente al Africa),
en las de Sonda, en las Molucas, en las Filipinas, en las del

archipiélago de San Lázaro, y en muchísimas del mar del Sur desde
dicho archipiélago hasta islas, que por su poca distancia de América
se creían poblados por americanos. La isla de Madagascar se pone
a 60 grados de longitud, y a los 268 se pone la isla de Pasqua o de
Davis, en la que se habla otro dialecto malayo, por lo que la exten-
sión de los dialectos malayos es de 208 grados de longitud. "[13]

     1.4. <u>The nineteenth century</u>. The 19th century marked
great advances both in linguistics and in Christian missions. Missionaries contributed greatly to the knowledge of foreign languages,
and linguists in turn developed concepts that were destined to have a
great influence upon both missionary work and biblical scholarship,
especially in the 20th century.

     1.4.1. <u>Language materials</u>. During the 19th century bibli-
cal translations were made in about 450 new languages and dialects,
or over six times as many as in the entire period prior to 1800.
Many of these languages were reduced to writing by missionaries,
and for many of them the biblical materials were the first or only
documents. Many missionaries who worked on these translations
also prepared word lists, grammatical materials, and other data on
the languages in question.

     Of great immediate relevance to the work of the 19th century
comparative linguists was the bringing to their attention of Sanskrit,
which had been discovered by missionaries of the preceding period.
At the outset of the modern Protestant missionary movement, which
is generally reckoned as beginning with William Carey, who went to
India in 1793, missionaries were working with Sanskrit and other
languages of India. Carey himself became an outstanding Bible translator and Bengali scholar, and in 1801 was appointed professor of
Sanskrit, Bengali, and Marathi at Fort William College in Calcutta.
One of his first accomplishments was a translation of the NT into
Bengali, published in 1801. Together with his colleagues Marshman
and Ward, and with the aid of qualified Indian helpers, Carey directed
the preparation of biblical translations in some 34 languages. These
include both Indo-European and Dravidian languages. He also left a
vast volume of data on the structural and comparative analyses of
languages of North India, having prepared, or helped to prepare,
grammars and dictionaries in Marathi, Punjabi, Bengali, Telinga,
and Bhotanta, as well as in Sanskrit.

M. Monier-Williams (1819-99), orientalist and Sanskrit scholar, was influenced by missionary motives and travelled extensively throughout India to study native religions. One of his works which is still relevant to the missionary is a brief treatise which demonstrates the value of a knowledge of Sanskrit for the Christian missionary in India. His linguistic works include: A Practical Sanskrit Grammar (1846; 4th ed. 1877); An English and Sanskrit Dictionary (1851); Introduction to Hindustani (1858); A Sanskrit and English Dictionary (1872; 2nd ed. 1899). The last named is based on the larger Sanskrit-wörterbuch of Boehtlingk and Roth, and is of value chiefly in that it makes some of the material of the German lexicon available to the English reader.

For Persian, there had been a translation of the Pentateuch made by Jews and published as early as 1546 in a polyglot edition with Hebrew, Chaldee, and Arabic; at the beginning of the 19th century Henry Martyn, colleague of Carey, directed the translation of the NT by Persian scholars, and himself made a careful study of the Persian language.

Modern missionary work among the Dravidian speaking peoples of India began even before the time of Carey, with the arrival of Lutheran missionaries in Tranquebar in 1706; the NT was published in Tamil in 1714-15. The NT in Telugu was translated by colleagues of Carey and published in 1818; the Gospels were published in Malayalam in 1811. An extensive treatment of the Dravidian languages was made by the English missionary, R. Caldwell, who wrote A Comparative Grammar of the Dravidian or South Indian Family of Languages (London, 1856; 3rd ed., abridged, 1913). Although hardly a comparative grammar in the modern sense of the term, it contains much valuable material on these languages.

In Burmese, the first western scholar to make an extensive study of the language was the American Baptist missionary Adoniram Judson. Beginning with a small dictionary and grammar made by Felix Carey (son of William Carey), Judson learned Burmese, translated the Bible into it (1835), and later prepared a Burmese grammar and dictionary which has been used both by missionaries and by other students of oriental languages. Judson also prepared a Pali dictionary sometime after 1834.

Robert Morrison was one of the first Europeans to seriously study Chinese; he went to China as a missionary and made a translation of the Bible which was published from 1810 to 1823, also preparing a dictionary, grammar and translations of the Chinese classics that were used by his successors. At about the same time Joshua Marshman and John Lassar, working with Carey in India, produced a translation of the Bible in Chinese, and Marshman prepared a Chinese grammar which was of aid to later scholars and missionaries. In the field of Chinese lexicography, the large dictionary written later by Mathews and since revised by Chao still appears to be considered as a standard work.

In Japanese, Karl F. A. Gutzlaff provided invaluable data, producing in Singapore a translation of the Gospel of John in 1837, twenty years before Japan was opened to foreigners.

For Africa there exist biblical translations in over 350 languages; in many of these the Scriptures and other Christian literature are the only materials published. Many of them were reduced to writing by missionaries, some of whom left grammatical materials and other language data as well. We can here do no more than cite a few of the 19th century missionaries who contributed to the study of African languages.

Johann Ludwig Krapf (1810-82), a German who went to East Africa under the Church Missionary Society in 1844, was the first European to make any adequate study of Swahili. He published a Swahili-English Dictionary (London, 1882), which has more recently been revised by Archdeacon Binns, translator of the Swahili NT, and is still a standard work. [14] Krapf also produced, in the field of Hamitic languages, a Vocabulary of the Galla Language (London, 1842), and had a part in the translation of biblical materials in some eight languages and dialects, including representatives of the Bantu, Hamitic, and Semitic groups.

J. L. Döhne, of the Berlin Missionary Society, who translated the Psalter into Kaffir (about 1841) and helped with the Psalter in Zulu (1850), produced a Zulu-Kaffir Dictionary (Cape Town, 1857). This dictionary contains one of the earliest attempts to describe the clicks of South African languages.

Alexander Mackay reduced the Ganda language of Uganda to writing about 1878, and together with R. P. Ashe published the first biblical selections in 1886. Mbundu of Loanda had been reduced to writing much earlier, by Jesuits who in 1641 issued a catechism in Latin, Portuguese, and Mbundu. Heli Chatelain, a Swiss-American missionary, made the first biblical translation (1888) and published a Grammar of Kimbundu.

Alexander Hetherwick, of the Church of Scotland Mission, translated the Gospels and Acts into Yao (1889), and produced an Introductory Handbook of the Yao Language. Rev. D. C. Scott, of the same mission, wrote An Encyclopaedic Dictionary of the Mananja Language of British Central Africa (1891) and translated parts of the NT into Nyanja (1893-94). Rev. Holman Bentley wrote a Dictionary of the Congo Language (1891), and translated the NT into Kongo (1893). A Grammar and Dictionary of the Bobangi Language (London, 1899) was written by Rev. John Whitehead. A vocabulary and short grammar of Shilenge, by Bishop Smyth and John Mathews, was published in 1902.

A Comparative Grammar of the South African Bantu Languages (1894, incomplete) was written by Father J. Torrend. A Comparative Handbook of Congo Languages was written by Rev. W. H. Stapleton, who also made biblical translations in Bangala, Kele, Western Swahili, and Heso.

I. G. Krönlein, who completed the NT in Nama, a Bushman language (1866), wrote Wortschatz der Khoi-Khoin (1889).

H. Goldie, of the United Presbyterian Church of Scotland, translated the NT into Efik of Nigeria (1862) and produced a Dictionary of the Efik Language. I. G. Christaller, translator of the Gospels in the Tshi dialect of Ashanti of the Gold Coast (1859), wrote A Dictionary of the Asante and Fante Language called Tshi (1881). R. Lepsius, who translated Mark into Nubian of Egypt (1860), wrote Nubische Grammatik, Mitre. Einteiling über die Völker und Sprachen Afrikas (1880). Nineteenth century missionary contributions to Hausa include a grammar (London, 1862) by J. F. Schön, of the Church Missionary Society, who also translated Matthew into Hausa (1857) and Mende (1871), revised parts of the NT in Ibo (1864-66), and helped edit the Yoruba NT (1862).

Leo Reinisch, who supervised the translation of Mark into Bogos (1882) and Falasha (1885), languages of Ethiopia, later published Die Somali Sprache (Vienna, 1900 et seq.) and Das persönliche. Fürwort und die Verbalflexion in den chamito-semitischen Sprachen (1909). A. C. Hollis, Secretary of the British East Africa Administration, translated Mark in Masai of Kenya and Tanganyika (1905); he is the author of The Masai (1905) and The Nandi: Their Language and Folklore (1909).

In the Western Hemisphere, the publication in 1851 of a grammar of Greenlandic Eskimo by the Moravian missionary Samuel Kleinschmidt, based not on Latin grammar but upon the language's own structure, was an important landmark in American linguistics (Rosing, pp. 63-65, and below, 2.2.).

In Middle and South American languages there was less new work done by missionaries in the 19th century than in the preceding period. Special mention, however, should be made of that done in Miskito of Nicaragua and Honduras, in which Alexander Henderson prepared a translation of some biblical selections and a grammar (1846) and Moravian missionaries were responsible for the Gospels (1889) and later the NT (1905).

For languages of the North American continent, important pioneering linguistic work was done by a number of early missionaries in the United States. Special mention should be made of that done about the middle of the 19th century by Cyrus Byington in Choctaw, R. M. Loughridge in Creek, and David Zeisberger in Onandaga. The Russian priest Ivan Veniaminov developed the alphabet which is still used for Aleut, and wrote an Aleut grammar (1846; see bibliography for 1944 edition).

The following languages of North America are listed by North as having biblical translations published in the 19th century for the first time: Aleut (3 dialects), Algonquin, Beaver, Blackfoot, Cherokee, Chipewyan, Choctaw, Cree (3 dialects), Creek, Dakota, Delaware, Eskimo (3 dialects), Haida, Hidatsa, Iroquois, Kwagutl, Maliseet, Micmac (2 dialects), Nez Percé, Nishga, Ojibwa, Oneida, Osage, Oto, Ottawa, Potawotami, Seneca, Shawnee, Slave, Tukudh, Zimshian. (Massachusetts is the only one listed prior to the 19th century.)

Languages of Middle and South America listed by North as having biblical translations in the 19th century are: Acawoio, Aymara, Carib, Guaraní, Maya, Miskito, Quiché, Warau, Yahgan. (He lists Arawak and Otomí as having biblical materials prior to the 19th century.)

1.4.2. <u>Theoretical work.</u> With the 19th century the relationship between linguistics and Christian missions begins to take on somewhat of an aspect of mutuality. Whereas in preceding periods the contributions were made for the most part from missions to linguistic knowledge, we now find the beginnings of a genuine two-way interchange. With the organization of the accumulated knowledge of languages (especially Indo-European) into a science for the first time by 19th century scholars in the field of historical linguistics, there began an influence upon Christian scholars that affected both biblical studies and the quality of Bible translation work. This influence began to be felt in the 19th century, especially in reference to the study of biblical languages and texts, and reached its fuller implications in the 20th century.

As Indo-European comparative linguistics developed in the 19th century, there was also extensive comparative study of Hebrew and related languages. With the discovery and study of other Semitic languages it was no longer possible to consider Hebrew as the original tongue, and thus the foundations were laid for applying more objective linguistic criteria to the study of Hebrew and to the interpretation of the OT documents.

The 19th century was also the great period of textual criticism of the Greek NT, in which techniques were developed that were later used by philologists and linguists on secular texts. NT scholars of the 18th century, including Richard Bentley, J. A. Bengel and J. J. Wettstein, had been interested in the variant readings in the text of the Greek NT and had proposed certain critical principles. These were further developed in the first part of the 19th century by Johann J. Griesbach, K. Lachmann, Samuel P. Tregelles and Constantine Tischendorf; the techniques were further refined and applied later in the century by B. F. Westcott, F. J. A. Hort, J. Weiss and others. (Parvis, pp. 603-14.)

The language of the Greek NT also became an object of serious study during this period. Lexical studies of about the middle of the 19th century led to the publication of Thayer's Greek-English Lexicon (1886), based on the work of C. G. Wilke and C. L. W. Grimm, which was the standard lexicon in English until the middle of the 20th century. The finding of the Egyptian papyri later in the 19th century led to the discovery of the Koine Greek as a language in its own right. Credit for this discovery goes primarily to Adolf Deissmann, whose outstanding work extends into the beginning of the 20th century but is a reflection of the preceding period. A. T. Robertson's extensive grammatical work, first published in 1914, was the result of a quarter century's work and was based primarily on the 19th century historical approach to linguistics.

1.5. <u>The twentieth century.</u> For this century the mutual influences between linguistics on the one hand and Christian scholars and missionaries on the other have reached a much fuller development, with 20th century structural linguistics now contributing heavily to the work of the Christians. We therefore begin this section with a statement (1.5.1.) of some of the contributions of linguistics in this situation, followed by a statement (1.5.2.—1.5.5.) of some of the more specific results for Christian missions, biblical scholarship, missionary language schools, and linguistic preparation for missionaries. We reserve for inclusion under 2.1—2.5. the treatment of the 20th century contributions of missionary translators and missionary linguists to linguistics in various specific aspects.

1.5.1. <u>Contributions of structural linguistics to 20th century Christian scholarship and missions.</u> The following dominant ideas, developed by 20th century linguists, have influenced the work of missionaries and biblical scholars in the 20th century:

(1) The concept of the phoneme (see 2.1. below).
(2) The emphasis upon structure, differentiating between historical and descriptive linguistics.
(3) Study of the dynamics of interaction between languages, with concepts of borrowing, prestige languages, etc. [15]
(4) Information theory, with its implications for translation.

We here mention briefly some of the linguists who had a special influence upon Christian missionaries during this period.

The work of Westermann and Meinhoff in Germany exerted a considerable influence on German missionaries, and helped to make many missionary translators in Africa more keenly aware of the relationships among African languages and of their distinctive characteristics.

In the meantime, the growth of the London School of Oriental and African Studies was having an increasing effect on missionaries particularly through the writings of Ida C. Ward, who for some time was director of the Africa Department; the book by her and Westermann on phonetics became especially important for missionaries in West Africa, and was widely used as a textbook by European missionary candidates. A. N. Tucker, also of the School of Oriental and African Studies, did extensive field work with missionaries in East Africa and thus influenced their work in that area.

C. M. Doke was a missionary and Bible translator who later became professor of Bantu in the University of Witwatersrand in Johannesburg. Besides his work on phonetics and his lexical work, he led the drive for conjunctive writing of Bantu languages, whose words had been badly cut up into meaningless strings of grammatical particles, since missionaries had usually analyzed the languages on the model of English or French rather than as languages having their own distinctive structures.

Daniel Jones and his school of English phoneticians had an important influence upon missionaries in all parts of the world, beginning in the pre-phonemic period of linguistics. The development, partly by them, of the alphabet of the International Phonetic Association enabled missionaries to transcribe languages more systematically, and Jones' book on phonetics was an important landmark in the field.

Edward Sapir and Leonard Bloomfield, with their writings and teachings in the United States, contributed perhaps more than any others to the approach now being used by missionaries in many parts of the world. This contribution has been mediated to missionaries and Bible translators in large measure through the Summer Institute of Linguistics, the Hartford Seminary Foundation, and the American Bible Society. Many of the contributions of missionaries to specific aspects of linguistics as mentioned below are traceable to these sources.

1.5.2. <u>Language materials</u>. The 20th century has marked a tremendous development in both the quantity and the quality of language materials produced by missionaries. Biblical translations have appeared in some 500 new languages, and at present the pace of both translation work and revision is greater than at any other time in history.

Missionaries are now working in over 300 more new languages, besides continuing work in many of the others. Many of these missionaries either have been prepared in descriptive linguistics or have received some linguistic orientation, and for this reason the materials now being produced are much more useful to linguists than ever before. Besides biblical translations and other missionary literature, and often prior to or in connection with the preparation of such materials, there have been prepared phonemic and grammatical sketches, lexical materials, and transcriptions of native text materials.

Besides this work in new languages, there is scarcely a major language in the world in which there is not a revision of the Bible under way at present. Such revision work reflects (1) the availability of better biblical texts in the original languages and (2) a greater sensitivity to linguistic problems such as grammar, orthography, and the nature of translation as effective communication.

We make no attempt at listing specific languages in which work has been done in this century, since for them the materials produced by missionaries include not only biblical translations but the other types of material mentioned above, much of which may be located by reference to contemporary bibliographies of the various areas. [16] A few of the outstanding contributions in certain fields will be mentioned in the following sections and included in the bibliography.

1.5.3. <u>Biblical scholarship in the 20th century</u>. There has been a greatly extended study by Christian scholars of the languages

of the Middle East, together with archaeological studies of the area.
Of special importance are the Tell-el-Amarna letters of Egypt, discovered by peasants in 1887. William L. Albright of Johns Hopkins
University is perhaps the best known biblical scholar in this field.
The Ugaritic texts discovered at Ras Shamra in Syria have made possible an important study of this language and its linguistic and cultural
affinities with the others of the ancient Middle East.

Work on the Qumran or Dead Sea scrolls, since their discovery in 1947, has been of special importance both in the field of
OT textual criticism and in matters of pronunciation, grammar and
lexicon of Hebrew, as well as for a study of Aramaic at an earlier
stage than was formerly possible. The bibliography on studies of
the Qumran materials has rapidly grown to many hundreds of items. [17]

Textual studies of the Greek NT have continued, with Herman
Von Soden's work early in the century and others who have continued
in this field. At present the Bible Societies, whose principal concern
traditionally has been the translation and distribution of the Scriptures
in various languages, have undertaken the sponsorship of these
studies on a scale far exceeding earlier programs.

Koine Greek studies in this century have been carried out
along structural lines, especially with the grammatical work of Moulton and of Blass and Debrunner. Outstanding lexical work has been
done in Moulton and Milligan's work on the papyri and by Bauer,
whose lexicon has now been translated and adapted into English by
Arndt and Gingrich.

The work of Black on Aramaisms in the NT is an important
linguistic approach to the 'translationisms' in Greek which reflect
idioms and constructions that were present in the spoken Aramaic of
Palestine and which affected the language of the Greek NT.

James Barr has now injected into biblical studies a healthy
corrective influence for some of the extravagant etymological meanings that were current in 19th century biblical scholarship and which
have been carried into our time by people working in the field of
biblical theology. This field, developed by theologians rather than
linguists (Barr, p. 21), has been heavily influenced by 19th century

Humboldtian ideas of the effect of language upon thought, and has tended to perpetuate mentalistic interpretations of the biblical documents and some rather extreme etymologizing in vocabulary studies of the Bible. Barr, influenced by Bloomfield and yet aware of the values of the Sapir-Whorf hypothesis, has endeavored to correct some of these tendencies and to direct biblical scholars toward a linguistically sounder approach to their materials.

1.5.4. Missionary language schools. Another result of 20th century linguistics has been the great development, within the last two decades, of missionary language schools in different countries, using modern methods and concepts. These followed upon the intensive language courses in the United States and Great Britain during World War II, and have applied their principles to teaching languages to missionaries.

Four of these schools deserve special mention. The one in San José, Costa Rica, sponsored by the United Presbyterian Church, gives an intensive course in Spanish to approximately 150 missionaries each year. A similar school in Campinas, Brazil, prepares missionaries in Portuguese. In Seoul, Korea, Yonsei University has over 60 missionaries studying Korean. The Inter-Mission Language School in Manila, headed by Donald Larson, prepares missionaries in Tagalog, Ilocano, and Cebuano.

1.5.5. Linguistic preparation for missionaries. Many present-day missionaries have received some preparation in linguistics and thus have a different outlook and approach to their language studies and translation work than formerly. Among Protestants in the United States some elementary linguistic studies were introduced into the curricula of a few seminaries, e.g. Hartford Seminary Foundation and the Biblical Seminary of New York, largely for the purpose of teaching missionaries how to learn foreign languages more satisfactorily. The greatest impetus to the use of modern linguistic methods in Bible translating and in the making of technical language analyses by missionaries came with the growth of the Summer Institute of Linguistics (also known as the Wycliffe Bible Translators), which was begun in 1935. At present it conducts summer training programs in Australia, England, Germany, and on the campuses of three universities in the United States. Through the years several thousand persons have taken the courses, and more than one thousand are now in the field working directly under the supervision of the Wycliffe Bible Translators. From the beginning the courses of these institutes have incorporated the results and insights of contemporary linguistic science into the program, with the result that not only have certain basic linguistic concepts been widely disseminated among missionaries, but a number of Bible schools and seminaries have now introduced courses which parallel the program of the Summer Institute of Linguistics and make use of their published texts.

The Translations Department of the American Bible Society has also developed a team of well trained linguists who have supplied technical help to Bible translators in more than sixty countries. These men conduct field institutes for translators, assist translators in linguistic and exegetical problems, and prepare published helps for translators, including books on Bible translating, introductions to descriptive linguistics, and techniques of language learning. They, as well as the missionaries of the Summer Institute of Linguistics, have also contributed a number of articles on linguistics to such journals as Language, International Journal of American Linguistics, Word, Lingua, The Bible Translator, and Practical Anthropology.

The Hartford Seminary Foundation has, under the leadership of H. A. Gleason, developed an increasingly effective program for the training of missionary linguists and Bible translators.

Among the Roman Catholics in the United States, Georgetown University has developed an outstanding Institute of Languages and Linguistics which has had considerable influence on linguistic studies and attitudes of Roman Catholic missionaries.

2. Fields of significant interchange between linguistics and Christian missions

2.1. Alphabets and phonemic analysis. Three of the alphabets mentioned above as developed by Christian missionaries from the early period stand out as having special interest. The Gothic alphabet invented by Ulfilas in the fourth century, based on Greek

and Runic characters, approaches a phonemic transcription sufficiently to make possible an accurate phonemic interpretation of the
Gothic records. The Armenian alphabet developed by Mesrop at the
beginning of the fifth century and based on Greek characters was also
a good representation of the language as was also that devised by
Cyril in the ninth century for Old Church Slavic, based on the Greek
letters with certain additions.

The orthographies used for aboriginal languages by Roman
Catholic missionaries in the 16th and 17th centuries and by Protestant
missionaries in the 19th century were for the most part quite inadequate when judged by today's standards of phonemics, modeled as
they were upon Latin or the alphabets of modern languages with little
or no modification to suit the aboriginal languages. If the sound system happened to be similar to that of the language which served as a
model, as Náhuatl sounds for example were fairly similar to those of
Spanish, the missionary alphabets were relatively successful; but
for the most part materials of this period are not very useful from a
phonemic standpoint.

There were a few exceptions to this, such as the use of diacritics by Ruíz for Guaraní and also the use of displaced punctuation
marks to indicate contrastive tone in Lisu of southwest China, devised by Protestant missionaries early in the 20th century. But the
development of orthographies for unwritten languages was largely a
hit-and-miss affair before the basic concepts of de Saussure, Sapir,
and Bloomfield on the nature of the phoneme. Westermann and Ward
had an important influence on the writing of some African languages,
and Doke's phonetic work mentioned above was important, but in many
parts of the world the writing of minor languages is still greatly
handicapped by inadequate orthographic conventions.

Since the 1930's, which saw the development of the concept
of the phoneme, many missionaries assigned to unwritten languages
have been encouraged to make a thorough study of the phonemic system as a basis for reducing the language to writing. The major influence for this has come via the Summer Institute of Linguistics in
the shape of Kenneth L. Pike's work and textbooks in phonetics, phonemics and tone languages, and via the American Bible Society through

Eugene A. Nida's work in conferences with Bible translators in many parts of the world.

The result of this has been to produce for aboriginal languages much more adequate orthographies, prepared primarily along phonemic lines but with two important qualifications: (1) The orthography resulting from a strictly phonemic analysis is adjusted as much as possible to the dominant language of the area (e.g. to Spanish in Latin America, to French in West Africa, to Arabic in the Sudan, to Thai in Thailand). (2) Certain morphophonemic concepts are introduced which result in orthographic modifications. For example, when phonologically conditioned changes are morphophonemically predictable, certain morphemes may be written in a unique form in order to preserve their unity graphemically. Phonemic tone and other suprasegmental phonemic features are often not written in such an orthography in languages where they are highly predictable.

Many persons engaged in Bible translating and other missionary work have thus not only produced biblical texts with greater linguistic value than in the pre-phonemic period, but their dictionaries, native text transcriptions, [18] and grammatical sketches are more valid and useful to the linguist. A number of missionaries have published phonemic sketches of their languages. [19]

2.2. Grammar (morphology and syntax). Missionary grammars of the pre-structural period, which continued into the first part of the 20th century, were based almost entirely upon foreign models, with the work of Roman Catholics generally following Latin grammar and that of Protestants following western European languages.

Early in the present century the influence of Ferdinand de Saussure, mediated through others, led to a few grammars by European missionaries in Africa and India along lines that reflected the structure of the languages themselves. Examples of this were the work of Edwin W. Smith in Ila of Rhodesia and of C. M. Doke in Zulu.

The German Moravian missionary Kleinschmidt's grammar of Greenlandic (1851) 'initiated the presentation of grammars of languages native to the Western Hemisphere in terms of their own

structures' (Rosing, p. 63, note by C. F. Voegelin). George R.
Heath, another Moravian missionary, published important material
on the grammar of Miskito during the early part of the 20th century
(1913, 1927). However, it was not until after the grammars of Boas
and his students, followed by the structural work of Sapir and Bloomfield, that American missionaries actually began to follow a structural approach to grammar.

This has been accomplished primarily as a result of the
influence of the Summer Institute of Linguistics and the Hartford
Seminary Foundation. Townsend's work in Cakchiquel, done in 1926
and used as a basis for his lectures to missionary candidates in the
Summer Institute of Linguistics in the 1930's (although not published
until 1960), was structurally oriented and contributed toward the
development of a descriptive approach to grammar on the part of
missionaries. Nida's textbook on morphology (1946) was prepared
with special concern for the needs of missionaries working in languages whose structures differ from Indo-European. Pike's important work on tagmemics (1954-55) arose out of a practical need for
teaching grammatical structure to missionary translators, and
Gleason's valuable textbook (1955) was also the outgrowth of his
experience in teaching linguistics to missionary candidates. The
more recent volume by Elson and Pickett (1962), which introduces
tagmemic theory to the beginning student, also reflects the practical
needs of the missionary.

Quite naturally the needs for translation of ideas and not
merely words have compelled missionary linguistics to become
keenly interested in discourse analysis and stylistic forms, for not
only the sequence of words and clauses is important for the translator,
but the sequences of sentence types and the interrelationship of sentence patterns are indispensable elements in any fully satisfactory
translation procedure.

Among the most significant missionary contributions in the
field of grammar have been the collection of a vast amount of data on
languages that are otherwise relatively little known, both in grammatical sketches and in the more recently produced religious texts,
whose quality has been greatly improved as a result of a more ade-

quate understanding of structure. A number of doctoral dissertations and other published grammatical materials on aboriginal languages by missionaries may be noted here. [20]

     2.3. Comparative linguistics. In the early days collections were made of comparative materials such as the Lord's Prayer in many languages and the polyglot biblical materials that have been mentioned earlier in this paper. There was an interest in preparing catalogs of the languages of the world, and men like Hervás y Panduro[21] made some significant observations as to their relationships. Pimentel's work (1862), which was the first serious attempt at comparing and classifying the languages of Mexico, was based on earlier Roman Catholic missionary sources consisting of grammars, dictionaries, and religious writings. Carey's work in India led to interest in the comparison of related languages, and the introduction of Sanskrit to European scholars by missionaries and others was a major factor in the development of Indo-European comparative linguistics.

     Much material of comparative nature was collected during the 19th century and later by missionaries in surveys conducted in West Africa and elsewhere to determine into which languages and dialects Bible translations were to be made. Roman Catholic work of comparative nature was developed by Fr. Wilhelm Schmidt and his colleagues, and although their theories of language relationships have not won very wide acceptance, their linguistic work deserves high commendation.

     The comparison of Semitic languages has been greatly accelerated in connection with biblical studies, as noted above.

     In the more recent period missionaries have provided scholars with many word lists and vocabularies for use in comparative studies and glotto-chronological work, especially of Malayo-Polynesian, Bantu, and American Indian languages. Some of the recent comparative work by missionary linguists has been of outstanding technical character, such as the studies by Gudschinsky and by Longacre, who have done much toward clarifying the relationships among some of the languages of Mexico.

2.4. <u>Lexicography</u>. The preparation of dictionaries by the earlier Roman Catholic missionaries, especially for Middle and South American languages, has been mentioned above. Some of these are very extensive and valuable lexical works. Since the beginning of the 19th century Protestants have contributed to the lexical knowledge of many languages, not only with published dictionaries but with many other word lists that were reproduced in mimeographed form in connection with missionary language training programs in Africa and elsewhere but never formally published.

In the more recent period there have appeared numerous dictionaries prepared by missionaries in phonemic orthography, with or without adaptations to the prestige language of the area. We may mention Sedat's dictionary of Kekchí (1955) and some 29 monograph-length dictionaries prepared by members of the Summer Institute of Linguistics from 1948 to the present. [22]

One aspect of dictionary making has of course developed along lines more related to semantics; some of the implications of this will appear in the following section.

2.5. <u>Translation.</u> As indicated above (1.1.2.), the principal Christian contribution toward a concept of meaningful translation in the early church period was made in the fourth century by Jerome, whose Latin Bible was in sharp contrast with the extremely literal Greek translation which Aquila made of the OT two centuries earlier. Most European translation work in the Middle Ages, however, was of religious essays rendered into stiff, ecclesiastical Latin.

In the Renaissance period, the dominant 16th century figure in the field of translation was Martin Luther, who insisted upon the importance of full intelligibility in translation and who carefully worked out the implications of his translational principles in such matters as (1) shifts of word order, (2) employment of modal auxiliaries, (3) introduction of connectives when required, (4) suppression of Greek or Hebrew terms which had no acceptable equivalent in German, (5) use of phrases where necessary to translate single words in the original, (6) shifts from metaphors to non-metaphors and vice versa, and (7) careful attention to exegetical accuracy and textual

variants.[23] His principles, which were similar to those stated outside of Christian circles by Etienne Dolet about the same time, greatly influenced other Bible translations, including those in English of
the years following.

At about this same time, English translators of the 16th and
17th centuries were translating secular literature with a type of freedom that made for a high degree of intelligibility and vividness of
style but which often left a good deal to be desired in terms of faithfulness to the original.[24] It is remarkable the degree to which Bible
translators of the period (including those of the King James Version
of 1611) avoided this pitfall, due at least in part to their high regard
for the original as an inspired document.

In 1789 George Campbell published an outstanding work on
the history and theory of translation, especially as related to the
Scriptures. In his two-volume work, of which the first is a 700-page
introduction to his translation of the Gospels, Campbell treated Bible
translation in a detailed and systematic way, with far greater breadth
and insight than anyone before had ever employed in dealing with the
problems. He took considerable pains to point out the inadequacies
of the King James Version; and both in minor details and in broad
principles he displayed an unusual combination of sound knowledge
and common sense. Campbell summarized the criteria of good translating under three principles (Campbell, pp. 445-46):

(1) To give a just representation of the sense of the original.
(2) To convey into his version, as much as possible, in
    consistency with the genius of the language which he
    writes, the author's spirit and manner.
(3) To take care that the version have 'at least so far the
    quality of an original performance, as to appear natural
    and easy'.

Using these fundamental principles, Campbell proceeded to point out
their implications, not only in the history of Bible translating, but in
the way in which the Greek text should be translated into contemporary
English. These principles are very similar to those enunciated by
Tytler in 1790, which came to have much influence in the secular
field of translation.

However, the implications of the principles used by Campbell and Tytler were not followed out in the 19th century as one might have expected. The classicist viewpoint of men like Matthew Arnold led to an emphasis upon technical accuracy, with the pendulum swinging back toward a literal and pedantic approach to translation of secular works. This attitude was shared by biblical scholars such as J. B. Lightfoot and B. F. Westcott,[25] who were among those who produced the English Revised Version of 1881 and the American Standard Version of 1901. These versions, although based upon more authentic originals than was the King James Version of 1611, were so highly literal that they were never widely accepted to replace that version as their translators had expected. In approaching the problem of 'determining the relative claims of faithfulness and elegance of idiom when they come into conflict' (Westcott, pp. 5, 6), they often preferred to maintain peculiarities of the source language even when these differ from idiomatic English.

Most missionary translations of the Bible during the 19th century and early 20th centuries tended to be highly literal, reflecting the influence of the King James Version and of the versions of 1881 and 1901. Judson's Burmese Bible (1835) was an exception to this; it was quite idiomatic, and is the only missionary translation from the early 19th century which has continued to enjoy popular demand without undergoing a major revision.

The 20th century has witnessed a very radical change in translation principles, in both secular and religious fields. Biblical translations in contemporary English such as the Twentieth Century New Testament (1898-1901) and the NT translations by Weymouth (1903), Moffatt (1913), and Goodspeed (1923) reflected a new attitude toward language, linguistics, and communication. These have been followed more recently by the translation by J. B. Phillips (the Epistles in 1947, and later the rest of the NT), E. V. Rieu (1952, the four Gospels), and the New English Bible New Testament, produced by a committee of scholars in 1961; all these translations have been strongly influenced by contemporary attitudes towards translation and communication.

This approach to translation has been brought to the attention of missionaries especially through the work of the linguistically

trained members of the Summer Institute of Linguistics and through
the program of the Bible Societies. The contributions of the latter
have included Nida's book on Bible translating (1947), the quarterly
The Bible Translator (published since 1950 by the United Bible Societies), and a handbook by Bratcher and Nida for translators of the
Gospel of Mark, besides personal contacts with translators all over
the world through visits, conferences, and correspondence. These
books and many of the articles in the The Bible Translator contain
materials on basic semantic concepts and problems involving the
relationship of language to culture, and include such matters as componential analysis of meaning and the relation of verbal symbols to
patterns of cultural behavior. Some of the concepts of information
theory have been brought to bear on the practical problems of mean-
ingfulness in translation, [26] and the contemporary approach to language
structure has been applied in such a way as to lead to translations
which communicate more satisfactorily while at the same time pre-
serving the content of the original message.

      2.6. Language learning. In the field of language learning
for missionaries, two basic patterns were followed in the period
prior to structural linguistics. In areas where there was already a
written language and a grammatical tradition, as in Chinese, Sanskrit, Persian, Arabic, etc., missionaries used the available materials and learned by the methods in vogue for the particular language.
But for the unwritten aboriginal languages, there was no method to
follow, and language learning was usually very chaotic. At an early
date language schools were set up by the various missions in Africa,
southeast Asia, and elsewhere, but due to the lack of a systematic
approach the results were often quite unsatisfactory.

      One of the first men to do something about this situation was
T. F. Cummings, a missionary in India who later set up a course in
phonetics and language learning at Biblical Seminary in New York.
His book on learning a language was used by missionaries and stimulated a more systematic approach to this problem.

      From 1935 onward, the Summer Institute of Linguistics has
exerted an important influence toward the application of contemporary
linguistic techniques to language learning, even though its own program has been more specifically directed toward the problems of

reducing languages to writing. The American Bible Society, through assistance given to the summer programs of the Toronto Institute of Linguistics since 1950 and of the Outgoing Missionary Conference of the National Council of the Churches of Christ in the U. S. A. since 1956, has helped orient missionary candidates for all parts of the world toward a better approach to learning foreign languages, and the language schools mentioned in 1. 5. 4. above have played an important role.

Nida's book on this subject (1950) has been widely circulated, and the recent manual by Smalley (1961-62), accompanied by extensive tape drills, is aimed at giving the missionary a practical background in phonetics that will help him learn a language.

3. Bibliography

We here list most of the works that have served as sources, plus selected ones from among those to which general allusion has been made or which provide additional source material or constitute important contribution in the fields discussed. No attempt is made to include the numerous biblical translations mentioned, dates for which are chiefly taken from North's book, nor to list exhaustively the missionary language materials which have been mentioned in the text above.

Anselm, St.
  1863 Dialogus de Grammatico, in Opera Omnia, Paris, cols. 561-82.
  1952 Also in Latin with Spanish translation in Obras Completas de San Anselmo, vol. 1, Madrid: Biblioteca de Autores Cristianos, pp. 439-83.
Arndt, William F. , and F. Wilbur Gingrich
         (see under Bauer, Walter).
Augustini, Sancti Aurelii
  1841 De Grammatica Liber, Principia Dialecticae, etc. in Opera Omnia, vol. 1. Paris. cols. 1385-1448.
  1947 De Magistro/ Del Maestro (Latin and Spanish, in Obras de San Agustín, vol. 3. Madrid: Biblioteca de Autores Cristianos, pp. 682-759.

Augustini, Sancti Aurelii
 1951   [Various letters to and from Jerome] in Obras de
         San Agustín, vol. 8. Madrid: Biblioteca de Autores
         Cristianos.
Bacon, Roger
 1928   Opus Majus, vol. 1, Robert B. Burke, tr. Philadel-
         phia.
Barr, James
 1961   The Semantics of Biblical Language. London: Ox-
         ford University Press.
Bataillon, Marcel
 1950   Erasmo y España. 2 vols. México: Fondo de Cul-
         tura Económica. (first edition was in French,
         Erasme et l'Espagne 1937)
Bauer, Walter
 1949-52 Greichisch-Deutsches Wörterbuch zu den Schriften
         des Neuen Testaments und der übrigen urchristlichen
         Literatur. 4th ed. , Berlin. English edition by
         William F. Arndt and F. Wilbur Gingrich under title
         of A Greek-English Lexicon of the New Testament
         and Other Early Christian Literature. Chicago:
         Univ. of Chicago Press, 1957.
Bendor-Samuel, John
 1961   The Verbal Piece in Jebero. Monograph 4, Supple-
         ment to Word 17.
Black, Matthew
 1946   An Aramaic Approach to the Gospels and Acts. Lon-
         don: Oxford. (2nd edition, 1954).
Blass, Friedrich and Albert Debrunner
 1961   Grammatik des neutestamentlichen Griechisch.
         Göttingen, 11th edition. English edition, translated
         and revised by Robert W. Funk under title of A
         Greek Grammar of the New Testament and other
         Early Christian Literature, Chicago: Univ. of
         Chicago Press, 1961.
Bloomfield, Leonard
 1933   Language. New York: Henry Holt and Co.
Boas, Franz
 1911   Handbook of American Indian Languages. BAE-B 40.

Bratcher, Robert G. and Eugene A. Nida
    1961   A Translator's Handbook on the Gospel of Mark.
           Leiden: E. J. Brill, for the United Bible Societies,
           London.
Burrows, Millar
    1956   The Dead Sea Scrolls, New York: The Viking Press.
    1958   More Light on the Dead Sea Scrolls. New York: The
           Viking Press.
Campbell, George
    1789   The Four Gospels, vol. 1. London: A. Strahan and
           T. Cadell.
Colwell, E. C.
    1962   The Greek Language in The Interpreter's Dictionary
           of the Bible, vol. 2 (E-J). New York: Abingdon
           Press, pp. 479-87.
Crawford, John C.
    1959   Pike's Tagmemic Model Applied to Mixe Phonology.
           University of Michigan diss. (microfilm).
Cross, Frank M. , Jr.
    1957   The Dead Sea Scrolls in The Interpreter's Bible, vol.
           12, New York, pp. 645-67.
    1958   The Ancient Library of Qumran and Modern Biblical
           Studies. New York: Doubleday and Co.
Cummings, T. F.
    1916   How to Learn a Language. Albany, New York:
           Frank H. Evory and Co.
de Saussure, F.
    1922   Cours de linguistique générale. Paris (2nd ed.).
Deissmann, Adolf
    1895, 1897 Bibelstudien. Published in English as Bible
           Studies, 1901.
    1909   Licht vom Osten. Tübingen. Published in English
           as Light From the Ancient East, 1908; rev. ed. ,
           New York, 1927.
Doke, C. M.
    1925   The Phonetics of the Language of the Chu Bushmen.
           Bantu Studies 2. 129-65.
    1926   The Phonetics of the Zulu Language. Johannesburg.
Doke, C. M. and B. W. Vilakazi
    1948   Zulu-English Dictionary. Johannesburg.

Elson, Benjamin
    1960   Sierra Popoluca Morphology, IJAL 26. 206-23.
    1960   Gramática del Popoluca de la Sierra. Xalapa,
            México: Universidad Veracruzana. (From Cornell
            University diss., 1956, microfilm).
Elson, Benjamin and Velma Pickett
    1962   An Introduction to Morphology and Syntax. Santa Ana,
            Calif.: Summer Institute of Linguistics.
Funk, Robert W.
            (See under Blass, Friedrich).
Gasquet, Cardinal
    1914   Roger Bacon and the Latin Vulgate in Roger Bacon
            Essays, ed. A. G. Little, pp. 87-99, Oxford.
Gleason, H. A., Jr.
    1955   An Introduction to Descriptive Linguistics. New York:
            Henry Holt.
Grant, Frederick C.
    1961   Translating the Bible. Greenwich, Conn.: The
            Seabury Press.
Gray, Louis H.
    1939   Foundations of Language. New York: Macmillan Co.
Grimes, Joseph A.
    1960   Huichol Syntax. Cornell University diss.
Gudschinsky, Sarah C.
    1959   Proto-Popotecan: A Comparative Study of Popolocan
            and Mixtecan. IUPAL 15.
Harris, C. R. S.
    1927   Duns Scotus, vol. 1 Oxford.
Haugen, Einar
    1953   The Norwegian Language in America: A Study in
            Bilingual Behavior. Philadelphia: Univ. of Penna.
            Press.
    1956   Bilingualism in the Americas: A Bibliography and
            Research Guide. Pub. 26 of the American Dialect
            Society. Univ. of Alabama Press.
Heath, George R.
    1913   Notes on Miskito Grammar and on other Indian
            Languages of Eastern Nicaragua. AA 15. 48-62.
    1927   Grammar of the Miskito Languages. Herrnhut.

Hervás y Panduro, Lorenzo
    1800-1805 Catálogo de las Lenguas de las Naciones Conoci-
               das. Vol. 1, Lenguas y naciones americanas; vol.
               2, Lenguas y naciones de las islas de los Mares
               Pacífico e Indiano Austral y Oriental, y del Conti-
               nente del Asia. Madrid.
Hess, Harold Harwood
    1962 The Syntactic Structure of Mezquital Otomí. Univer-
          sity of Michigan diss. (microfilm).
Hirsch, S. A.
    1914 Roger Bacon and Philology in Roger Bacon Essays,
          ed. A. G. Little, pp. 101-151. Oxford.
Humboldt, W. von
    1845 Betrachtungen über die Verschiedenartigkeit des
          Naturgenusses. Gesammelte Werke, 1 Band, Kosmos
          1. Stuttgart.
Isidoro de Sevilla
    1951 Etimologías. Madrid: Biblioteca de Autores Cris-
          tianos.
Jones, Daniel
    1922 Outline of English Phonetics. 2nd ed., Leipzig and
          Berlin.
Latourette, Kenneth Scott
    1938 A History of the Expansion of Christianity, vols. 1-2.
          New York.
Lightfoot, J. B.
    1872 On a Fresh Revision of the English New Testament.
          London: Macmillan.
Longacre, Robert E.
    1957 Proto-Mixtecan. Indiana University RCPAFL 5.
    1962 Amplification of Gudschinsky's Proto-Popolocan-
          Mixtecan, IJAL 28.227-42.
Longacre, Robert E. and Cornelia Mak
    1960 Proto-Mixtec Phonology, IJAL 26.23-40.
Luther, Martin
    1530 Ein Sendbrief vom Dolmetschen. Werke. English
          translation by W. H. Carruth under title Luther on
          Translation. Open Court 21.465-71 (1907).
McHenry, J. Patrick
    1962 A Short History of Mexico. New York: Doubleday.

McKaughan, Howard P.
    1958   The Inflection and Syntax of Maranao Verbs. Manila:
            Institute of National Language.
Metzger, B. M.
    1955   Bible Versions in Twentieth Century Encyclopedia of
            Religious Knowledge, vol. 1 (Aachen to Kodesh).
            Grand Rapids: Baker Book House, pp. 137-53.
    1962   Ancient Versions in The Interpreter's Dictionary of
            the Bible, vol. 4 (R-Z). New York: Abingdon Press,
            pp. 749-60.
    1962   Medieval and Modern Versions in The Interpreter's
            Dictionary of the Bible, vol. 4 (R-Z), New York:
            Abingdon Press, pp. 771-82.
Moulton, James Hope
    1908   A Grammar of New Testament Greek. Edinburgh:
            T. and T. Clark, vol. 1.
    1929   Vol. 2.
Moulton, James Hope and George Milligan
    1930   The Vocabulary of the Greek Testament Illustrated
            from the Papyri and other Non-literary Sources.
            London.
Müller, Max
    1881   Lectures on the Science of Language, vol. 1. New
            York.
Nida, Eugene A.
    1946   Morphology: The Descriptive Analysis of Words.
            Ann Arbor: Univ. of Michigan Press.
    1947   Bible Translating. New York: American Bible
            Society.
    1950   Learning a Foreign Language. New York: Commit-
            tee on Missionary Personnel, Div. of Foreign Mis-
            sions, Nat'l Council of the Churches of Christ in the
            U.S.A. Revised ed. , 1957.
    1958   Analysis of Meaning and Dictionary Making, IJAL
            24. 279-92.
    1959   Principles of Translation as Exemplified by Bible
            Translating in Brower, Reuben A. , ed. , On Trans-
            lation. Cambridge: Harvard Univ. Press, pp. 11-
            31. (Rep. in The Bible Translator 10. 148-64, 1959).

North, Eric M.
   1938   The Book of a Thousand Tongues. New York: Harper.
Parvis, M. M.
   1962   NT Text in The Interpreter's Dictionary of the Bible,
           vol. 4 (R–Z), New York: Abingdon Press, pp. 594-
           614.
Pedersen, H.
   1931   Linguistic Science in the Nineteenth Century, trans.
           J. Spargo, Cambridge, Mass.
Pickett, Velma B.
   1959   The Grammatical Hierarchy of Isthmus Zapotec.
           Univ. of Michigan diss. (microfilm).
Pike, Kenneth L.
   1943   Phonetics. Ann Arbor: Univ. of Michigan Press.
   1945   The Intonation of American English. Ann Arbor:
           Univ. of Michigan Press.
   1947   Phonemics: A Technique for Reducing Languages to
           Writing. Ann Arbor: Univ. of Michigan Press.
   1948   Tone Languages. Ann Arbor: Univ. of Michigan
           Press.
   1954-55 Language in Relation to a Unified Theory of the
           Structure of Human Behavior. Glendale, Calif.:
           Summer Institute of Linguistics.
Pimentel, Francisco
   1862   Cuadro Descriptivo de las Lenguas Indígenas de
           México. México, 3 vols. Rep. in Obras Completas
           de D. Francisco Pimentel, vols. 1 and 2. México,
           1903.
Pittman, Richard S.
   1954   A Grammar of Tetelcingo (Morelos) Náhuatl. Lan-
           guage Dissertation 50 (Supplement to Lg. 30).
Roberts, B. J.
   1951   The Old Testament Text and Versions. Cardiff:
           Univ. of Wales Press.
   1962   OT Text in The Interpreter's Dictionary of the Bible,
           vol. 4 (R–Z). New York: Abingdon Press, pp. 580-
           94.
Robertson, A. T.
   1914   A Grammar of the Greek New Testament in the Light
           of Historical Research. New York. (4th ed. , Nash-
           ville, 1923.)

Rosing, Otto
    1951   Kleinschmidt Centennial II: Samuel Petrus Klein-
             schmidt, IJAL 17.63-65.
Rubio, Angel
    1939   De la Obra Cultural de la Antigua España. Trabajos
             Filológicos en Indias durante los Siglos XVI, XVII,
             y XVIII. Panamá.
Sapir, Edward
    1921   Language: An Introduction to the Study of Speech.
             New York: Harcourt, Brace.
Sayce, A. H.
    1883   Introduction to the Science of Language, vol. 1.
             London.
Schmidt, Wilhelm
    1926   Die Sprachfamilien und Sprachencreise der Erde.
             Heidelberg.
    1939   The Cultural Historical Method of Ethnology, trans.
             S. A. Sieber. New York.
Sedat, Guillermo
    1955   Nuevo Diccionario de las Lenguas K'ekchi' y Española.
             Chamelco, A. V., Guatemala.
Shell, Olive A.
    1950   Cashibo I: Phonemes, IJAL 16, 198-202.
    1957   Cashibo II: Grammemic Analysis of Transitive and
             Intransitive Verb Patterns, IJAL 23.179-218.
    1952   (after Buell Quain). Grammatical Outline of Kraho
             (Ge Family), IJAL 18.115-29.
Slocum, Marianna C.
    1948   Tzeltal Noun and Verb Morphology, IJAL 14.77-86.
Smalley, William A.
    1953   A Programme for Missionary Language Learning.
             The Bible Translator 4.106-12.
    1961   Outline of Khmu' Structure. New Haven: American
             Oriental Society.
    1961   Manual of Articulatory Phonetics. New York: Com-
             mittee on Missionary Personnel, Div. of Foreign
             Missions, NCCC; Part 1.
    1962   Part 2 and Workbook.
Smith, Edwin W.
            A Handbook of the Ila Language.

Summer Institute of Linguistics
    1960   Twenty-fifth Anniversary Bibliography, Glendale,
            Calif.
Thayer, Joseph H.
    1886   A Greek-English Lexicon of the New Testament.
            New York: Harper.
Thomson, S. Harrison
    1940   The Writings of Robert Grosseteste. Cambridge.
Townsend, W. Cameron
    1960   Cakchiquel Grammar in Mayan Studies I. Norman,
            Oklahoma: Summer Institute of Linguistics, Univer-
            sity of Oklahoma, pp. 1-79.
Turner, Glen D.
    1958   Jivaro Phonology and Morphology. Indiana Univer-
            sity diss.
Tytler, Alexander F.
    1790   Essay on the Principles of Translation. London:
            J. M. Dent and Co.
Venlaminov, I.
    1846   Opyt grammatiki aleutsko-lis'yevskogo yazyka.
            St. Petersburg. English translation by R. H.
            Geoghegan, The Aleut Language. Washington:
            U. S. Dept. of the Interior, 1944.
Waterhouse, Viola
    1962   The Grammatical Structure of Oaxaca Chontal.
            Indiana University RCPAFL 19.
Weinreich, Uriel
    1953   Languages in Contact. New York: Linguistic Circle
            of New York.
Westcott, B. F.
    1897   Some Lessons of the Revised Version of the New
            Testament. London: Hodder and Stoughton.
Westermann, Diedrich and Ida C. Ward
    1933   Practical Phonetics for Students of African Lan-
            guages. London: Oxford University Press.
Wevers, J. W.
    1962   Septuagint in The Interpreter's Dictionary of the
            Bible, vol. 4 (R-Z), New York: Abingdon Press,
            pp. 273-78.

Winny, James, ed.
    1960   Elizabethan Prose Translation. Cambridge.
Wonderly, William L.
    1946   Phonemic Acculturation in Zoque, IJAL 12.92-95.
    1951-2 Zoque: Phonemics and Morphology, IJAL 17.1-9,
            115-23, 137-62, 235-51; 18.35-48, 189-200.
    1952   Semantic Components in Kechua Person Morphemes.
            Lg. 18.366-76.
    1961   Some Factors of Meaningfulness in Reading Matter
            for Inexperienced Readers in A William Cameron
            Townsend en el 25° Aniversario del Instituto Lingüís-
            tico de Verano. México, pp. 387-97.
Würthwein, Ernst
    1957   The Text of the Old Testament, tr. Peter R. Ackroyd.
            Oxford Basil Blackwell.

NOTES

[1] References in parentheses to author and/or pages are to works listed in the bibliography at the end of this article.

[2] A series of papers on linguistics as related to various religions, especially in the field of translation, is scheduled to appear in Babel, vol. 9, Nos. 1-2 (1963), constituting a special issue on The Translation of Religious Texts and including articles on Hinduism, Buddhism, Islam and Christianity.

[3] Throughout this paper we abbreviate OT for Old Testament, NT for New Testament.

[4] Letter 57 to Psammachius on the Best Method of Translating, from A Select Library of Nicene and Post-Nicene Fathers, translated by Schaff and Wall, Volume 6, Jerome: Letters and Select Works. (See also Grant, p. 36.)

[5] See discussions of these differences in Schwarz, especially chapter 2.

[6] See now Leo Pap, review of Arno Borst, Der Turmbau von Babel. Band 1 and Band 2, Teil 1 and 2 (Stuttgart, 1957-59), in Lg. 38.400-04 (1962); references are made to early and medieval beliefs about language origins and the relationships between languages. Borst's work would appear to be relevant to a number of matters

touched upon in our sections 1.1.2 and 1.2.2, but we have not had opportunity to consult it.

[7] As for example, homo _man_ < ab humo _from clay_; oculi _eyes_ < oculunt _they cover_ (referring to the eyelids) or lumen ocultum _hidden light_ (referring to something contained in the eyes).

[8] Harris, p. 136; a footnote cites Werner, Die Sprachlogik des Duns Scotus, which we have not had the opportunity of consulting.

[9] See review by Pap cited in fn. 6 above.

[10] For more detail on this Masoretic work on the Hebrew vowels, see Roberts, 1951, pp. 47-63; 1962, pp. 586-88; Würthwein, pp. 17-20.

[11] Figures in this and the succeeding paragraphs are from the work by Rubio listed in the bibliography.

[12] Quoted in Schwarz, p. 155. For a lengthy discussion of Erasmus' views and also those of Teuchlin, see Schwarz, pp. 61-166.

[13] Hervás y Panduro, vol. 1, p. 30; vol. 2, p. 10, quoted in Müller, pp. 141-42.

[14] Encyclopedia Britannica, 14th ed., vol. 21, p. 629.

[15] These concepts have been developed especially by Haugen and Weinreich (see bibliography).

[16] The Summer Institute of Linguistics bibliography as of 1960 (see under S.I.L. in our bibliography) lists materials in 140 aboriginal languages and dialects produced by members of that organization; the titles include elementary reading materials, non-linguistic materials and technical linguistic materials, but exclude reading materials of biblical and other religious nature, and also exclude technical materials published in The Bible Translator and Practical Anthropology.

[17] Among the best general treatments are those of Burrows and Cross; see bibliography.

[18] See for example the Linguistic Series published by the Summer Institute of Linguistics of the University of Oklahoma (Nos. 1-7, Norman, 1958-1962), which contains texts in Comanche, Pocomchi, Mixteco, Populuca. (For dictionaries and grammatical sketches, see the following sections.)

[19] The Summer Institute of Linguistics bibliography as of 1960 lists phonemic studies of some 42 languages prepared by members of that organization; 27 of these, on American languages, were published in IJAL. Some of the more important phonemic sketches are included in the bibliography to our present paper.

[20]Such dissertations include items in bibliography under Bendor-Samuel (1961), Crawford (1959), Grimes (1960), Elson (1960), Hess (1962), McKaughan (1958), Pickett (1959), Pittman (1954), Smalley (1961), Turner (1958), Waterhouse (1962), Wonderly (1951-52). See also items by Shell and by Slocum, and listings in Summer Institute of Linguistics bibliography as of 1960.

[21]See above, 1.3.2.

[22]Mostly published by the Summer Institute of Linguistics; the 29 languages are: Cashibo, Chinanteco, Cora, Huasteco, Huave, Huichol, Mazahua, Mazateco, Mixteco, Náhuatl (2 dialects), Mayo, Movima, Negrito, Otomí, Pocomchí, Popoloca, Popoluca, Seri, Tagabili, Tarahumara, Tojolabal, Totonaco, Tzeltal, Tzotzil, Zapoteco (3 dialects), and Zoque.

[23]For a supplementary discussion of these matters see Edward H Lauer, Luther's Translation of the Psalms in 1523-24, Journal of English-Germanic Philology, 14.1-34 (1915), and Heinz Bluhm, The Evolution of Luther's Translation of the Twenty-Third Psalm, Germanic Review, 26.251-58 (1951).

[24]See the discussion in Winny, pp. xii-xxi. A glaring example of this tendency may also be seen in the translation of Don Quijote by Peter Motteux which appeared in 1700 and still forms the basis for some of the popular English editions in use today.

[25]Their views and approach to translation appear especially in their books listed in the bibliography.

[26]See for example Wonderly, 1961.

12 Implications of Contemporary Linguistics for Biblical Scholarship

Philology and Linguistics

Within the last two decades biblical scholars have become increasingly aware of linguistics as a discipline which seems to hold considerable promise in the area of exegesis, lexicography, and discourse structure. At the same time, however, a great deal of confusion has arise because of the proliferation of different schools of linguistics (e.g., tagmemic, stratificational, and generative-transformational), the formidable algebraic symbolism employed by many linguists, and the fact that linguists rarely deal with specific texts of literary importance and practically never with biblical materials. If, however, one is to appreciate certain of the implications of contemporary linguistics for biblical scholarship, one must understand not only the relation of linguistics to philology, communication theory, anthropology, psychology, and philosophy, but also the manner in which linguistics may provide insights into such practical problems as text criticism, authorship, exegesis, language teaching, and Bible translation. In order to do this, one should view the problems of meaning and grammatical relations from more than the standpoint of the biblical languages themselves. Only from the perspective of the ordinary use of language in present-day contexts can the relevance of corresponding biblical usage be fully appreciated. Accordingly, in this paper illustrative data are drawn from various sources, and in general nonbiblical data are cited first so that one may see more clearly the linguistic relevance of the problems. Corresponding illustrative data from biblical materials are then cited to show parallel tendencies or structures. By means of this approach the reader may comprehend better the way in which the broader framework of linguistics provides a basis for analyzing certain problems of biblical scholarship.

In order to understand properly the implications of present-day linguistics for biblical scholarship, one must first distinguish carefully between philology and linguistics. Philology, in the more generally accepted use of this term, tends to focus attention primarily upon particular texts and documents, usually of literary value; and from the perspective of historical development it treats the vocabulary, discourse structure, themes, and motifs, principally from the standpoint of their content. In contrast to this philological approach, linguistics is concerned with the structure of language, not as used in particular texts, but as illustrative of what can be and is used in all types of verbal communication. For the linguist all texts in a language are of interest, including those of literary value, but his concern is not so much with the contents of such texts as with their formal structures. The perspectives of linguistics are threefold: historical, comparative, and descriptive; but the subject matter is the structure of language, with constant emphasis upon the relationship between (1) language competence, i.e., the overall structure of language as it is internalized for the speaker, and (2) language performance, i.e., the particular manner in which an individual speaker actualizes this competence in the production of a particular discourse.

There are three principal areas in which the interests and concerns of linguists and philologists overlap and are interrelated: (1) the semantic structure of linguistic units (usually, words), (2) the analysis of texts as examples of the discourse structures of particular languages, and (3) the relation of language to thought. Linguists generally recognize the immense value of much that philologists have done in the careful analysis of literary texts, in the tracing of historical developments in features of form and content, and in the editing and interpretation of these materials. Precisely such literary concerns have contributed to man's interest in language generally and even to the field of linguistics itself. It would be wrong, however, to consider linguistics as merely some late appendage to philology or to think of philology as having been swallowed up by the larger discipline of linguistics. Both disciplines have their important and legitimate fields of scientific inquiry.[1] Developments in present-day linguistics cannot be understood, however, without due regard for the contributions from and interactions with other disciplines in addition to philology.

Communication Theory and Linguistics

Linguistics has been influenced by and has greatly influenced several other fields of scientific endeavor. In the first place, communication theory, especially in the form of information theory, has made several important contributions to linguistic insights.[2] The fact that language in discourse is approximately fifty percent redundant, whether on the phonological, syntactic, or semantic levels is important, and this helps one to realize why verbal communication cannot be one hundred percent efficient. Such a measure of redundancy is essential if verbal communication is to overcome physical and psychological "noise." This also means that the rate of flow of information in the average discourse is essentially the same for all languages. This being the case, we recognize more readily why it is that all good translations tend to be longer than the original texts from which they have been made. This does not mean, of course, that all longer translations are good translations—only that good translations tend to be longer. A more detailed examination of this situation may prove helpful, and we may illustrate the essential problems by diagraming certain of the fundamental features and relations.

From the standpoint of information theory, any discourse has two important measurements: length (l) and difficulty (d). Any well informed discourse, i.e., any message (M) which has been properly encoded to meet the needs of a particular group of receptors, will have a component of difficulty which is more or less equivalent to the channel capacity of the receptors, as indicated in Figure 1.

If, however, one attempts to translate a discourse literally, i.e., word for word from one language into another, thus producing a

Language A

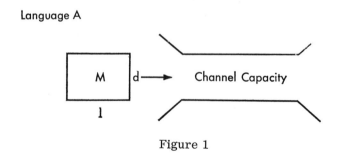

Figure 1

message of essentially the same length, it is almost inevitable that the difficulty will proportionately increase. At the same time, the channel capacity of the receptors in the "new language" is generally much narrower than that of the original receptors, since these second-ary receptors do not share with the original encoder the common information which is an inevitable part of any actual communication. A literal translation thus involves greater inherent difficulty in its structure, for which the receptors have a more limited capacity to interpret, as illustrated in Figure 2.

Language B

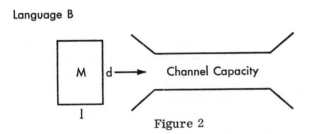

Figure 2

The solution to this problem is to build into the communi-cation the necessary redundancy so that the communication may be appropriately decoded by the secondary receptors within the limits of their channel capacity. This may require not only (1) the lengthen-ing of the text itself, e.g., supplying names of participants rather than using pronominal references and identifying overtly elements which are left covert in the original text, but also (2) supplementation of the text by certain marginal helps, which will provide the necessary back-ground information indispensable to a proper understanding of the text. Such a technique may be illustrated by Figure 3.

Language B

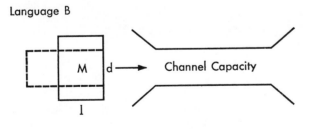

Figure 3

It is on the basis of communication theory that the Bible
Societies have recently developed a number of basic texts on trans-
lating: Toward a Science of Translating, Bible Translations for
Popular Use, and The Theory and Practice of Translation. [3]

Anthropology and Linguistics

Anthropology has made very important contributions to modern linguistics, especially in the field of semantics, which has been
revolutionized by the development of componential analysis. The
techniques of componential analysis were first introduced by linguist-
anthropologists for the analysis of kinship systems, but the significance
of determining meaning by such techniques was quickly recognized
and componential analysis was rapidly extended to other areas of
vocabulary, particularly those domains in which one could readily
describe the contrasts in the practical (non-linguistic) world and correlate these with distinctions in linguistic usage. [4] By means of these
techniques one can see how in Motilone, an Indian language of Colum-
bia, what appear to be three different homophonous words, meaning
"to hatch out eggs," "to commit suicide," and "to fry corn cakes,"
are really only one verb, specifying activities involving egg-shaped
objects (after death bodies are always wrapped in egg-shaped bundles
and corn cakes are normally egg-shaped).

Concern for language as a part of the total culture has also
resulted in a greater emphasis upon the context of a word. The individual word is thus largely meaningless apart from context and it is
only within the various contexts that the semantic structure of any
word or semantic unit can and must be defined.

Psychology and Linguistics

There was a time when modern linguistics reacted so strongly
against improper psychologizing about language that linguistics tended
to reject any and all efforts to relate language to thought processes.
At the same time, doctrinaire behaviorist theories preferred to
describe the mind as a kind of tabula rasa and to depict the learning
of a language as merely the result of accumulated impressions. There

is no generally recognized psychological theory which is adequate to explain all that is involved in language acquisition, competence, and performance, but it is quite clear that many universal features of language point to a number of what may be called "predispositions" of mental activity and structure.[5] The recognition of these "patterns of the mind," if one may employ such a terminology, has important implications for the biblical exegete and translator. In the first place, these newer insights attack some of the misconceptions about words and concepts (as though people have no concepts unless they have specific words to identify them) and do much to explain the translatability of texts. It has been found, for example, that in all languages there are four principal semantic categories: objects, events, abstracts (that is, qualities and quantities of objects and events), and relations. Moreover, these four basic semantic classes tend to be reflected quite systematically in the so-called kernel structures of languages and are basic to the "deep structures," as described in generative-transformational linguistics. Such universal features and the recognition of their importance are not, however, dependent upon any one linguistic theory, but are increasingly recognized by those working with the semantic structures of language.

Philosophy and Linguistics

The concern of philosophy for problems of symbolization and communication has inevitably had important implications for linguistics.[6] Such distinctions in meaning as syntactic, cognitive, and pragmatic have produced important insights; and the emphasis upon symbolic logic[7] has likewise stimulated a good deal of response from linguists. At one time the construction of mathematical philosophers of "logical languages" seemed to be an important area for linguistic insights, but scholars soon discovered that "natural languages" are so different from artificially constructed ones that a comparison is really not very fruitful for understanding the processes of communication. In contrast to those who constructed logical languages, the so-called linguistic analysts rejected structures as such and sought to focus attention upon the form of philosophical statements rather than upon their contents. This likewise has proven interesting to linguists, but unfortunately not too productive, since the rejection of language structure as a basic framework for analysis has limited the range and depth of these philosophical inquiries.

Some persons have reacted against present-day developments in linguistics because of the seeming multiplicity of "schools" and the divergent views expressed by different linguists. However, the differences in possible "models" for the description of language structures reflect a very healthy development in linguistics—not too different from what exists in the field of physics. In fact, linguistics is at the present time in one of its most productive phases and is perhaps contributing more than any other discipline to the basic theory in behavioral science. Despite the differences between linguistic theories and the highly technical manner in which linguistic results are often described, there are many solid, verifiable results for the scientific analysis of language—the area of human behavior which is the most intricately structured and of which man is the least consciously aware.

For biblical scholars, however, what is of direct concern in present-day development of linguistics is not those contributions which have come from other disciplines, but the ways in which linguistics itself may contribute to biblical studies. The following discussions of certain problems of text, authorship, exegesis, lexicography, language teaching, and Bible translating are designed to suggest at least some of the significant results which may be derived from the application of certain linguistic techniques.

Linguistics and Problems of Text

For many years textual critics have generally followed the principle that the more difficult reading is more likely to be the right one. To some persons this has seemed to be mere perversity on the part of the critics, but linguistics, with special help from information theory, is in a position to explain just why this preference for the more difficult reading is justified. Information theory, which is based upon the concept of entropy (represented in the Second Law of Thermodynamics), helps to explain how the forms of language adjust to the context. The easier reading is the one which fits the context best and it is the one toward which scribes tend to move when they make unconscious modifications. In other words, the context is maximized at the expense of the individual linguistic units.

Linguistics and Problems of Authorship

While most studies of authorship have concentrated upon statistical comparisons of vocabulary and grammatical forms, linguistic analyses of a text suggest that there is a very important area which has been for the most part overlooked, probably because of its essentially negative character. This is the nonspecification of shared information. As an analogy to the First Law of Thermodynamics, dealing with the conservation of energy, one may show how in actual communication the source does not make overt that information which is shared by the source and the receptor. To do so would not only be a waste of energy, but would also be a symbol of psychological distance. Going into detail about common information immediately creates a barrier to real communication, since it suggests to the receptor that the source and he do not have much in common after all or that the message is really being directed to someone else. Linguistic analysis of texts soon shows that tantalizing omissions are one of the principal marks of genuineness. Compare, for example, First Timothy with Philemon, or Ephesians with First Corinthians.

One of the principal difficulties with statistical analyses of words and grammatical forms is that the texts which we possess are too limited to provide verifiable bases. One must have a far larger corpus to be certain of statistical analyses of isolated features. On the other hand, generative-transformational linguistics[8] suggests that there exists a far more satisfactory manner in which to analyze distinctive features than by counting so-called surface phenomena. If one makes a careful study of the relations between deep, or kernel, phenomena (the selection of either the deep or the kernel levels will not make much difference) and the resulting transformations on the surface level, the distinctive features of the different sources are far more readily recognized. The recent article by Y. T. Radday on "Two Computerized Statistical-Linguistic Tests Concerning the Unity of Isaiah"[9] is an interesting confirmation of this use of relations between deep and surface structures. He discovered that the proportion of nominalized verbs (which is only one of the typical transformations in Hebrew structure) proved to be highly distinctive between the first and second parts of Isaiah.

Linguistics and Grammatical Exegesis

Regardless of the particular linguistic model which one may
wish to employ as a basis for descriptive analysis, one must recognize
that there is no one-to-one correlation between the semantic level and
the actual syntactic structures of the discourse. This means that the
same underlying structure may give rise to more than one form of
expression and that seemingly identical forms of expression may go
back to quite different underlying structures. The proper understanding and appreciation of this fact is essential for exegesis, and it is
perhaps in this field that present-day linguistics can make a major
contribution to biblical studies.

In several different respects the Greek text of Rom 1:5 illus-
trates a number of the problems of linguistic levels and the manner
in which linguistic techniques may be used to explicate some of the
essential problems of language structure and meaning. Rather, however, than use the Greek text of this passage, it is more convenient
to employ a typical literal translation as a basis for analysis, since
in the use of transformational techniques we can so much more readily
see these in English than we could in Greek:

> Through whom we have received grace and apostleship
> unto the obedience of faith among all nations
> for his name's sake.

If, however, we compare a translation of this verse in the New English Bible ("Through him I received the privilege of a commission in
his name to lead to faith and obedience men of all nations") or in
Today's English Version ("Through him God gave me the privilege of
being an apostle, for the sake of Christ, in order to lead people of all
nations to believe and obey"), we immediately note that the form in
present-day English is quite different from a literal translation. Are
there valid reasons for such interpretations and renderings? Is there
any set of rigorous procedures which may be employed to show precisely how one can move systematically from the Greek text to what
may be regarded as justifiable present-day English equivalents?
Within the brief statement of the problem in this paper, it is quite
impossible to outline in detail all the necessary steps or the full implications of each procedure, but enough will be evident to suggest

that there are systematic ways of dealing with such matters and that these methods provide much greater insight than procedures which have often been primarily impressionistic and intuitive.

The following analysis employs an adaptation (largely for the sake of simplicity) of a generative-transformational linguistic model, though other linguistic models could also be employed, and highlights the kinds of questions which linguistics would ask of such a Greek text (as reflected in the literal English translation) and how they would attempt to determine precisely what are the underlying semantic features of the grammatical structure. [10] Note, however, that in this analysis no attempt is made to deal with referential components of the lexical units. We are not so concerned at this point with the distinctive NT meanings of such words as grace, apostleship, faith, obedience, name, etc., as with the manner in which these words are related to one another grammatically.

The linguist would never, of course, attempt to analyze the meaning of this verse apart from its total context, including not only the entire Epistle to the Romans but also the other Pauline writings. Moreover, he would want to have as background all the available information about the uses of the words employed in this verse and also any special characteristics of style reflected in the epistolary formula in which this clause is embedded. Then, with all this as background, he still has some important questions to ask, primarily about certain so-called kernels, as these reflect even deeper semantic structures. He recognizes that through whom we received grace is a kind of "substitute passive." Though received is formally an active verb, it is in this context a substitute for a passive. We is really not the agent of the action, but the goal of an event. Moreover, on the basis of background information, he soon realizes that this we is only an epistolary substitute for I. But if I is the goal of the action, who is the agent? (The preposition through [Greek dia] indicates not primary agency, but secondary agency.) As is typical of many similar passages in the Pauline corpus, it is God who is the primary agent of the grace; but God is implicit, not explicit, in this clause.

The next major problem involves the relation between grace and apostleship. The grammatical structure with and (Greek kai) would suggest that these are two coordinate events (or activities).

But note that God is the agent of grace, while Paul is the one who is the apostle. Structurally, apostleship serves as a combined event-object word, i. e., "to serve as an apostle." The fact that God is the agent of grace and that Paul is the agent of being an apostle should immediately suggest that what seems to be syntactically coordinate cannot be such, since there are two quite different agents. Moreover, the term apostleship designates a particular aspect of grace (or gift). Hence, what appears syntactically as coordinate is semantically actually subordinate, with the second element defining more precisely the content of the first, hence, the translations "the privilege of a commission" or "privilege of being an apostle."

When we examine the phrase, the obedience of faith, we are faced with another syntactic problem. What is the relation between these two event words? One could, of course, regard faith as the body of doctrine, and then people would be expected to obey the doctrine (i. e., what was expected to be believed); but this interpretation is not in keeping with the context nor with the position of this epistle in the Pauline corpus. A more meaningful approach to this difficulty is to ask ourselves, "Who is the agent of the obedience and who is the agent of faith?" In both instances, the answer is those among all nations. These are the ones who believe and obey. Furthermore, we soon recognize in this hypotactic construction obedience of faith the underlying verbal expression from which it is derived, viz., "believe and obey." (Similarly, the baptism of repentance [Mark 1:4] is equivalent to "repent and be baptized.") Though we can, of course, say in English "obedience of faith" and "baptism of repentance," neither of these constructions, in which the second noun specifies an event coordinately preceding the first, is normal English. They are Greek and have for a long time been imposed upon English translations of the NT, with the result that many persons have completely failed to comprehend what is the actual meaning of this construction.

It is important to note that the syntactically coordinate construction grace and apostleship is semantically subordinate. Conversely, the syntactically subordinate construction obedience of faith is semantically coordinate. These facts, however, only become fully evident when one analyzes the surface structures in relation to the underlying semantic base.

As already noted, the phrase among all nations specifies the
agent of the events of believing and obeying. The final phrase for his
name's sake poses problems in a literal English translation, since
the relation of this phrase to the preceding expression is far from
clear. Surely, for his name's sake cannot apply to among all nations.
Moreover, it is not a qualification of believing or obeying. It does,
however, go with apostleship. Most modern translations delete the
term name, since it is only a substitute term for the person himself,
already identified by his, the closest equivalent being for his sake.

There is, however, one more problem, namely, the relation
between being an apostle and the people among all nations believing
and obeying. The Greek preposition eis "unto" only suggests in a very
general way what is involved, traditionally defined as purpose or result. But an examination of the semantic structures shows clearly
that between Paul's activity as an apostle and the people's believing
and obeying there is a causative relationship. Paul is thus the causative agent, and this may be made explicit by some such expression as
to lead to or to cause to.

Up to this point we have not attempted to deal with levels of
language, style, or lexical adequacy. We have only been concerned
in a very general way with the problems of grammatical meaning. It
would be possible to outline these procedures in rigorous detail, but
this does not seem necessary or advisable. What is important is that
one recognize that beneath the surface phenomena of language there
are important structural relations which are amenable to systematic
analysis and exposition. Of course, the application of such a methodology may point clearly to a structural ambiguity, in which case one
can define the ambiguity with much greater certainty. On the other
hand, there may not be sufficient evidence in the original text for one
to define the nature of the ambiguity; the forms may constitute simply
a grammatical obscurity. But even then the methodology will make
it possible for one to describe the precise limits of the obscurity.

In a time when the Bible was thought to be written in a kind
of Holy Ghost language, the only criterion to exegetical accuracy was
the pious hope that one's interpretations were in accord with accepted
doctrine. At a later period, when grammar was viewed almost exclusively from an historical perspective, one could only hope to arrive

at valid conclusions by "historical reconstructions," but these often
proved highly impressionistic. At present, linguistics has provided
much more exact tools of analysis, based on the dynamic functioning
of language, and it is to these that one ought to look for significant
developments in the future.[11]

       One of the severe handicaps to objective analysis of grammat-
ical structures has been the mistaken concept that there is something
so uniquely individual about the grammatical structure of each language
and so intimately connected with the entire thought processes of the
speakers of such a language, that one cannot really comprehend the
meaning of a message without being immersed in the syntactic formulations. Moreover, the grammar of a language has been regarded by
some as being a model of a people's world view. This is simply not
true. The idea that the Hebrew people had a completely different
view of time because they had a different verbal system does not stand
up under investigation.[12] It would be just as unfounded to claim that
people of the English-speaking world have lost interest in sex because
the gender distinctions in nouns and adjectives have been largely eliminated or that Indo-Europeans are very time conscious, because in
so many languages there are tense distinctions in the verbs. But no
people seems more time-oriented than the Japanese, and their verbal
system is not too different from the aspectual structures of Hebrew.
Furthermore, few peoples are so little interested in time as some of
the tribes in Africa, many of whose languages have far more tense
distinctions than any Indo-European language has. It simply is not
sufficient to note differences of language structure in Greek and Hebrew
and to correlate these with seeming differences in philosophical orientation or personality types of the speakers. Such analogies may be
ingenious, but they have not been proven. The only way in which correlations between languages and world views could be made would be
to distinguish all those languages which have a certain structure from
all those languages which do not have it (or which have the converse
of it), and then to make similar comparisons between all the different
peoples involved. All the attempts by anthropologists to discover such
correlations on a cross-cultural basis have resulted in complete failure, and there is no indication that further investigations in this direction would produce any other results. In fact, the lack of correlation
is so striking as to show quite conclusively that those who have postu-
lated determinative relations between linguistic structures and world

views have simply been deluded. The implications of this for future biblical studies, whether in the area of grammar or lexicography, are of enormous importance.

Attempts to link grammatical features and national characteristics or world view are doomed to failure, largely because grammatical features are all arbitrary, "fossilized" structures. They may have represented alternative choices some thousands of years ago, but they must be arbitrary and conventional if they are to function satisfactorily in providing a structure which is sufficiently redundant to be usable and sufficiently supple to make it possible for people to say something which they have never heard before. The requirement that language provide for novelty means that conceptual determinism based on syntactic forms is basically false.

Linguistics and Lexicography

The rapidly developing field of structural semantics has a great deal to contribute to the lexicography of biblical languages, but unfortunately a number of biblical scholars have been held back in their understanding of lexicography by three serious misconceptions. In the first place, there has been the tendency to regard the "true meaning" of a word as somehow related to some central core of meaning which is said to exist, either implicitly or explicitly, in each of the different meanings of such a word or lexical unit. It is from this central core of meaning that all the different meanings are supposed to be derivable. In reality, however, the different meanings of single words may contain no such central core or common denominator of meaning. Note, for example, the different meanings of charge in such contexts as charge the bill, charge his account, charge the enemy, charge the battery, put him in charge, a charge of murder, and the preacher accepted his new charge. There is no common denominator of meanings in this series of meanings of charge, but there are a number of links between the meanings in the common and diagnostic components which bind together what may be called a "chain of meanings." One might argue that a common denominator of meaning would be "to place a burden upon," something which one who is familiar with the historical derivation might well think of. But this would be skewing the linguistic facts, for such a common denominator would have to be understood in quite a different manner in various contexts. In fact, it could only be understood in an entirely figurative sense in most of the contexts and, even then, in different figurative senses. "Placing a burden upon" cannot be a diagnostic component of meaning of these various uses of charge, any more than "heavy" can be a common component of the meaning of the Hebrew root *kbd in all of its range of meanings.

In the second place, a common mistake has been to regard the presumed historical development of meaning as reflecting the "true meaning" of a word. That is to say, the so-called etymology of a word is supposed to contain the key to the proper understanding of all its meanings. However, in English the average person is not aware that goodbye is derived from God be with you, and it would be entirely erroneous to assume some religious "hangover" in this farewell expression. On the other hand, most speakers equate the occurrences of by in the words bylaw, bypath, and byproduct as representing historically the same element in each case and signifying simply a subordinate or derivative feature, but historically the by in bylaw is derived from burgh, i. e. , the law of a burgh (or borough) rather than that of the county or state, and the by in bypath and byproduct is the preposition-adverb. Etymologies, whether arrived at by historical documentation or by comparative analysis, are all very interesting and may provide significant clues to meaning, but they are no guarantee whatsoever that the historical influence is a factor in the people's actual use of such linguistic units. Valid lexicography must depend in the ultimate analysis upon patterns of co-occurrence in actual discourse.

The third impediment to satisfactory lexical studies of biblical vocabulary is the prevailing unsatisfactory system of classifications of meaning. Perhaps nothing is quite so confusing as most classifications of meanings, even many of those in Bauer's dictionary of the New Testament vocabulary (e. g. , treatments of ἔχω, ἡμέρα, κατά, and πνεῦμα). In fact, there are often four different criteria of classification, employed in different orders and arrangements. These involve (1) presumed historical derivation, (2) logical connections between meanings, (3) occurrence in certain grammatical forms, and (4) occurrence in certain lexical contexts. Such classifications often result in a presentation of information which is poorly designed to reveal the actual semantic structures involved.

If this state of affairs is to be rectified, quite new approaches to lexicology must be introduced. In the first place, critical studies of meaning must be based primarily upon the analysis of related meanings of different words, not upon the different meanings of single words. Only by the study of related meanings of different lexical units within well-defined lexical domains can one really succeed in determining the significant common, diagnostic, and supplementary components of meaning. There are, of course, some very important reasons for this approach by domains, but most important is the fact that related meanings of different words are much closer in semantic space than are different meanings of the same word. For example, related meanings of run, walk, hop, skip, and crawl are much closer in semantic space and hence more amenable to structural analysis than are different meanings of a word such as run, e.g., he ran home, he ran the business, a run on the bank, and a run in her stockings. Lexicographers of biblical languages have imagined, however, that they could not treat the differences in meaning between pneuma, psychē, nous, and kardia until first they had classified all the diverse meanings of these terms. On the contrary, it is only after carefully distinguishing between the related meanings of these terms within the different semantic domains in which they occur that one can set up really relevant subdivisions of meaning for different terms.

The basis for the classification of meanings must be co-occurrences, thus recognizing the pre-eminence of the context. Moreover, a series of meanings of a particular term will be arranged essentially in terms of a series of more and more rigidly "marked" meanings, that is to say, meanings which are conditioned by their co-occurrence with other lexical units.

This process of maximizing the context is fully in accord with the soundest principles of communication science. As has been clearly demonstrated by mathematical techniques in decoding, the correct meaning of any term is that which contributes least to the total context, or in other terms, that which fits the context most perfectly. In contrast to this, many biblical scholars want to read into every word in each of its occurrences all that can possibly be derived from all of its occurrences, and as a result they violate one of the fundamental principles of information theory. Perhaps this error is in some measure related to the false notion that when words are put

together they always add their meanings one to another. The very
opposite is generally the case. For example, green may denote a
color, a lack of experience (he is green at the job), and unripe (green
fruit); and house may indicate a dwelling, a construction for storing
objects (warehouse), a lineage (the house of David), a legislative body,
and a business establishment; but in the combination green house the
meanings of both green and house are restricted to only one each of
these meanings. On the other hand, in the compound greenhouse the
meanings of both green and house are somewhat different from what
they are in green house. But in neither instance does one add all the
meanings of green to all the meanings of house. In such instances
there is a mutual restriction of meaning. Moreover, in combinations
such as green house and greenhouse one must not attempt to see implied in the component parts all the related meanings which these
terms have in other combinations. That is to say, words do not carry
with them all the meanings which they may have in other sets of co-
occurrences. Unfortunately, however, this is precisely what some
students of the Bible would seem to imply by their treatments of
meaning. For example, some persons would like to think that in
every occurrence of the root dik-, in such forms as dikaios, dikaioō,
and dikaiosynē, all of the diverse meanings are in some way or other
implicit. This would amount to saying that essentially there are no
differences between the Matthean and Pauline uses, or that despite
the differences all the related meanings are still to be found embedded in each usage. For the Greek root dik- one might possibly argue
for such a position, but surely with the Hebrew root *kbd, which in
different contexts may carry such widely diverse meanings as "heavy,
much, many, slow, dull, grievous, difficult, burdensome, wealth,
riches, prestige, glory, honor," it would be folly to support such a
"syncretistic" view of semantic structure.

Linguistics and Language Teaching

Considerable strides have been made since World War II in
many aspects of language teaching. No longer does the student merely
learn about a language, i.e., memorize the rules of grammar, but he
actually learns the language. By concentrated approaches to the total
structure of a language and with emphasis upon the distinctive features
of language rather than on the subordinate mass of details, students

have gained remarkable facility in modern languages. There is absolutely no reason why the biblical languages cannot be equally well
taught, but in so many instances they are not. It is no wonder that
students increasingly depreciate the study of biblical languages and
administrative officers are accused of cooperating in eliminating
Greek and Hebrew as required courses. If such languages are not
taught any better than they usually are, then they ought to be eliminated, since they tend to be such an appreciable waste of the students'
time.

        Two of the important aspects of present-day research in the
field of language learning are the recognition that not all people learn
languages in the same way, and that no one method is going to be of
maximal efficiency for all persons. Nevertheless, there are a number
of important innovations which teachers of modern languages have
employed, and unless these are taken over at least in part (with the
recognition, of course, that the student of biblical languages is more
concerned with decoding than with encoding) then further attrition in
the learning of Greek and Hebrew is inevitable.

                   Linguistics and Bible Translation

        Perhaps one of the most conspicuous influences of linguistics
upon the biblical field has been in the area of translation. The Bible
Societies have been particularly concerned that the advances and insights from the science of linguistics be made available to Bible translators in various parts of the world. It has been quite obvious that
one cannot depend upon traditional views and attitudes toward translation if people are really to understand what the biblical text means.
For example, in most European languages an overwhelming percentage
of persons have consistently misunderstood the rendering of Rom 1: 17,
"the righteousness of God is revealed from faith to faith." Almost
without exception the average person has thought that the righteousness spoken of here is God's own personal righteousness, rather than
what he has done to put men right with himself. But many Bible translators have been loathe to restructure the Greek syntax so that it will
communicate what the text actually means. In fact, one committee
refused on the ground that if the laity could understand the Bible so
readily, then what would the preachers have to do? However, a

rendering which does not communicate the sense of the original is
simply not a translation but a string of words, and any legitimate
analysis of the adequacy of a translation must accept as a primary
criterion of correctness the manner in which such a translation is
understood by the majority of persons for whom it is designed. Fundamentally, this means that the Bible Societies have based their view of
translational adequacy upon the elementary principles of communication theory in developing what has been termed "dynamic equivalence" in translation. Perhaps this may be most adequately described
by the use of a diagram, as in Figure 4.

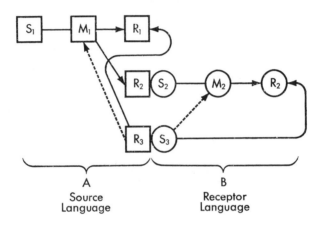

Figure 4

        The components of S_1, M_1, and R_1 stand for the source,
message, and receptors of the original communication. The enclosing
squares, in contrast with the circles in the second line, are designed
to highlight the differences in linguistic and cultural contexts of the
communication. The translator, R_2-S_2, is both square and circle,
in that he decodes the message given in the first cultural context, and
then encodes this in a different linguistic form (M_2) for receptors
(R_2) who live within a quite different linguistic and cultural context.
In the past, any judgment as to the adequacy of a translation depended
primarily upon the opinions of some other person or persons (R_3-S_3)
who could compare the two forms of the message (M_1 and M_2) and
could determine whether there was sufficient formal agreement as to

warrant one's regarding the second as a translation of the first (broken lines leading from R_3-S_3). There is, however, a very grave difficulty involved in such a procedure, primarily because the critic knows both languages too well, and regardless of the form of M_2 he knows what it should mean because he also understands M_1. Such an approach to translation is simply not adequate. A much more satisfactory approach is to be found when the critic analyzes precisely what R_2 understands by the message which he receives (suggested by the solid line R_3-S_3 to R_2). That is to say, what is the meaning of the passage as understood by a monolingual who does not have the original message to refer to? If receptors in the second language consistently misunderstand the intent of the message as they read it, obviously this is not a legitimate translation, regardless of the extent to which the translator may defend his linguistic usage.

It would be quite wrong to imagine that the average reader of a translation will understand precisely what the original receptors understood. This is impossible. For one thing, the receptors in the second language simply do not share with the original source all the common experiences which were so important a part of the total setting of the communication. Furthermore, one must assume that in all translations there is bound to be some loss of information and impact. However, if the receptors in the second language consistently fail to grasp the proper sense or if the renderings simply make no sense at all to them, certain significant restructuring of the translation must be introduced. The particular techniques which must be employed are fully outlined in the books on Bible translating, listed in note 3.

As part of the program of the Bible Societies to apply certain aspects of linguistic insights to various phases of biblical studies, a number of different types of projects have been undertaken. First, there are the textual studies, including The Greek New Testament published by United Bible Societies, together with A Textual Commentary on the Greek New Testament, which gives the reasons for the UBS committee's decisions on various NT textual problems. At present the Bible Societies are sponsoring the work of an international and interconfessional committee studying the major textual problems of the OT so as to provide translators working on the OT with something similar

to what has been done for the NT. Secondly, there are a series of
Translator's Handbooks, a quarterly journal The Bible Translator,
a number of basic texts and theoretical works, and several volumes
dealing with material which is supplementary and complementary to
the translator's task in the fields of anthropology, communication,
comparative religion, and language learning, [13] all of which are
designed to help Bible translators appreciate and apply in their work
the results of present-day developments in related fields of scholarship.

It would be quite wrong to suggest that all the major problems
of biblical scholarship can be resolved merely by the application of
linguistic procedures, but it would be equally wrong to neglect the use
of techniques which are proving so indispensable in so many phases
of scientific inquiry involving communication.

NOTES

[1] Of special interest in this connection is Reuben A. Brower
(ed.), On Translation (Cambridge, Mass.: Harvard, 1959), and
Thomas E. Sebeok (ed.), Style in Language (Cambridge, Mass.:
MIT Press, 1960).

[2] For an introduction to certain aspects of communication
theory, one may profitably consult Norbert Wiener, The Human Use
of Human Beings: Cybernetics and Society (New York: Houghton
Mifflin, 1954), and Colin Cherry, On Human Communication (New
York: Wiley, 1957).

[3] Eugene A. Nida, Toward a Science of Translating (Leiden:
Brill, 1964); William L. Wonderly, Bible Translations for Popular
Use (London: United Bible Societies, 1968); and Eugene A. Nida and
Charles R. Taber, The Theory and Practice of Translation (Leiden:
Brill, 1969).

[4] Important articles on componential analysis include Floyd
G. Lounsbury, "A Semantic Analysis of the Pawnee Kinship Usage,"
Language 32 (1956) 158-94; Ward H. Goodenough, "Componential
Analysis and the Study of Meaning," Language 32 (1956) 195-216;
Harold C. Conklin, "Lexicographical Treatment of Folk Taxonomies,"
Problems in Lexicography (eds. Householder and Saporta; Publication
21; Bloomington: Indiana Univ. Research Center in Anthropology,

Folklore, and Linguistics, 1962) 119-41; Eugene A. Nida, "Analysis of Meaning and Dictionary Making," International Journal of American Linguistics 24 (1958) 279-92; Charles O. Frake, "The Ethnographic Study of Cognitive Systems," Cognitive Anthropology (ed. Stephen A. Tyler; New York: Holt, Rinehart and Winston, 1969) 28-40.

[5] Several important contributions to the field of psychology and language include those of Noam Chomsky, Review of B. F. Skinner, Verbal Behavior (New York: Appleton-Century-Crofts, 1957), Language 35 (1959) 26-57; Lev Semenovich Vygotsky, Thought and Language (Cambridge, Mass.: MIT Press, 1962); Willard V. Quine, Word and Object (New York: Wiley, 1960); George A. Miller, "Language and Psychology," New Directions in the Study of Language (ed. Eric H. Lenneberg; Cambridge, Mass.: MIT Press, 1964) 89-107.

[6] See especially Jerrold J. Katz, The Philosophy of Language (New York: Harper and Row, 1966); Charles Morris, Signification and Significance (Cambridge, Mass.: MIT Press, 1964).

[7] For an introduction to symbolic logic, see Hans Reichenbach, Elements of Symbolic Logic (New York: Macmillan, 1947).

[8] Generative-transformational linguistics, of which Professor Noam Chomsky of MIT is the leading proponent, is based on the concept that underlying the surface phenomena of actual language usage lies the deep structures of meaning, and that by a series of "transformational rules" the deep semantic structure can be transformed into surface structure. Such a model treats language as a dynamic structure, and the linguist is not concerned so much with describing a corpus of texts as with determining the competence of speakers to produce and to understand utterances, many of which are entirely new to them.

[9] JBL 89 (1970) 319-24.

[10] For a more systematic and detailed analysis of such transformational techniques, see Eugene A. Nida and Charles R. Taber, The Theory and Practice of Translation, 33-35.

[11] For an introduction to some of the major elements in generative-transformational grammar one should consult Noam Chomsky, Aspects of the Theory of Syntax (Cambridge, Mass.: MIT Press, 1966); Emmon Bach, An Introduction to Transformational Grammars (New York: Holt, Rinehart and Winston, 1964); Roderick A. Jacobs and Peter S. Rosenbaum, English Transformational Grammar (Waltham, Mass.: Blaisdell, 1968); and Charles J. Fillmore, "The Case for Case," Proceedings of the 1967 Texas Conference on Language

Universals (eds. E. Bach and R. Harms; New York: Holt, Rinehart
and Winston, 1967); Terence D. Langendoen, Study of Syntax: The
Generative-Transformational Approach to the Structure of American
English (New York: Holt, Rinehart and Winston, 1969).

[12]See James Barr, The Semantics of Biblical Language
(London: Oxford University Press, 1961); B. Siertsma, "Language
and World View (Semantics for Theologians)," The Bible Translator
20 (1969) 1-21.

[13]Eugene A. Nida, God's Word in Man's Language (New York:
Harper and Row, 1952); Customs and Cultures (New York: Harper
and Row, 1954); Message and Mission (New York: Harper and Row,
1960); Religion Across Cultures (New York: Harper and Row, 1968);
Eugene A. Nida and William A. Smalley, Introducing Animism (New
York: Friendship Press, 1959); William A. Smalley, Articulatory
Phonetics (Yonkers, N. Y.: Practical Anthropology, 1962); and
Eugene A. Nida, Learning a Foreign Language (Santa Ana, Cal.:
Summer Institute of Linguistics, 1950); Kurt Aland et alii, The Greek
New Testament (London: United Bible Societies, 1969); Bruce M.
Metzger, A Textual Commentary on the Greek New Testament (London
and New York: United Bible Societies, 1971).

Author's Postscript

A collection of anyone's writings covering a decade or so of research will inevitably involve three liabilities: significant changes in point of view, repetition of illustrative data, and obsolescence of certain information. An awareness of these liabilities made me hesitate at first to respond positively to Professor Anwar Dil's invitation to have a selection of my articles published in the series on Language Science and National Development. However, I am glad that the articles in this collection are now made available in a single volume, since several of them were published in journals and books which are not easily accessible to most scholars and students. Much of what I have written on translation theory is now best summarized in the volume The Theory and Practice of Translation, and various aspects of semantic analysis are more fully developed in Componential Analysis of Meaning, a volume scheduled for publication by Mouton in the fall of 1974.

As will be evident from some of my more recent articles, my viewpoint and emphasis have undergone change, so that if I were now to rewrite some of the earlier articles in this series, I would have to make some substantial changes in them. However, rather than undertake a detailed statement of present-day differences in opinion and judgment, I believe it will be more helpful to the readers of this collection if I outline certain of my primary concerns and attitudes toward research and communication.

Over the years, my central interest in language has shifted from the analysis of formal structures, principally morphology and syntax, to an analysis of semantic structures. This shift was an almost inevitable result of an increasing concern with translational equivalence. In relation to translational equivalence, I have greatly appreciated the contributions of symbolic logic, yet these have proved to be grossly inadequate in dealing with the larger units of discourse and with stylistic subtleties. Propositional paraphrases are quite insufficient for measuring many of the important semantic differences. Accordingly, I have been concerned to describe and explain the function of semantic elements which are not properly treated by propositional logic.

While I have consistently employed various models in attempting to explicate structure, I have always strongly resisted the tendency to become enamored with or attached to a single linguistic model. Models are best treated as elaborate scientific metaphors. They may provide important insights as to the nature of linguistic phenomena, but they cannot take the place of the language structure itself. A viable model is an important tool for explaining certain aspects of reality, but there is a danger in attempting to push the model too far. For example, a competence model of language structure is important, but overemphasis on competence, almost to the exclusion of performance, has seriously handicapped a good deal of generative transformational investigation. It is entirely too easy to neglect the facts of language revealed in performance and thus to restrict unduly the basis for judging important aspects of language structure itself.

My basic eclecticism with respect to linguistic models parallels to some extent my conviction concerning the nonorthogonal character of language itself. In the final analysis, language structure is not completely uniform; there are always aspects of language which may be said to be "out of balance," in that they reflect competing analogies and alternative patterns of usage and explication. If that were not the case, languages would not experience the kinds of changes to which they are constantly subject.

One of my most basic concerns has been communication— communication not only in terms of translational equivalence, but also in terms of clear expositions of insights concerning language structure and behavior. Any really significant insights about language can certainly be explained in intelligible language. Accordingly, I have attempted to keep technical vocabulary to a minimum and to employ abundant illustrative data. The fact that scientific truths can

normally be stated in simple language is strikingly illustrated in the
history of descriptions of planetary movements. The pre-Copernican
statements concerning the movements of the planets were indeed basically accurate, because by means of them the position of the planets
in the visible heavens could be predicted; but these formulations were
terribly complicated. After Copernicus discovered the true relation
between the sun and the planets, the formulations became amazingly
less complex. To a large extent, the same is true of language: correct interpretations are relatively simple, and therefore one tends to
become suspicious of explanations which seem to require the use of
highly esoteric symbols and numerous neologisms.

My interest in Bible translation goes a long way beyond the
academic, even though in the long history of Bible translation, in its
occurrence in more than 1,500 languages, and in its unusual breadth
of literary genres, I find an abundance of fascinating data to engage
my academic concerns. Despite the many problems involved in the
literary history of this collection of ancient writings, the Bible still
constitutes a highly relevant document for modern man.

New York City
September 1974

Bibliography of Eugene A. Nida's Works

Compiled by Anwar S. Dil

List of Abbreviations:

BUBS	Bulletin of United Bible Societies
IJAL	International Journal of American Linguistics
Lg	Language
LL	Language Learning
PA	Practical Anthropology
TBT	The Bible Translator

1945   Linguistics and ethnology in translation problems. Word
1.194-208. [French version: Lexique, traduction et
anthropologie culturelle. La Lexicologie, No. 2 of Series
A, "Initiation a la linguistique"—lectures edited by Alain
Rey, 265-268. Paris: Klincksieck, 1970.]

1946   Morphology; the descriptive analysis of words. Ann Arbor,
Michigan: University of Michigan Press. [Second edition,
1949.]

1947 a.   Bible translating: an analysis of principles and procedures.
New York: American Bible Society.

     b.   Field techniques in descriptive linguistics. IJAL 13.138-46.

     c.   Linguistic interludes. Glendale, California: Summer
Institute of Linguistics. [Turkish version: Dilbilim üzerine
tartismalar. Translated by Özcan Baskan. Istanbul,
Turkey: Istanbul Üniversitesi, Edebiyat Fakültesi Basimevi,
1973.]

1948 a. The analysis of grammatical constituents. Lg 24.168-77.
     b. The identification of morphemes. Lg 24.414-41.

1949   Approaching reading through the native language. LL 2.
         16-20.

1950 a. Difficult words and phrases. TBT 1.25-29, 72-74, 116-21,
         158-62.
     b. Equivalents of the genitive in other languages. TBT 1.70-
         71.
     c. Learning a foreign language. New York: Friendship Press.
         [Revised edition, 1957.]
     d. New help on old problems. TBT 1.2-6.
     e. Orthographic problems in Yipounou. TBT 1.110-16.
         [Reprinted in Orthography studies: articles on new writing
         systems, ed. by William A. Smalley, 148-55. London:
         United Bible Societies, 1963.]
     f. Questions and answers. TBT 1.34-37, 63-67.
     g. The most common errors in translating. TBT 1.51-56.
     h. (With C. Moisés Romero). The pronominal series in Maya
         (Yucatan). IJAL 16.193-97.
     i. The translator's problems. TBT 1.41-50.
     j. Training the translation helper. TBT 1.56-62.
     k. Translation or paraphrase. TBT 1.97-106.

1951 a. A system for the description of semantic elements. Word
         7.1-14.
     b. New help on old problems. International Review of Mis-
         sions 40.190-96. [This article is different in content from
         1950 d.]
     c. Problems of revision. TBT 2.3-17.
     d. Proofreading. TBT 2.18-24.
     e. Questions and answers. TBT 2.93-95, 133-37.
     f. Report on the Reina-Valera Spanish revision. TBT 2.
         168-77.

1952 a. A new methodology in Biblical exegesis. TBT 3.97-111.
     b. God's word in man's language. New York: Harper & Row.
         [Sections reprinted as: Robert Morrison, pioneer transla-
         tor in China. The Fields, February 1967, p. 5. William

1952 b.   Carey, Wycliffe of the East. The Fields, April 1967, p. 6.
           Bound by the Holy Scriptures. The Fields, April 1968, pp.
           8-9. Lord, open the king's eyes. The Fields, May 1968,
           pp. 8-9.]
      c.   How the word is made flesh (communicating the gospel to
           aboriginal peoples). Princeton Pamphlets—No. 7. Prince-
           ton, New Jersey: Princeton Theological Seminary.
      d.   Questions and answers. TBT 3.87-89, 131-34.
      e.   Selective listening. LL 4.92-101.

1953 a.   Fundamental problems involving revisions of the Bible.
           BUBS 14.5-8.
      b.   What is phonemics? TBT 4.152-56. [Reprinted in Ortho-
           graphy studies: articles on new writing systems, ed. by
           William A. Smalley, 18-21. London: United Bible Socie-
           ties, 1963.]

1954 a.   Checking a translation for consistency. TBT 5.176-81.
      b.   Customs and cultures. New York: Harper & Row. [=
           Customs, cultures, and christianity. London: Inter-
           Varsity Press, 1963.]
      c.   Practical limitations to a phonemic alphabet. TBT 5.35-
           39, 58-62. [Reprinted in Orthography studies: articles
           on new writing systems, ed. by William A. Smalley, 22-
           30. London: United Bible Societies, 1963.]
      d.   What is a primitive language? TBT 5.106-12.

1955 a.   A changing Africa. BUBS 23.3-7.
      b.   Cross-cultural communication of the Christian message.
           PA 2.36-42.
      c.   Identification, a major problem of modern missions. PA
           2.90-95.
      d.   Problems in translating the Scriptures into Shilluk, Anuak
           and Nuer. TBT 6.55-63.
      e.   Tribal and trade languages. African Studies 14.155-58.

1957 a.   Bible translation in Latin America. BUBS 29.21-24.
      b.   Language, culture and theology. Gordon Review 3.151-67.
      c.   Mariology in Latin America. PA 4.69-82. [Reprinted in:
           Practical anthropology supplement, ed. by William A.

1957 c.   Smalley, 7-15. Tarrytown, New York: Practical Anthro-
          pology, 1960. Readings in missionary anthropology, ed.
          by William A. Smalley, 17-25. Tarrytown, New York:
          Practical Anthropology, 1967.]

     d.   Meaning and translation. TBT 8. 97-108.

     e.   Motivation in second language learning. LL 7 (3 & 4). 11-16.

     f.   Religion and anthropology. PA 4. 63-64.

     g.   The role of language in contemporary Africa. PA 4. 122-
          37. [Reprinted in: Practical anthropology supplement, ed.
          by William A. Smalley, 30-38. Tarrytown, New York:
          Practical Anthropology, 1960. Readings in missionary
          anthropology, ed. by William A. Smalley, 135-43. Tarry-
          town, New York: Practical Anthropology, 1967.]

     h.   The Roman Catholic, Communist, and Protestant approach
          to social structure. PA 4. 209-19. [Reprinted in: Practi-
          cal anthropology supplement, ed. by William A. Smalley,
          pp. 21-26. Tarrytown, New York: Practical Anthropology,
          1960. Readings in missionary anthropology, ed. by Wil-
          liam A. Smalley, pp. 31-36. Tarrytown, New York:
          Practical Anthropology, 1967.]

     i.   Working out a cooperative answer (In reply to 'Should we
          attend Indian ceremonials?'). PA 4. 59-62.

1958 a.   Analysis of meaning and dictionary making. IJAL 24. 279-
          92. [In this volume, pp. 1-23.]

     b.   Marginal helps for the reader. TBT 9. 1-21.

     c.   Some contemporary translations in French. TBT 9. 151.

     d.   Some psychological problems in second language learning.
          LL 8 (1 & 2). 7-15.

     e.   The relationship of social structure to the problems of
          evangelism in Latin America. PA 5. 101-23. [Reprinted
          in Readings in missionary anthropology, ed. by William A.
          Smalley, 37-51. Tarrytown, New York: Practical Anthro-
          pology, 1967.]

1959 a.   Are we really monothesists? PA 6. 49-54. [Reprinted in
          Readings in missionary anthropology, ed. by William A.
          Smalley, 223-28. Tarrytown, New York: Practical
          Anthropology, 1967.]

     b.   Drunkenness in indigenous religious rites. PA 6. 20-23.

278 Language Structure and Translation

278 Language Structure and Translation

1959 b. [Reprinted in Readings in missionary anthropology, ed. by
         William A. Smalley, 103-106. Tarrytown, New York:
         Practical Anthropology, 1967.]
     c. Illustrations for "primitive" peoples. BUBS 38.65-72.
     d. Indians of the Americas face the future. (Address given at
         Triennial Conference of the National Fellowship of Indian
         Workers at Estes Park, Colorado, July 1958.) National
         Fellowship of Indian Workers, News Letter No. 71, Spring
         1959, pp. 1-3.
     e. (With William A. Smalley). Introducing animism. New
         York: Friendship Press.
     f. Principles of translation as exemplified by Bible translating.
         On translation, ed. by Reuben A. Brower, 11-31. Cam-
         bridge, Mass.: Harvard University Press. [= TBT 10.
         148-64.] [In this volume, pp. 24-46.]
     g. Review of The Christian faith and Non-Christian religions,
         by A. C. Bouquet. PA 6.283-85.
     h. (With Ann Beardslee). The missionary role in "marriage
         palavers." PA 6.231-34. [Reprinted in Readings in mis-
         sionary anthropology, ed. by William A. Smalley, 282-85.
         Tarrytown, New York: Practical Anthropology, 1967.]
     i. The role of cultural anthropology in Christian missions.
         PA 6.110-16. [Reprinted in Readings in missionary anthro-
         pology, ed. by William A. Smalley, 307-13. Tarrytown,
         New York: Practical Anthropology, 1967.]
     j. Translation and word frequency. TBT 10.107-10.

1960 a. A synopsis of English syntax. Norman, Oklahoma: Sum-
         mer Institute of Linguistics. [Revised edition: The Hague:
         Mouton, 1966.]
     b. Do tribal languages have a future? TBT 11.116-23.
     c. Message and mission. New York: Harper & Row. [Paper-
         back edition: Pasadena, California: William Carey Lib-
         rary, 1972.] [Chapter 7 "Psychological relationships in
         Communication " reprinted as: Psychological relationships
         in the communication of the Christian faith. Occasional
         Bulletin 11.1-18. New York: Missionary Research Lib-
         rary.]
     d. Religion: communication with the supernatural. PA 7.97-
         112.

1960 e. The Bible translator's use of receptor-language texts.
         TBT 11.82-86.
     f. The translation of 'leprosy'. TBT 11.80-81.
     g. The ugly missionary. PA 7.74-78.

1961 a. (With Robert G. Bratcher.) A Translator's handbook on
         the Gospel of Mark. Leiden, The Netherlands: E. J.
         Brill.
     b. Christo-paganism. PA 8.1-15.
     c. Communication of the Gospel to Latin Americans. PA
         8.145-56.
     d. Kerygma and culture. Underlying problems in the commu-
         nication of the Gospel in Spanish-speaking Latin America.
         Lutheran World 8.269-80.
     e. New help for translators. TBT 12.49-60.
     f. New translations in the new world. BUBS 47.103-107.
     g. Reina-Valera Spanish revision of 1960. TBT 12.107-19.
     h. Review of The mission of the Church, by Charles Couturier,
         S. J. PA 8.93-96.
     i. Review of Myth and mythmaking, ed. by Henry A. Murray.
         PA 8.140-41.
     j. Review of Sandals at the mosque, by Kenneth Cragg. PA
         8.139.
     k. Review of The New English Bible: New Testament (Oxford
         University Press; Cambridge University Press.). BUBS
         46.65-66.
     l. Review of The status seekers, by Vance Packard. PA
         8.141-43.
     m. Tearing the thought curtains. PA 8.281-82.
     n. Some problems of semantic structure and translational
         equivalence. A William Cameron Townsend en el XXV
         aniversario del I. L. V., ed. by Benjamin Elson, 313-25.
         Mexico, D. F.: Instituto Lingüistico de Verano.
     o. The indigenous churches in Latin America. PA 8.97-105.
         110.
     p. Typography: elements and principles. BUBS 46.52-55.

1962 a. Akamba initiation rites and culture themes. PA 9.145-50,
         153-55.
     b. (With Fred C. C. Peng). An alternate analysis of Akamba
         themes. PA 9.151-53.

1962 c. Diglot scriptures. TBT 13.1-16.
      d. Linguistic and translation consultants. BUBS 51.99-103.
      e. Opportunities in the field of Bible translating. TBT 13.193-200.
      f. Review of Pentecost and missions, by Harry R. Boer. PA 9.189-90.
      g. Semantic components. Babel 8.175-81.

1963 a. (With William L. Wonderly). Linguistics and Christian missions. Anthropological Linguistics 5.104-44. [= TBT 15.51-69; 107-16; 154-66 (1964) = Volume 15 (1964)] [In this volume, pp. 192-247.]
      b. Bible translating and the science of linguistics. Babel 9.99-104.
      c. (With William L. Wonderly). Cultural differences and the communication of Christian values. PA 10.241-58.
      d. Reading in existentialism (reply to Donald M. Vesey). PA 10.279.
      e. Review of Scientia missionum ancilla, ed. by Loffeld and John Wils. PA 10.283-85.
      f. Review of The missionary nature of the church, by Johannes Blauw. PA 10.237-38.
      g. (With William L. Wonderly). Selection, preparation, and function of leaders in Indian fields. PA 10.6-16.
      h. The church and its ministries (reply to question). PA 10.233-36.
      i. The translation of religious texts. Babel 9.3-5.

1964 a. (With Henry Torres). Cultural independence and response to the message. PA 11.235-38.
      b. Linguistic and semantic structure. Studies in languages and linguistics; Festschrift in honor of Charles C. Fries, ed. by Albert H. Marckwardt, 13-33. Ann Arbor, Michigan: The English Language Institute of the University of Michigan. [In this volume, pp. 47-70.]
      c. Review of The church and cultures: an applied anthropology for the religious worker, by Louis J. Luzbetak, S. V. D. PA 11.285-88.
      d. Review of A factual study of Latin America, by W. Stanley Rycroft and Myrtle M. Clemmer. PA 11.189-91.

1964 d.   Toward a science of translating. Leiden, The Netherlands:
          E. J. Brill.

1965 a.   Culture and church growth. PA 12.22-37.
     b.   Review of Ecumenics: the science of the church universal,
          by John A. Mackay. PA 12.237-39.

1966 a.   African influence in the religious life of Latin America.
          PA 13.133-38.
     b.   Language husks or spiritual food? Interlit 4(2).1,11,12.
     c.   Missionaries and anthropologists. PA 13.273-77, 287.
     d.   Review of Syntactic translation, by Wayne Tosh. Lg
          42.851-54.
     e.   Bible translation in today's world. BUBS 65. 22-27.
          (= TBT 17.59-64.)

1967 a.   Difficulties in translating Hebrews 1 into Southern Lengua.
          TBT 18.117-22. [In this volume, pp. 71-78.]
     b.   Readjustment—an even greater problem. PA 14.114-17.
     c.   Bible translation—fascinating! Royal Service, May 1967.
     d.   Translating the New Testament into Haitian Creole. TBT
          18.27-30.

1968 a.   From gods to ghosts. World Vision, April 1968, pp.
          10-13.
     b.   From medieval to modern man. PA 15.170-76.
     c.   Religion across cultures. New York: Harper & Row.
     d.   Oversättning som vetenskap, som teknik och som konst.
          Svensk Teologisk Kvartalskrift, Årgång 44, pp. 204-21.
          [Swedish version of the original unpublished manuscript:
          Translation: a science, a skill, and an art.]

1969 a.   Communication of the Gospel in Latin America. Cuernava-
          ca, Mexico: Centro Intercultural de Documentación. [Re-
          vised version: Understanding Latin Americans. South
          Pasadena, California: William Carey Library, 1974.]
     b.   Science of translation. Lg 45.483-98. [In this volume,
          pp. 79-101.]
     c.   (With Charles R. Taber). The theory and practice of
          translation. Leiden, The Netherlands: E. J. Brill.

1970 a.   Formal correspondence in translation. <u>TBT</u> 21.105-13.
     b.   (With Harold W. Fehderau). Indigenuous pidgins and
          koinés. <u>IJAL</u> 36.146-55. [In this volume, pp. 131-46.]
     c.   Semantic components in translation theory. <u>Le langage et</u>
          <u>l'homme,</u> June 1970, pp. 42-46. Bruxelles: Institut
          Libre Marie Haps. [Reprinted in <u>Applications of linguistics,</u>
          ed. by G. E. Perren and J. I. M. Trim, 341-48. Cam-
          bridge: The University Press, 1971.]

1971 a.   (With William L. Wonderly). Communication roles of lan-
          guages in multilingual societies. <u>TBT</u> 22.19-37. [A shorter
          version appeared under the same title in <u>Language use and</u>
          <u>social change,</u> ed. by W. H. Whiteley, 57-74. Oxford: The
          University Press, 1971.] [In this volume, pp. 147-73.]
     b.   Language and communication. <u>No man is alien: essays</u>
          <u>on the unity of mankind,</u> ed. by J. Robert Nelson, 183-202.
          Leiden, The Netherlands: E. J. Brill. [German version:
          Sprache und Kommunikation. <u>Um Einheit und Heil der</u>
          <u>Menschheit; Festschrift for Willem A. Visser 't Hooft,</u>
          ed. by J. Robert Nelson and Wolfhart Pannenberg, 181-
          200. Frankfurt am Main: Verlag Otto Lembeck, 1973.]
     c.   New religions for old: a study of culture change. <u>PA</u> 18.
          241-53. [Reprinted as: "New religions for old: a study
          of culture change in religion" together with "Some comments
          made during discussion sessions." <u>Church and culture</u>
          <u>change in Africa,</u> January 1971, pp. 9-44, 94-99.]
     d.   Our mission: to introduce men to Jesus Christ. <u>The</u>
          <u>Church Herald,</u> November 5, 1971, pp. 10-11, 21-22.
     e.   Review of <u>From English to Slovenian: problems in trans-</u>
          <u>lation equivalence,</u> by Joseph Paternost. <u>General Linguis-</u>
          <u>tics</u> 11.131-32.
     f.   Sociopsychological problems in language mastery and re-
          tention. <u>The psychology of second language learning,</u> ed.
          by Paul Pimsleur and Terence Quinn, 59-65. Cambridge:
          The University Press.

1972 a.   (With Barclay M. Newman). <u>A translator's handbook on</u>
          <u>The Acts of the Apostles.</u> London: United Bible Societies.
     b.   Communication and translation. <u>TBT</u> 23.309-16.
     c.   Linguistic theories and Bible translating. <u>TBT</u> 23.301-308.

1972 d. Linguists and translators. TBT 23.225-33.
  e. (With Charles R. Taber). Semantic structures. Studies
      in linguistics in honor of George L. Trager, ed. by M.
      Estellie Smith, 122-41. The Hague: Mouton. [In this
      volume, pp. 102-30.]
  f. (Ed.). The book of a thousand tongues, 2nd edition. Lon-
      don: United Bible Societies.
  g. The fifth point of the compass. PA 19.274-79.
  h. Varieties of language. TBT 23.316-22. [In this volume,
      pp. 174-83.]
  i. Implications of contemporary linguistics for Biblical
      scholarship. Journal of Biblical Literature 91.73-89.
      [In this volume, pp. 248-70.]
  j. Linguistic models for religious behavior. PA 19.13-26.
  k. Why translate the Bible into "new languages"? TBT 23.
      412-17.

1973 a. (With Barclay M. Newman). A translator's handbook on
      Paul's Letter to the Romans. London: United Bible Socie-
      ties.
  b. (With Jan de Waard). A translator's handbook on the Book
      of Ruth. London: United Bible Societies.
  c. Bible translating in today's world. The Bible is for all,
      ed. by Joseph Rhymer, 54-74. London: Collins.

1974 a. What are literacy selections? TBT 25.201-206.
  b. The Book of Life. How to understand the Bible, by Ralph
      Herring, Frank Stagg, and others, 13-25. Nashville,
      Tennessee: Broadman Press.
  c. Words and thoughts. TBT 25.339-43. [In this volume,
      184-91.]
  d. A new epoch in the Bible Societies. BUBS 96.8-9.
  e. Review of La Linguistique du XXe Siècle, by Georges Mounin.
      TBT 25.360-61.
  f. Translation. Current trends in linguistics, ed. by Thomas
      A. Sebeok, 12.1045-68. The Hague: Mouton.

1975 a. Exploring semantic structures. München: Wilhelm Fink
      Verlag.
  b. Semantic structure and translating. TBT 26.120-32.
  c. Componential analysis of meaning. The Hague: Mouton.

Nida, Eugene A.   1914-
        Language structure and translation:
essays by Eugene A. Nida. Selected and
Introduced by Anwar S. Dil. Stanford, California:
Stanford University Press [1975]
        xvi, 284 p.   24cm.
(Language science and national development series,
Linguistic Research Group of Pakistan)
        Includes bibliography.
I. Dil, Anwar S., 1928-   ed.
II. (Series) III. Linguistic Research Group of Pakistan